T0323689

The Strategy for Korea's Economic Success

THE STRATEGY
FOR KOREA'S
ECONOMIC SUCCESS

Hwy-Chang Moon

OXFORD
UNIVERSITY PRESS

OXFORD
UNIVERSITY PRESS

Oxford University Press is a department of the University of Oxford. It furthers
the University's objective of excellence in research, scholarship, and education
by publishing worldwide. Oxford is a registered trade mark of Oxford University
Press in the UK and certain other countries.

Published in the United States of America by Oxford University Press
198 Madison Avenue, New York, NY 10016, United States of America.

© Oxford University Press 2016

First Edition published in 2016

All rights reserved. No part of this publication may be reproduced, stored in
a retrieval system, or transmitted, in any form or by any means, without the
prior permission in writing of Oxford University Press, or as expressly permitted
by law, by license, or under terms agreed with the appropriate reproduction
rights organization. Inquiries concerning reproduction outside the scope of the
above should be sent to the Rights Department, Oxford University Press, at the
address above.

You must not circulate this work in any other form
and you must impose this same condition on any acquirer.

Cataloging-in-Publication data is on file at the Library of Congress
ISBN 978–0–19–022879–8

9 8 7 6 5 4 3
Printed by Sheridan, USA

CONTENTS

LIST OF FIGURES

LIST OF TABLES

PREFACE

This book provides an explanation of Korea's economic growth over the last 50 years. While scholars have attempted to pinpoint the factors of Korea's success based on existing theories, they have not been able to holistically explain Korea's "miraculous" growth from its war-stricken days in the 1950s. Today, Korea is renowned for its significant economic growth and globally recognized firms such as POSCO, Samsung, and Hyundai—a result that seemed implausible 50 years ago.

In analyzing competitiveness, Western theories place an emphasis on factors such as advanced technologies and cheap labor. Through this analytical framework, for example, Western scholars attribute the success of the United States to its advanced technologies and the success of Korea to its cheap labor. What existing theories cannot explain is why certain countries experience more success relative to their counterparts that have similar factor conditions. The ABCD model that is introduced in this book provides a clear analytical framework that answers this fundamental question.

Western economics also emphasizes the importance of innovation, based on raw intelligence and brainpower, to be competitive among similarly advanced countries. This book will show that raw intellect and innovation are not required to achieve sustainable competitiveness. In fact, several case studies will show that many of today's most successful firms are not the "first movers" in their respective industries and do not employ state-of-the-art technologies.

The book will start off by introducing the background behind Korea's rapid growth. The new ABCD model will then be introduced and juxtaposed to existing economic theories. I will also use the ABCD model to analyze several past and present Korean case studies to demonstrate the practicality of the model. The book will then address the effects of internationalization, offer guidelines for Korea's future growth, and ultimately apply the ABCD model to other countries.

While the ABCD model was originally created to identify the factors that have contributed to Korea's economic success, I have come to realize that the real value of the ABCD model lies in its applicability to other countries. No matter what their stage of economic development is, other countries can also benefit from the guidelines of the ABCD model. It can serve as a playbook to successful growth for emerging economies and also serve as a strategic framework for advanced countries that are losing competitiveness.

In completing this project, I would especially like to thank my research assistants, who spent countless hours conducting research and revising the manuscript. Special thanks to Yeon W. Lee, who has made enormous contributions to this project from start to finish. I would like to thank Wenyan Yin and John Yang for their thoughtful insights, critiques, and edits. Thanks also go to my former assistants, Dr. Jimmyn Parc and Dr. Sohyun Yim, for their contributions in the early stages of this book and their valuable comments on the final manuscript. I also would like to thank Ted Moon, Jane Ng, and Oxford University Press reviewers for their reviews and helpful comments.

For the publication of this book, I am particularly grateful to my editor, Scott Parris, who recognized the value of this book and provided many insightful suggestions and Cathryn Vaulman, who helped with many things, particularly the communication with the design and editorial staff. In addition, I thank the project manager Alphonsa James, the copy editor Lynn Childress, the design team, and the entire editorial staff at Oxford University Press for their support. I also hereby acknowledge that this work was supported by Laboratory Program for Korean Studies through the Ministry of Education of Republic of Korea and Korean Studies Promotion Service of the Academy of Korean Studies (AKS-2015-LAB-2250003). Finally, I would like to thank my family, who provided support with encouragement and ideas. Without their help and love, I could not have done this.

Hwy-Chang Moon
Graduate School of International Studies
Seoul National University

The Strategy for Korea's Economic Success

Introduction

A. A DIFFERENT START IN KOREA'S ECONOMIC DEVELOPMENT

In May 2012, the Korean Peninsula was hit by a major dry spell that lasted for months, breaking the national record for the worst drought in over 100 years. To remedy this nationwide catastrophe, the government organized disaster-control centers, mobilized water tank trunks, developed new water sources, and increased the budget for other drought-relief measures. Within the following months, the seasonal rain front arrived northward onto the peninsula, slaking the record-high dry spell and preventing further hazards.

Throughout world history, droughts have been the cause of poor harvest and famine, causing various policies to be implemented to subdue natural hazards. Toward the end of the *Joseon* Dynasty from 1882 to 1910 (the period known as the Greater Korean Empire), there were continuous droughts that lasted for 29 years. In an effort to resolve this disaster, King Gojong, who was considered the rightful son of God by the people, held a rain-calling ceremony to pray to the gods at the *Wongudan* Altar.

During this same period, Los Angeles was also experiencing a serious dry spell. However, contrary to King Gojong's rain-calling ceremony, decision-makers in Los Angeles responded with a more scientific and economic approach. William Mulholland, the engineer and superintendent of the Los Angeles Water Department, carried out several massive water projects, one of which involved building a 233-mile-long aqueduct to deliver water from the Eastern Sierra to the metropolis. Its construction spanned over five years and required over 5,000 workers before it was completed in 1913.[1] This particular project was historic because it was the first aqueduct built in California. Alongside this modern achievement, significant effort was geared toward connecting the waterways of Sacramento in Northern California and San Diego in southern California. This massive initiative transformed Southern California from an arid desert into a globally competitive region for agriculture, catalyzing Los Angeles to emerge as a large industrial district.

Over the next 50 years, Korea and the United States headed down different paths. Korea, which depended on superstitious rituals to combat natural hazards such as droughts, became a colony of Japan and suffered from the Korean War, making it one of the poorest countries until the 1960s. The United States, on the other hand, which approached issues scientifically, became the world's strongest economic and military power. The varying approaches of these two nations reveal important implications for national emergency programs against natural hazards. The juxtaposition of the two varying responses shows how government goals and policies can affect national development. It is clear that the country that depended on superstition was not able to escape poverty, whereas the country that employed constructive solutions to combat its issues showed advancement. Korea has since been successful in overcoming its desolate conditions and has become one of the most dynamic and fastest-growing nations. In this light, it is meaningful to examine how Korea, once one of the poorest countries, achieved economic success in such a short period.

According to classical economics, a nation's prosperity is primarily determined by the abundance of factor endowments (i.e., inherited resources such as land, population, and natural resources). Based on this approach, many countries in Asia, Africa, and Latin America should experience great prosperity due to their abundant land, large populations, and ample natural resources. However, in reality, countries with rich natural endowments are often not the wealthiest countries. In fact, many of the advanced countries in Europe and Asia (e.g., Japan, Singapore, and Korea) have fewer inherited natural resources but remarkably higher national income.

Table I.1 shows an overview of major countries' factor endowments and wealth. From this table, it is apparent that inherited factors have not contributed much to increasing the wealth of nations. When the rankings of the first three columns (land size, population, and oil reserves) are compared with that of the last column (GDP), many countries that possess inherited advantages are not among the economies that are experiencing prosperity.

Conversely, there are six countries included in the top 15 of the GDP rankings (Germany, France, United Kingdom, Italy, Spain, and South Korea) that lack such endowments but have succeeded in becoming the

Table I.1 TOP 15 COUNTRIES BY LAND SIZE, POPULATION,
OIL RESERVES, AND GDP

Rank	Land Size	Population	Oil Reserves	GDP
1	Russia	China	Saudi Arabia	United States
2	Canada	India	Venezuela	China
3	China	United States	Canada	Japan
4	United States	Indonesia	Iran	Germany*
5	Brazil	Brazil	Iraq	France*
6	Australia	Pakistan	Kuwait	United Kingdom*
7	India	Nigeria	United Arab Emirates	Brazil
8	Argentina	Bangladesh	Russia	Russia
9	Kazakhstan	Russia	Libya	Italy*
10	Algeria	Japan	Nigeria	India
11	Congo	Mexico	Kazakhstan	Canada
12	Greenland	Philippines	China	Australia
13	Saudi Arabia	Vietnam	Qatar	Spain*
14	Mexico	Ethiopia	United States	South Korea*
15	Indonesia	Egypt	Brazil	Mexico

* Wealthy economies without large inherited advantages in land size, population, and oil reserves.
Source: Land size from UN Statistics Division (2013), population from CIA World Factbook (2013), oil reserves from OPEC Statistics Bulletin (2013), GDP from World Bank (2013).

world's most prosperous economies. Very few countries that have abundant natural resources are a part of today's wealthiest economies. This fact highlights the need to investigate new critical factors for economic success that traditional economic theories have failed to recognize.

B. THE NEED FOR A NEW FRAMEWORK

For centuries, scholars and economists have dedicated their efforts to explaining the sources of national growth and competitiveness. Early economic theories began with mercantilism in the sixteenth and seventeenth centuries, followed by Adam Smith's theory of absolute advantage in the eighteenth century, which was further developed into David Ricardo's theory of comparative advantage. Most of these earlier theories attempted to analyze the dynamics of trade by attributing economic strengths to the abundance of inherited resources. During the 1930s, however, the Heckscher-Ohlin model received much recognition for effectively explaining the modern economy with the emergence of technology and the manufacturing sector.

The Heckscher-Ohlin model was highly acclaimed for being practical and virtually self-evident. However, in 1953, Russian economist, Wassily Leontief empirically tested Heckscher-Ohlin's theorem and showed results that were contrary to what the theorem had predicted. In his famous demonstration (known as the Leontief paradox), the United States was shown to export more labor-intensive goods and import more capital-intensive goods despite being one of the most capital-abundant countries in the world. Since this Leontief study, much effort was directed at improving existing theories and models of trade, as scholars began to recognize the increasing complexity of international commerce.[2]

Toward the 1980s, one of the hottest fields of research in economics and industry growth was corporate strategy. As the capitalist system became deeply embedded in Western economies following the end of World War II, business schools, consulting firms, and the private sector began to flourish. Also, as competition among firms heightened, there arose a demand for superior management strategies, which gave birth to many theories and models. One of the most widely accepted theories of business strategy in the modern era is the industry-structure view. This theory emphasized the influence of industry structure on firm performance, meaning that the sustainability of a firm's performance is determined by the industry structure in which the firm competes. However, this approach was soon challenged by the resource-based view, which paid greater attention to the firm's endogenous factors in gaining competitiveness. According to this view, firms that possess critical resources and capabilities that are valuable, rare, inimitable, and non-substitutable, called VRIN, can obtain above-average returns against rivals.

However, as the resource-based view only considered firms' competitive advantages within a static business context, the dynamic-capabilities view was developed to address this limitation. According to this dynamic perspective, a firm's competitive advantage is determined by its capability to build, integrate, and reconfigure internal and external resources in a rapidly changing environment. Still another important approach within the field of business strategy is the institution-based view. Although this approach is not as widely used by scholars and business practitioners relative to the other three approaches, it is important because it can better explain the competitive advantages of the firms in less developed nations where institutions play a greater role and have more influence on business.

Along with these academic efforts, Michael Porter (1990) introduced a systematic framework for national competitiveness—the diamond model—in his book titled, *The Competitive Advantage of Nations*. This book was intended to succeed *The Wealth of Nations*, written by Adam Smith

([1776] 1937), by redefining the foundations of national wealth. Porter's original diamond model was subsequently extended in two directions. The first incorporated multinational activities and influenced the creation of other related models such as the double diamond model (Rugman 1991; Rugman and D'Cruz 1993) and the generalized double diamond model (Moon, Rugman, and Verbeke 1995, 1998). The second extension added human factors to develop the nine-factor model (D. S. Cho 1994). Finally, a new comprehensive model was introduced by integrating concepts from both of these extensions of the diamond model (Cho and Moon 2013b).

In short, starting from Adam Smith, scholars have come up with multiple theories in an attempt to better explain the economic performance of both developed and developing nations. However, none of these models could adequately explain the success of Asian economies. This is primarily because Asian nations have a different economic and social structure compared to the more developed nations in the West. Although newly developed models are more comprehensive and systematic than previous methods, they are still based on the identification of traditional resources (e.g., technology, market sophistication, and advanced infrastructures and systems) and therefore have a limited ability to explain the dynamics of the unique cases of Asian countries, particularly Korea.

C. DEVELOPING A NEW MODEL

Several studies on East Asia, particularly on Korea, attribute their success to cultural factors such as collectivism (e.g., Hofstede and Bond 1988; Moon and Kim 2006a) and strong authoritarian leadership (e.g., Inglehart 1997). However, an in-depth evaluation of the factors behind this region's growth suggests that there is much more to the region's success story than what these studies have identified. Existing models that aim to analyze East Asian development are limited because they are based on a partial understanding of the region's success factors. The earlier frameworks neither sufficiently detail the cause of success nor provide satisfactory implications for scholars and policymakers.

To this end, this book introduces success factors that have been overlooked but that have enabled Korea's tremendous and accelerated economic growth. This book also aims to provide important lessons to other countries, especially the developing countries in Asia, Africa, Eastern Europe, and Latin America. Korea's success story holds great value and provides practical lessons for developing countries given that Korea's economic growth was achieved within the last 50 years. Korea's rather late start in global competition shows that it is possible for other developing countries to implement similar strategies and achieve significant economic development in a short period of time. For developing countries that did not enjoy a rich history of wealth, many Western solutions are too radical, exhaustive, and unrealistic. This is because they are often based on a Western-style economic and social system. This book illustrates that the Korean model can provide more practical implications for other developing countries to learn and embrace.

The structure of this book is designed as follows. Part I (chapters 1 through 3) explains the miraculous growth of the Korean economy. Chapter 1 deals with the fundamental elements of Korea's economic performance. By focusing on the essential role of education, chaebol, and government policies in improving human resources, capital formation, and total factor productivity, respectively, this chapter takes a foundational approach to Korea's economic growth. Chapter 2 shows how each successive government of Korea designed and implemented development policies to catalyze economic growth. Along with the government leadership on national growth, chapter 3 discusses the business leadership of the founders of Korea's three top companies—POSCO, Samsung, and Hyundai—in enhancing the competitiveness of the private sector in Korea.

Part II (chapters 4 through 6) introduces and applies the newly developed ABCD model. Chapter 4 explains this new model, which is composed of four factors and eight subfactors that served as the key drivers of Korea's rapid development. The ABCD model shows how Korea's (1) agility (speed and precision), (2) benchmarking (learning and best practice), (3) convergence (mixing and synergy creation), and (4) dedication (diligence and goal orientation) have enhanced national competitiveness. Chapter 5 illustrates the theoretical background of the ABCDs by referring to the mainstream theories on economic development and business competitiveness. This chapter then describes the distinctive approach of the ABCD model by comparing it to existing literature. In chapter 6, the model is applied to explain the success of the three Korean firms, POSCO, Samsung Electronics, and Hyundai Motor.

Part III (chapters 7 through 9) brings in a key area of focus by highlighting the importance of internationalization, which is an important element for enhancing competitiveness of both nations and firms. The methods for successful internationalization are discussed by emphasizing the effective utilization of international resources for creating and maintaining competitive advantage. In this regard, chapters 7 and 8 deal with the role of internationalization combined with the ABCDs as solutions to enhance competitiveness of nations and firms, respectively. As a nation's economic prosperity also depends on culture, chapter 9 explores the role of the ABCDs in improving the productive economic and business culture, which further contributes to increasing the efficacy of internationalization.

The book concludes with Part IV (chapters 10 through12), which discusses Korea's current challenges and provides general guidelines for further development using the ABCD model. Chapter 10 discusses Korea's three critical challenges today: (1) an unproductive service sector, (2) sociopolitical problems, and (3) an aging population, and shows how these three challenges could be tackled using the ABCD model. Chapter 11 introduces how Korea can further advance by transitioning from a catch-up country to an innovative one by upgrading the ABCDs. The final chapter, chapter 12, closes the book with a generalization of the ABCD model by applying the model to other nations and firms at both developed and developing stages.

The contents of this book are extensions of my earlier studies published in books (particularly *K-Jeonryak*), academic journals, and periodicals (e.g., *Dong-A Business Review, Korean Economic Daily*). The extensions cover four areas: (1) an intensive literature review for the theoretical background of the ABCD model, (2) updated data and case studies to prove the validity of the model, (3) applications to new areas such as service, sociopolitical system, and aging, and (4) implications for gaining and sustaining competitive advantages.

My hope for this book is to help both scholars and practitioners better understand the new paradigm of competitiveness, which could be applied to various levels of development at both the national and firm levels. In particular, I hope this methodology will provide can-do confidence for economic development and a practical framework for those who do not currently possess significant competitive advantages.

PART I

The Miracle of Korea

In the 1960s, Korea was as poor as Ghana, one of the world's poorest countries. These two countries' exports consisted primarily of agricultural and mining goods, and both received a similar amount of foreign aid. However, since then, the two economies grew at significantly varying rates. Korea entered into heavy and chemical industries such as steel, machinery, electronics, shipbuilding, and petrochemicals while Ghana continued to focus on agriculture and mining. Over the span of 50 years, Korea gradually upgraded its industrial structure, transforming itself from a poor agricultural nation into a global leader in multiple advanced industries.

Alongside Korea's industrial development, the Korean government accelerated open-door policies in various areas beginning in the 1990s. In 1992, Korea's capital markets were opened to foreigners for the first time. In 1995, Korea joined the World Trade Organization (WTO), and subsequently joined the Organization for Economic Cooperation and Development (OECD) in the following year. Korea's economy surged due to expanded internationalization through newly implemented open-door policies, until all activities took a hit during the 1997 Asian Financial Crisis. Despite this setback, Korea managed to overcome the financial crisis and has continued to show strong growth to this day. Today, Korea is one of the G20 countries leading the global economy. Along with economic development, Korea has been one of the few Asian countries to achieve democratization.

In chapter 1, the foundations of Korea's economic development will be discussed to show how all these achievements were made possible by focusing on the essential roles of human resources, capital resources, and total factor productivity. Chapters 2 and 3 continue the discussion by examining the factors behind Korea's success with specific examples at both the national and corporate levels.

CHAPTER 1

Foundations of Korea's Economic Development

Despite scarce natural resources, Korea successfully developed its economy and rose up from two nation-wrecking events: Japanese colonialism (1910–1945) and the Korean War (1950–1953). How can we explain Korea's rapid economic success? One explanation can be found in the role of human capital, which is a nation's endowment of educated, trained, and healthy workers that determine economic productivity.[1] As the productivity of human capital is directly related to education, the contribution of education to the development of East Asia appears highly significant. This is why many studies on East Asian economies, including Korea, overwhelmingly support the human capital theory.

Along with human capital that emphasizes education and vocational training, the second popular factor is the ability for capital accumulation. Scholars in this field have conducted cross-country studies to examine a variety of macroeconomic relationships, including the one between financial development and long-term growth.[2] The general argument is that higher levels of financial development are significantly correlated with faster rates of economic growth.[3] Furthermore, the role of capital is highly connected to the advancement of technology because new technology can be introduced into the production process through large investments in research and development (R&D), technological infrastructure, and production facilities.

The efficient mobility of human and capital resources then leads to the third fundamental factor, total factor productivity (TFP). Despite some of the controversies on its measurement, TFP is critical in economic development because the productivity of human and capital resources is what truly generates added value, growth in income, and prosperity for a country. This is why scholars (e.g., Porter 1990) have emphasized the importance of creating value from the efficient use of resources on top of increasing the volume of resources. In fact, countries that utilized human and capital resources most productively are the ones that ultimately demonstrated rapid growth. Korea, in this sense, was able to grow at a fast pace because it learned how to productively utilize its human and capital resources. To get a basic understanding of Korea's development, this chapter is dedicated to unfolding the three foundational elements of the Korean economy—human resources, capital resources, and TFP. Accordingly, education and the *chaebol* structure are examined as the most representative factors that enhance human and capital resources, while the role of government policy is used to explain how Korea was able to enhance TFP for a greater increase in productivity. Although there are many other variables that affect and explain these three areas, the ones presented here best represent the construct of these three foundations. The detailed rationale is provided in what follows.

1.1 HUMAN RESOURCES

The rapid expansion of education in Korea is exceptional and has played a key role in upgrading the quality of its human resources, which in turn contributed to its economic development. The hype and prioritization of education in Korea (often referred to as "education fever") is widely recognized, and many believe that education has served as the backbone to Korea's success. In particular, scholars from the West have attributed this intriguing achievement in education to strong Confucian values. This argument appears to be plausible as other East Asian countries (namely the "Four Asian Tigers" and Japan) share the heritage in Confucian values and show similar educational achievements. In a way, Confucianism is related to the dedication and achievements in education. For example, Korean students have continued to achieve the top scores in reading, science, math, and problem solving in the OECD's Program for International School Assessment (OECD 2014b). Furthermore, the difference between the upper and lower five percentiles for Korean students is much smaller than the OECD average, showing that the average level of Korean education is relatively high.

Koreans' prioritization of education is regarded as the product of Confucian attitudes and in that regard, a higher education level promises greater economic success. Indeed, Korea is one of the most relentless devotees of Confucianism, and it has maintained these fundamental values throughout its intellectual history since the *Joseon* period. For example, Vogel (1991) explained the rapid economic development of East Asian countries in terms of Confucian traditions and political factors (e.g., strong leadership, effective policy, state planning, and talented bureaucrats). Similarly, the Confucian tradition is used to explain educational development.

The influence of Confucianism is quite broad and embedded in many facets of the Korean society. Therefore, one can justifiably conclude that Confucianism played a pivotal role in fostering Korea's educational system and development. However, Confucianism alone did not generate the entirety of the success that Korea and other East Asian economies now enjoy. The role of education has been much more responsive to the surrounding environment, and growth in education has been an outcome of other factors such as the economy and government policy. In this light, the following section shows a new perspective to explain how Korea's educational values and systems have been shaped to the current standard, and why they served as an important resource for Korea.

1.1.1 Korean Education in the Developing Stage

Education played a pivotal role in Korea's transformation by promoting the development of human resources (*Economist* 2011). In 1945, the literacy rate of Korea was a mere 22%, and less than 20% of children attended secondary school. Within a few decades, however, the numbers shifted dramatically; enrollment rates reached 90% for primary school in 1964, and the same occurred for middle and high schools in 1979 and 1993, respectively (UNESCO 2000).

Fortunately, each phase of investment in education fueled Korea's economic growth. For example, the development of primary education following the Korean War supplied workers for the labor-intensive industries of the 1960s. The expansion of secondary education contributed to the development of the capital-intensive industries in the 1970s and 1980s. In addition to having an impact on output growth, the emphasis on providing universal access to primary and secondary schools promoted social mobility and income equality (Koh et al. 2010). Eventually by the 1990s, the focus shifted to expanding tertiary education, laying the foundation for Korea's success in the information technology (IT) industry and knowledge-based economy (Jones 2013).

One striking feature of Korea's developmental history is that the educational revolution immediately began and continued during the post-liberation years amidst instability, poverty, and the highly destructive wartime period. It is also important to note that it preceded Korea's much praised economic development. By the time Korea's economic takeoff began in the early 1960s, education started to expand rapidly at all levels, and primary education soon became available nationwide. Furthermore, educational development, as measured by enrollment levels and teacher training, continued to keep pace with national growth. Korea had higher levels of school enrollment than any other developing nation with similar GDP per capita by the 1970s.

1.1.2 Distinctive Features of Korean Education for Improving Human Resources

(1) Lecture-Based Learning and Rote Memorization

The two well-known characteristics of Korea's education system are lecture-based learning and rote memorization. These attributes from the pre-twentieth-century culture remain unique characteristics of Korea's schooling. This form of teacher-centered schooling strongly emphasizes memorization and choral repetition. However, this methodology was criticized for limiting the development of cognitive creativity and liberal attitudes. Despite these criticisms and efforts for change, Western teaching methods had little impact on Korean education, and lectures, recitation, and memorization remained the norm. One reason for this is that Western pedagogical philosophies were difficult to understand for non-Western people. In addition, the time and means to disseminate knowledge via the Western approach were limited. Furthermore, students, parents, and teachers were more concerned with conforming to the standards of achieving better exam scores. Therefore, although a number of Korean educators were enthusiastic about introducing the progressive methods of the West, the actual pedagogy and administration showed little change.

However, are these methods truly ineffective and harmful for the learner? Contrary to the popular view, these two traditions have many benefits and have produced good results. First of all, lecture-based learning allows the transfer of knowledge to a greater number of people in a shorter amount of time. In terms of knowledge transfer, traditional lectures heighten productivity by encouraging greater concentration for both the teacher and student. There are no distractions from engaging others' opinions which can often be subjective, poorly explained, and abstract. Therefore, when distributing factual information or mainstream theories, learning solely from the teacher can be more effective; it allows for faster and more accurate learning. Furthermore, these methods help students develop their memorization skills when they learn from lectures or textbooks. Particularly during the initial phase of Korea's development where there were a large number of students and a limited number of teachers, this was the best strategy for Korean schools.

The deficiencies of lecture-based learning and rote memorization would have become apparent if this continued in advanced studies. However, these methods are highly efficient and productive in the early stage of education where solid knowledge foundations must be established prior to advanced studies and sophisticated learning (Moon 1999). The Korean education system put great emphasis on these two valuable traditions to facilitate faster learning and meet the huge demand for education.

(2) Learning from the West, While Maintaining Asian Values

Among different perspectives on higher education in Korea, the most prominent approach incorporates the Western university system with Confucian values. Although higher educational institutions have existed for a long time in Korea (e.g., *Sungkyunkwan* established in 1398), Western university ideas were imported into Korea in the early twentieth century. German, English, and French university philosophies were starting to influence Korea even before the colonial periods. Western methods of governance, administration, and academic culture proved to be highly influential in developing Korea's current university structure. These new ideas were mixed with existing educational and cultural traditions to produce the current state of universities in Korea.

Korea's modern higher education system became a hybrid of the European model (via the Japanese) and the US model (e.g., Altbach 1989; Kim 2007). With regards to European influence, policymakers considered all universities as equals and the government tried to implement standardized admissions policies to prevent institutional diversity (Shin et al. 2007). Korean universities also adopted the American department system, course-based credit hours, and tuition fees. On the other hand, Korean educators continued to maintain the traditional lecture and memorization-based methods.

Today, Korea stands at a critical crossroad, and many agree that the education system needs improvement. Memorization-focused education, based on Asian ideals of discipline, has lacked meaningful advancement and innovation. This is evident when comparing the achievements of Western and Eastern education systems. Western countries like the United States, with their stronger academic programs at the higher level, have more competitive tertiary institutions and produce more sophisticated groups of learners. In contrast, Eastern countries such as Korea have a more competitive population in the primary and secondary levels, resulting from their focus on accumulating knowledge. The future of Korea's education depends on how to harmonize these different systems to the best needs of educating human resources in a changing economic environment.

(3) Mobilizing Different Actors and Approaches

With proper engagement, Korea's private education sector—including private schools, tutoring services, and *hagwons* (private institutions that provide various academic or non-academic supplementary education)—are effective means to increase the quality and opportunity of education by promoting competition in the education market. This also strengthens the degree of risk-sharing between the government and private sector in terms of education (Patrinos et al. 2009; Lewis and Patrinos 2011). In the case of Korea, meeting the social demand for schooling was a critical factor amidst its remarkable educational expansion. This burden, which is normally imposed on the government, had been significantly reduced due to the rise of the private education sector.

Although the socioeconomic impacts of the private sector sparked greater controversy among the public, the role of the private education sector cannot be ignored when analyzing the growth of education in Korea. For instance, the fact that half of all high schools and the majority of universities were private enabled the government to devote only a modest portion of its resources on education during the initial phase of Korea's economic development. Parents, rich or poor, were willing to make enormous sacrifices to put their children through education.

With greater responsibility for both formal and supplementary education directed to the private sector, the government was able to focus on developing vocational training schools. With increased popular motivation to pursue higher scholastic education, there was comparatively less enthusiasm to become a technician. As a result, the government made a greater effort to coordinate education with industrialization during the early stages of development. Vocational education programs mirrored the nation's drive toward industrialization of the heavy and chemical industries in 1973. Education campaigns reflected the nation's export reorientation from textiles and light industry toward automobiles, heavy equipment, steel, ships, and petrochemicals. The proportion of the budget allocated for vocational education doubled between 1970 and 1979, with the biggest increases in the years immediately following the announcement of the heavy and chemical industries program in 1973. Accordingly, the government issued the Industrial Education Promotion Law, which attempted to align vocational high schools toward industrial needs by systematizing on-the-job training programs.

(4) Embracing the Growing Demand for Education

The root causes of the Korean education fever are quite complex. For one, years of Japanese restrictions on educational opportunity led to pent-up demand for education. The limited opportunities for higher education under Japanese rule were especially frustrating, because it condemned most of the population to lower status and privilege. Since Confucian values equated education with rank and prestige, barriers placed by the colonial government were a cruel reminder of Koreans' lack of power (Seth 2002).

Traditionally, Korea had a centuries-old tradition in which formal learning and scholarship played a central role in society. Education in traditional Korea was valued both as a means of self-cultivation and a method of achieving status and power. While education was recognized as an end in itself by emphasizing the spirit of scholarship, in practice, it was generally seen as a means for upgrading social status. In the Joseon dynasty (1392–1910), a series of highly competitive examinations served as the mode of selection for prestigious government positions. Even today, Korea is often portrayed as an exam-centric nation. Public examinations act as the main selection method for a limited number of government posts, and formal education is largely organized around preparation for these exams.

After the end of World War II and the collapse of the colonial regime, the postwar chaos and subsequent outbreak of the Korean War uprooted millions of Koreans and broke down the old social order that restricted higher education to the hereditary elite. Previously, the *yangbans*, the Korean aristocrats whose titles were conferred on a hereditary basis, were the only group that could receive decent education and enter high ranks in politics or the military. Having been heavily suppressed under this social hierarchy, millions of ordinary Koreans saw the opportunity to improve their lives through education when the class system was dismantled.

Therefore, under the liberalized status and chance for social mobility, a large number of Korean people made zealous efforts for education. The popular phrase *"sadang orak"* (pass [the exam] with four [hours of sleep], fail with five [hours of sleep]) reflects the degree of goal orientation and determination of these people.

1.1.3 Education to Improve Human Resources for Korea's Economic Growth

The United States once had the most highly educated populace in the world with the highest percentage of citizens with a high school diploma. Unfortunately, the United States has been losing education spirit (Thomson 1989). Former President Clinton may have been correct when he said the United States would not be the leading economy in 50 years unless its students graduated high school with an excellent, world-class education (Haynes and Chalker 1998). President Obama also acknowledged the successful role of education in Korea's development and showed deep concern for the future of education in the United States. More specifically, what President Obama wished to emphasize was the importance of valuing education for the future. By referring to Korea's teachers as "nation builders," he highlighted the role of education in national competitiveness.

Although many people, both Koreans and non-Koreans, are interested in the education of Korea, most do not fully understand its essence and role in economic growth. I was recently interviewed on this topic by a Singaporean newspaper to provide suggestions for solving Singapore's education problems. Apparently, many doubt the effectiveness of Korea's private education institutions (i.e., hagwons), and many East Asian countries share similar problems of intensifying competition and financial burdens for parents. On the question of whether private education markets should be restricted through government intervention, my answer was simple: governments should promote, not contain, competition to weed out inefficient players and systems. Korea benefited immensely from the dual system of private and public education, along with policies aimed at improving academic and vocational education. Competition between and within public and private institutions has increased the quality and efficiency of education while expanding the scope of the available educational commodities for both the rich and the poor.

Korea, once a closed and stratified economy, experienced decades of colonial rule and was eager to escape poverty and social discrimination soon after democratic and egalitarian values were adopted.

The opportunity seemed open to all who worked hard, or at first, studied hard to pass a series of exams. Many Koreans undervalue this motivation by calling the system a *"testocracy"* (a system where merit is based on test scores), and frankly it is true that exams have been overemphasized in certain areas. However, it is equally true that the system was created to satisfy popular demand and that the competitive nature of education propelled Korea to the current level of success. In a society with few qualified teachers and a huge influx of students demanding public education, lecture-based and memorization approaches were the only viable way to serve the large student pool. Also, this type of learning is more effective than discussion-based classes, at least in the early phase of development in delivering the basics of knowledge. The four characteristics of Korea's education explained above show how Korea utilized its educational values to create an effective system for raising human resources to meet the need of economic development.

1.2 CAPITAL RESOURCES

Along with improvements in human resources through education, the process of economic development requires capital resources for investment in infrastructure and industry. Although capital accumulation alone is not sufficient for economic development, it plays a significant role in improving all facets of the economy. In the process of Korea's rapid economic development, Korean conglomerates, or chaebol, emerged as the most effective and productive vehicle for accumulating and utilizing capital resources for a country with few natural resources. Accordingly, this section focuses on the political economy of chaebol formation and its role in mobilizing financial resources.

1.2.1 Korean Chaebol in the Developing Stage

Capital-scarce Korea was able to accumulate a sizeable amount of capital in a short span of time through domestic savings and foreign borrowings in the early stage of economic development. By contrast, the flow of foreign investment into Korea was relatively small. Most investment in Korea was concentrated in the private sector to support large firms that could make better use of financial resources. This section will show how Korea transformed quickly in spite of its limited capital resources. An important reason is that with these valuable capital resources, the government was able to finance targeted firms and industries to speed up the process of industrialization.

One of the first tasks undertaken by the Park Chung-hee government in 1961 was to nationalize the commercial banks in Korea. In 1962, he assumed the power to appoint the heads of all commercial banks and to control the allocation of capital resources. It is no exaggeration to say that these banks, commercial as well as special purpose, served as government tools for allocating financial resources. They were nothing like the banks of the market-based financial system of the West (Woo 1991; Lee, Lee, and Lee 2002) or the internal banks formed by Japanese conglomerates.

1.2.2 Distinctive Features of Korean Chaebol for Accumulating Capital Resources

(1) Government to Target and Reward the Winners

Overall, the government policies were based on the assumption that the private sphere should play a major role in expanding the industrial sector. However, the government also believed that effective capital accumulation could not be reaped from the private sector alone and that firms needed to be nurtured by means beyond free market incentives. The government policy was thus a selective intervention (e.g., Westphal 1990) that fostered the growth of private enterprises and supported the industries deemed to be beneficial to the national economy. For nearly three decades, the Korean government selectively intervened to promote targeted infant industries, by supporting the creation of large-scale establishments by chaebol that imitated the Japanese zaibatsu. At their inception, targeted firms received priority access to preferential credit as well as reductions or exemptions on taxes and tariffs.

In line with the government's aim to promote exports, firms were chosen based on their export performance. Firms that wished to receive support were required to exceed a specific export target, and to get more privileges, firms had to work hard to compete with each other and foreign businesses (Kim, Shim, and Kim 1995). In this way, the Korean government maintained an efficient allocation mechanism and was able to reduce the risk of a government-initiated market failure or interventionist approach (Cho and Kim 1995). In particular, the designated chaebol trading companies, such as Samsung, Hyundai, and Daewoo, served as the government's vehicles for decentralizing export incentives and promoting the activities needed to strengthen Korea's export-marketing capabilities (Westphal 1990).

Under conditions favorable to the best performers in the industry, firms that properly understood government targets grew faster and emerged as conglomerates. This is an entirely different scenario from many other cases of developing countries, where governments support uncompetitive firms to which they have personal ties. Chaebol were successful not only because they received special privileges and benefits from the government, but because they knew they would not be able to maintain cooperative relationships with the government if they were not competitive. For firms, demonstrating their ability to perform well under this relationship was critical as the government was the best or often the sole source of capital, with private banks tightly managed by the government that had high targets for national growth. In essence, both the government and large conglomerates fulfilled their unique roles in the nation's economy and satisfied each other's needs.

(2) Selective Assimilation of Japanese Conglomerates

The group that benefited the most from the government financial incentive program was undeniably the chaebol. They also held major shares of business savings in the country. The emergence of the chaebol continues to be one of the most popular topics in analyzing Korea's development because they commanded monopolistic or oligopolistic influences in their respective industries. Contrary to popular economists' views that monopolies disrupt the economy and cause market failure, however, Korean conglomerates were highly effective in creating new sustainable markets. How the chaebol was created and operated with respect to capital formation is worth examining, especially by drawing comparisons to other similar business conglomerates such as the Japanese zaibatsu (or the current keiretsu).

The Korean chaebol most closely resembles the original form of zaibatsu in Japan. A zaibatsu was usually organized around a single family, and it effectively operated companies in all major economic sectors by using its contacts within the government to secure lucrative monopolies, subsidies, and tax concessions (Morikawa 1992). One of the defining characteristics of a zaibatsu was the organization of banks and trading companies (*sogo shosha*) at the epicenter of finance. As the Japanese name suggests (*zai* meaning money and *batsu* meaning clique), a zaibatsu constituted the financial inner circle that depended on a corporate bank to back its business functions.

With the turn of events following World War II, zaibatsu were broken down and reorganized, losing some of their unique characteristics such as family ownership and strong central autocracy. However, their structure and internal bank-centered financing remained much the same, and these are the biggest differences between Japanese and Korean conglomerates. The successors to the zaibatsu—the keiretsu—continued to work closely with the banks and government while establishing their own strong distribution channels with smaller loyal retailers. The Korean government and businessmen closely examined these large Japanese cliques and tried to imitate their success, particularly as general trading companies. These enterprises specialized in importing raw materials for domestic industries and exporting manufactured goods. They were efficient in facilitating trade and capital flow because they maximized price margins through available global intelligence networks. Furthermore, they performed important functions in the short-term financing of foreign trade (Johnson 1987).

(3) Efficient Capital Approbation and the Role of Chaebol

Unlike Japanese conglomerates that controlled their own financial institutions, the Korean government officially made firm ownership of corporate banks illegal, and strictly controlled all other types of internal financing sources. Instead, the government introduced debt-based industrial financing, creating incentives for households to save through the banking system. The government-controlled banks redistributed these savings as loans to the conglomerates. In this manner, the Korean government's control of bank credit and access to foreign borrowing served as the most potent instrument for implementing economic policies. The government unilaterally sourced capital through this banking channel for corporate financing (Mason 1980; Johnsons 1987). Therefore, the chaebol's interests were heavily controlled and managed by the government's economic goals (Tu, Kim, and Sullivan 2002). It is this government-controlled credit institution that encouraged efficient competition and determined which industry leaders to support. The government even ordered firms to merge or be acquired based on the performance of large groups throughout the 1970s and 1980s.

The present-day chaebol consist of independent groups of vertically and horizontally integrated firms. The activities of these firms are relatively unrelated with one another, with the only common link being ownership. Because of this, internal trading among member companies is relatively high. Expansion also occurred as a result of the government's industrial policies. Supported by such policies, chaebol often entered a new business in its infancy. The uncertainty of supply and demand prevented economies of scale and posed tremendous opportunity costs, and this forced the chaebol to integrate vertically according to the needs of the particular business. One of the benefits of this type of business structure is the creation of synergies by carrying out both unrelated and related diversification. In the earlier phase of economic development, Korean chaebol were able to develop competences in new areas while simultaneously improving competences in existing fields. Since these activities were performed concurrently in a short period, the chaebol used affiliated firms as platforms to accumulate and configure resources, and to maximize their sales and market share.

(4) Cohesive Organizational Culture toward a Single Goal

One final important feature of Korean chaebol is the vigorous and hard-working culture that helps increase the engagement and productivity of employees. Korea is widely known as one of the hardest-working countries in the world. Koreans work on average 44.6 hours a week, which is the most out of the 34 OECD countries (OECD 2013d). Triggered by the call to diligence through the *Saemaul* (or New Community) movement in the 1970s, Korea developed its reputation as hard-working people. However, what appears to be an innate quality of Confucian values should not be taken for granted because Koreans were not always diligent.

Laziness was typical among the uneducated masses before they were mobilized through the Saemaul movement. The movement was first a community development program intended to improve the economy of rural villages. Later, the programs were expanded to the urban areas, ultimately impacting the entire country. Propelled by President Park Chung-hee's avid efforts to enlighten and mobilize the people, Korean workers were soon transformed into one of the most diligent labor forces in the world. During this period, office buildings were always lit with people working incessantly through the night. Moreover, employees even declined vacations to work more for the company.

The dedication of the Korean labor force was due to the highly motivated goal of firms to become general trading companies to receive government tax reductions and other incentives. During the 1970s when successful business groups had not yet been formed, the "too-big-to-fail" notion became their goal and drove many potential business groups to strive for growth. With the focus on increasing market share and firm size rather than profits, all members of the firm from executives to general employees were eager to work. Although this kind of organizational motivation also produced insolvent firms such as the Daewoo Group, the Korean firm that could efficiently motivate its members toward a unified goal became a successful chaebol.

1.2.3 Chaebol to Maximize Capital Formation for Korea's Economic Growth

Until the 1960s, Korea was one of the most dislocated and poorest economies in the world. It was the impoverished half of a small former colony, a possessor of few natural resources and a nation ravaged by a bitter war that destroyed much of its physical infrastructure. Moreover, many people believed that Korea had limited capacity to absorb capital, especially in the industrial sector. Few dared to predict that Korea would become a successful industrialized economic power by the end of the twentieth century. Despite the seemingly insurmountable obstacles and naysayers, the Korean economy occupied the fast lane of economic growth and developed rapidly through the emergence of key chaebol (Chung 2007).

Korea was able to accumulate a sizeable amount of capital in a short period of time. As the government enacted a series of programs to secure business-friendly environments for firms, the private sector proliferated and dominated the share of investment in Korea. The alliance between the government and the burgeoning business beneficiaries was simple: as long as the business contributed to the country's economic growth, the government was willing to provide numerous financial favors. Korean firms, in this regard, strived to mobilize both human and financial resources to grow by working hard and setting high business goals. There was a high degree of interplay and synergies that facilitated the cooperation between government and business while encouraging competition among the firms to win favorable conditions.

1.3 TOTAL FACTOR PRODUCTIVITY (TFP)

The previous sections showed how Korea raised the necessary human and capital resources for economic growth, but what about Korea's productivity? Was Korea's growth based solely on quantitative increases in these two production factors, or were there other important determinants such as technology development? In order to explain this question, economists developed a concept called TFP in order to connect growth to input factors. According to this view, economic growth is a function of a country's resource endowments and their productivity. Therefore, any increase in productivity that cannot be explained by an increase in inputs is measured as TFP (World Bank 1993), including intangible assets such as technology innovation, improved organizational efficiency, gains from economies of scale and scope, and other managerial improvements.[4] This section explains how TFP has affected Korea's economic growth.

1.3.1 Korean Government Policies in the Developing Stage

TFP has been an important consideration in discussions of East Asian development because human and capital resources only accounted for two-thirds of total growth in the region until the 1990s (Page 1994). According to the standard neoclassical growth model (Solow 1956), input-driven growth is not sustainable because there are limits to factor mobilization and growth in inputs is subject to the law of diminishing returns. Thus, if there is no technological progress and if growth results exclusively from the accumulation of resources, growth will slow down and eventually stop.

In general, studies that investigated the sources of Korea's economic growth concluded that Korea demonstrated a high level of input-driven growth (Young 1992; Lewis 2004). Paul Krugman, the Nobel Prize winning scholar in economics, reached the same conclusion when he compared Asian growth to that of Western countries—Asia grew through input-driven "perspiration," whereas the West was led by productivity-driven "inspiration" (Krugman 1994). In the end, Krugman claimed that the Asian miracle would be short-lived. This argument seemed valid, especially with the outbreak of the Asian Financial Crisis in 1997. However, this view neglected important differences between the West and the East (and Korea in particular). Korea and Western countries have taken disparate paths to development, and the unique developmental capabilities of Korea are not captured in Western economics. To fully understand how Korea enhanced its productivity, the following four dimensions need to be explored and incorporated into the model of economic development.

1.3.2 Distinctive Features of Korean Government Policies for Enhancing Efficiency

(1) Economic Development Plans for Accelerated Growth

The series of five-year plans for economic development initiated by the Korean government, especially during the Park Chung-hee administration, are well-known for being highly aggressive and growth-oriented. These plans focused on creating and directing the conditions to foster capital investment, production, and exports. Japan's Ministry of International Trade and Industry had already pursued similar policies with its developmental programs (Johnson 1987), and Korea followed suit by establishing the Economic Planning Board in June 1961.

Officially, the five-year plans continued through the late 1990s with the seventh Five-Year Economic and Social Development Plan. However, due to the different nature and context of development in the 1990s, only the first five will be mentioned here. The first five plans are differentiated by their fast pace and clear focus on accelerating growth. The Park administration aggressively restructured industries, such as defense and construction, sometimes to stimulate competition and other times to reduce or eliminate it. The Economic Planning Board established export targets that, if met, granted additional government-subsidized credit and wider access to the growing domestic market. Conversely, failure to meet such targets led to credit withdrawal. By setting clear goals for firms, the government was able to raise the confidence of both foreign and domestic businesses to invest in the industries targeted by the government.

Also, similar to other high-performing Asian economies, Korea first underwent an import-substitution phase, but immediately switched to export-oriented policies. Initially, Korea implemented wide-ranging import liberalization measures after joining the General Agreement on Tariff and Trade in 1967, and imports continued to expand at a greater rate than exports. Thus, Korea first needed to develop import-substitution industries in order to reduce the increasing trade deficit. However, the policy shifted toward export expansion to accelerate the speed of industrialization. As Korea's changing trade pattern reveals, the country was able to move from import substitution to export promotion quickly and with precision. This was possible because there was a well-designed plan in place by the government.

(2) Learning through Trade-Oriented Policies

Most East Asian governments have pursued sector-specific industrial policies to some degree. The best known instances include Japan's heavy industry promotion policies of the 1950s and the subsequent imitation or learning of these policies by Korea. The import of machinery and production programs was then complemented by an intense domestic effort to make the most efficient use of imported knowledge. Learning imported technology is in fact the most efficient way of creating new technology through improvement. For instance, Hyundai Motor was eventually able to develop new powerful engines after the company learned the basic technology from Mitsubishi Motor of Japan and improved it. Hyundai Motor's tremendous effort of learning from its predecessors and improving upon existing technologies is one of the key factors for its success as a major international exporter.

Scholars (e.g., Lawrence and Weinstein 1999) revealed that higher levels of imports are associated with greater productivity growth; on the other hand, sectors that start with export strategies record lower rates of productivity growth. Korean firms, however, countered this statement with their successful export strategies. Like the five-year plans, export-oriented policies were quite effective in delivering growth to Korea. They pushed firms to learn the best practices of existing business players in order to become competitive in the world market. Since Korea had a relatively small domestic market, the government from the onset pressured firms to target the global market so that they could expand investment and achieve economies of scale. In order to further encourage the firms to expand outwards, the government maintained a low currency value and vigorously conducted monthly trade promotion meetings, on-the-spot guidance, and episodic purges of unsuccessful firms (see Chang 2003a, b).

(3) Structural Transformation and Spillover Effects

The relationship between economic growth and structural transformation remains a primary concern of development economics (Fagerberg and Verspagen 2002). Schumpeter (1934) emphasized the importance of technical innovations in guiding fundamental changes in economic growth and structure. Beginning with Clark (1940), several economists called attention to the importance of structural transformation through theories such as the big push (Rosenstein-Rodan 1943), balanced growth (Nurkse 1952), unbalanced growth (Hirschman 1958; Singer 1964), dual economies (Nurkse 1953; Lewis 1954) and stages of economic growth (Rostow 1960). Subsequently, global institutions, such as the United Nations and World Bank spearheaded these efforts, and scholars such as Kuznets (1966) and Chenery (1975) concluded that high rates of growth underlined substantial changes in economic structure.

Among East Asian countries, Korea is an outstanding example. It has successfully transformed its economy from low-income to upper-middle-income level, and its production structure shows high technological sophistication. Industrialization in Korea began in response to new opportunities of changing technologies and increasing export demand. Korea's industrial sector witnessed substantial structural changes during its technological catch-up and learning, and effectively responded to these changes to enhance its international competitiveness.

A notable goal by the Korean government in this regard was the development of the iron and steel industries. As the basis for other industrial commodities, steel and metal were critical resources. This was the central motivation behind the Korean government's initial focus on the steel industry. Successful development of steel allowed subsequent entry into industries such as automobiles and shipbuilding. When these sectors matured, the government built international-scale industrial complexes in petrochemicals, electronic components, and machinery. Some of these complexes built in the late 1960s have grown to become the world's largest industry clusters. Government policies of promoting key industries such as steel and the establishment of world-class industry clusters significantly enhanced the productivity of labor and capital, and transformed industrial structure to a more advanced level.

(4) Enhancing National Goals through Modernizing Rural Areas

There were two important effects of the *Saemaul* movement; one was to enhance the work ethic of urban workers and the other was to improve the living standards of rural farmers. The first effect was discussed in the previous section and this section will deal with the second effect. The *Saemaul* movement originally aimed to develop and modernize rural areas of Korea by evoking the spirit of diligence, self-help, and cooperation. The *Saemaul* movement began in 1971 when Korea faced economic disparities between rural and urban areas due to the prioritization of export-oriented industrialization. As the income gap between rural and urban communities grew wider, there was a mass exodus of youths to urban areas. Consequently, villages were deprived of laborers, and cities faced significant population pressure.

Moreover, at that time, Korean farmers were idle and lax during non-farming seasons in which they often turned to heavy drinking and gambling. In fact, from the period of the *Silla* Kingdom to the recent premodern past, Korea was known for its culture of drinking, singing, and dancing. The *Saemaul* movement thus aimed to enlighten rural people and change their views on poverty through "community education." These programs promoted the values of clear goal orientation while helping villagers develop various craft and construction skills. By proclaiming that "not even the state can help the lazy," the government raised appreciation for diligence and its contribution to a better livelihood.

Another intention of the government was to mobilize farmers and direct their efforts toward national development goals. The *Saemaul* movement successfully helped farmers overcome the "non-economic" psychological issues and achieve increased productivity and prosperity in the rural areas, through the methodology of "spiritual training" (Han 2004). Between 1970 and 1979, Korean farmers' average household income grew by more than five times from $825 to $4,602 (UNESCO 2012). The changing attitude of the rural people was further enhanced as they could also find opportunities to work in newly developed, local industry clusters; they did not have to leave their towns. As a result, the income gap between the rural and urban populations was significantly reduced and some rural populations even exceeded the urban populations in income.

1.3.3 Government Initiation to Enhance TFP for Korea's Economic Growth

The popular view that productivity gains are grounded mainly on technology imports and efficient allocation of capital to high-yielding investments may be incomplete. Particularly in Korea, strong governmental leadership was geared to speed up industrialization through export-oriented policies. Exports allowed firms to learn and catch up to the best practices and technologies of major global players. This knowledge was then quickly applied to manufacture goods for export. This played a pivotal role in promoting the private sector while transforming the industry structure, through enhancing input-driven productivity.

What is also important, and which is often missing in other studies, is that Korea's TFP was further enhanced by improving the productivities of human and capital resources, and related infrastructure through the government policy of industry clustering. The industry clusters played an important role by efficiently linking infrastructure and other related industries. Clusters enabled firms to reduce transportation and transaction costs, while encouraging both competition and cooperation. The *Saemaul* movement then helped the effectiveness of industry clustering by providing regional industry complexes with a motivated workforce educated by the campaign of the movement.

In essence, Korea's TFP growth was rendered by more than what existing studies found on various government policies which were effective in enhancing the productivities of human, capital, and other resources for economic development. Chapter 2 will detail specific government policies and describe how each of Korea's presidential administrations managed to overcome obstacles and create new competitive advantages. Observing the full picture of how these factors were utilized is the key to understanding Korea's productivity and economic growth.

CHAPTER 2

Korean Government Leadership for National Growth

When Korea's liberal, democratic government was first established in 1948, the country was one of the poorest in the world with a GDP per capita below $70.[1] However, to the amazement of observers worldwide, Korea demonstrated continuous growth into the twenty-first century and raised its per capita income remarkably to almost $28,000 by 2014—approximately 400 times that of the 1948 level. Another notable aspect is that Korea displayed transformative growth by developing new industries every decade, from the agricultural sector to labor-intensive manufacturing industries to capital-intensive industries and to more advanced technology-intensive industries. In particular, the industrial structure had been upgraded significantly by the 1980s, at which point Korea worked on enhancing the competitiveness of its existing industries in addition to developing new high-tech industries such as semiconductor components and specialized chemicals.

To analyze this success story, the US Congress published a report titled "The Korean Economy in Congressional Perspective" on October 27, 1986. This report begins by highlighting four reasons that explain how Korea was able to experience such rapid economic development: (1) the collective effort of the Korean people, (2) political leadership, (3) domestic market expansion, and (4) export promotion policies (United States Congress 1986). However, if these four factors are examined more thoroughly, the collective effort of the people is the outcome of political leadership (particularly at the early stage), domestic market expansion is the result of increased income, and the export promotion policy only constitutes one part of the government's economic planning. In fact, all four reasons are related to the role of government. This calls for the need to thoroughly grasp the essence of the Korean government's role in developing the economy in order to examine Korea's success comprehensively.

Throughout various social science disciplines, there have been a number of studies regarding the role of the government in achieving economic development, and these are primarily centered on two topics. The first is whether the government is a determining factor in economic development and the second discusses how the government carries out relatively effective policies to sustain growth.[2] These two questions reflect the fundamental concerns on the role of the government, and they require serious attention when trying to describe the trajectory of growth in developing countries, particularly the Asian newly industrialized economies (NIEs).

Although the two questions seem to describe a similar perspective, there is a distinct difference between the two. The former emphasizes the "what" factor and focuses on the government's interventionist policies as an important factor of economic growth. However, the problem with this approach is that it cannot explain why countries that pursue seemingly similar government policies or growth strategies show divergent economic performances. Such limitations can be resolved by the second approach, which discusses "how" governments have implemented development policy. Korea's economic growth can be better explained with the "how" approach versus the "what" approach, as will be discussed in the following section.

2.1 THE DEVELOPMENT STRATEGY OF KOREAN GOVERNMENTS

Political leadership under an effective governmental system is important in improving national competitiveness. However, many eminent scholars (e.g., Porter 1990) argue that the government only plays an exogenous role in creating and maintaining national advantages. Despite these views, the role of government, particularly in developing countries, is more important than is understood by Western scholars. The main purpose of governmental policies is to allocate national resources to sectors that have the highest productivity to maximize value creation and optimize value distribution. This type of government capability has taken precedence in Korea as well as other East Asian countries, and this is the key to properly understanding the role of government in these economies.

Korea gained independence from Japanese colonial rule in 1945, but the takeoff of its rapid economic growth did not occur until the early 1960s under President Park Chung-hee. The following section will dive into how Korean presidents have dealt with economic issues since the 1960s by observing the mainstream economic policies of Korea throughout its developmental history. Although brief, the review of the Korean economy in the last half century will show important strategies pursued by the Korean government—some successful and some not. This overview can provide useful benchmarks for developing countries that want to learn from Korea's experience of economic development. In particular, it would be interesting to see how each government contributed to not only solving the problems at the time but also creating new competitive advantages for the future.

2.1.1 Nation-Building Stage

(1) President Rhee Syng-man (1948–1960)

In 1948, Korea's first president Rhee Syng-man was inaugurated after the three years of *de jure* sovereignty of the United States. However, the joy of self-governance was short-lived as Korea quickly faced immense domestic problems that required immediate government action. The political and social instability, in addition to the North–South divide, caused industrial decline and high inflation, which were detrimental to the nation's economy and people. From a policy standpoint, land reform and the breakup of former Japanese properties were the two most urgent tasks of the government.

During this period, the northern part of the Korean peninsula was more industrious than the agriculture-based South. This was due to abundant underground minerals and hydraulic power resources in the North, which could be utilized for manufacturing. The electricity, metal, and cement necessary for basic construction were all processed in the North, while the southern region, with its climatic and geographic advantage, focused on agriculture, textiles, wood products, and smaller scale manufacturing which only required basic machinery.

Before the peninsula was divided, this division of labor was logical and efficient. However, with the new divide, both sides suddenly needed to supplement the resulting production imbalance. Unfortunately, the outbreak of the Korean War dismantled the government efforts that had begun to stimulate employment and market growth while enacting land reform. The war destroyed manufacturing facilities and crucial infrastructure such as roads, bridges, and ports, which were already poorly established in the South. This further depleted the low supply of agricultural products and other farming essentials. Inevitably, Korea entered a period of economic stagnation with soaring inflation due to the unstable political situation.

After the Armistice Agreement on July 27, 1953, the government slowly got back on track to restore the economy of the war-torn South, and with the aid of the United States, production lines steadily recovered momentum. Until 1961, Korea received approximately $3.2 billion of foreign aid in three different forms (Chung 2007). The first was given immediately after the Korean War as relief measures and included items such as food, clothing, and medicine. The second was given for national security in addition to helping war victims. The third type of aid provided by the United States consisted of development loans, which later turned into grants. All in all, US foreign aid was helpful in propelling Korea's development. However, the aid consisted mostly of basic food and products for short-term relief to stabilize the turbulent social and economic situation. With a weak political system and corrupt bureaucracy, the Korean economy during the 1950s did not see much improvement in its struggle to escape poverty.

2.1.2 Fast-Growing Stage

(1) President Park Chung-hee (Phase 1: 1963–1971)

Unlike the preceding administration which focused on the unification of the Korean Peninsula, President Park Chung-hee declared that the most important task was to create a modern nation through economic development. However, by the time President Park was inaugurated, the United States had reduced its aid to Korea significantly, and this limited the ability to use foreign aid to carry out economic policies (Haggard 1990). At the time, the central issues consisted of: (1) domestically versus internationally oriented development, (2) the promotion of agriculture versus manufacturing, (3) capital formation through foreign investment versus foreign loans, and (4) balanced versus unbalanced growth.[3]

While the government was contemplating the national goals for production, it carefully examined domestic and foreign consumption patterns. Overall, the limited size of the domestic purchasing power prompted the government to shift outward and promote export-oriented policies that were grounded on modern industrialization strategies. With the search for a global, wider market for Korean products, exporting was a good means to obtain foreign currency (Lee 2005; IMF 2006). During this period, "national building through export promotion" became the nation's basic philosophy in all sectors and economic activities (Harvie and Lee 2005). Therefore, the previous import-substitution growth strategy was shifted to an export-oriented growth strategy.

This naturally led to other key decisions to target industries and pursue unbalanced growth. Up to this point, the agricultural sector was significantly stronger than manufacturing. However, investment in agriculture required more time to realize returns on investment. Since Korea needed faster returns, the government chose to focus on the manufacturing industry primarily to increase exports. Given the comparative advantage of abundant, cheap, and well-disciplined labor, Korea first concentrated on developing light manufacturing industries, such as textiles and other labor-intensive goods. This had the added benefit of employing more workers, as high unemployment had been a serious problem in Korea due to its rapid population growth.

In order to promote export-oriented industries, the government realized the importance of controlling the financial sector. By allocating limited capital resources to targeted companies, the government was able to obtain firms' compliance with its economic objectives and easily control firms' activities. Accordingly, the government implemented a series of reforms including the nationalization of commercial banks, an increase in private interest rates to promote household savings, and the devaluation of the currency to increase exports. However, domestic capital accumulation through savings was not enough to satisfy the demands of domestic firms' investment. Therefore, the Korean government obtained capital through foreign public and commercial loans and offered them to selected firms at low interest rates (Gereffi and Wyman 1990; Lee 2005; Park et al. 2007).

Another notable policy under Park's rule was to cultivate large enterprises, or *chaebol*. President Park realized that relying on small and medium-sized enterprises (SMEs) would not achieve his goal of building a modern industrialized economy in a short period (Kim and Park 2011). Therefore, he chose to allocate capital efficiently to selected large firms, which would benefit from scale and be more competitive. The government only provided preferential treatment to firms that satisfied the goals set by the government, thereby avoiding the moral hazards of misusing capital. This facilitated the allocation of scarce resources to the most competitive firms for exports. The export-oriented growth strategy achieved great success at the early stage of Korea's economic development. The government initially adopted an unbalanced growth approach with the hope of increasing the spillover effects from the growth of targeted areas. The focus on the manufacturing sector and large companies promised faster and higher employment, quicker returns on investment, and quicker catching up on technology. This showed how the government had a clear vision and was decisive in its actions.

(2) President Park Chung-hee (Phase 2: 1972–1979)

The 1960s witnessed considerable economic growth in Korea due to the aforementioned government policies. However, since most of the raw materials and machinery for the manufacturing sector were dependent on foreign imports, there were limits on improving the economy beyond this initial growth. As the volume of Korea's exports grew, there was corresponding growth in imports of intermediate goods and raw materials, and this resulted in a large increase in the nation's trade deficit. At the same time, Korea's market position in light industries weakened as the entry of other developing countries increased competition and heightened trade conflicts.

In order to find a new source of competitiveness, the Korean government focused on six strategic industries: steel, nonferrous metals, machinery, shipbuilding, electronics, and chemicals. This selection clearly shows the government's intention to foster the heavy and chemical industries (HCIs) (Lee 2005; IMF 2006). In order to achieve economies of scale, only a few large firms were given licenses for doing business in the HCIs. This policy further encouraged the growth of large firms throughout the 1970s. Unlike the labor-intensive light industries that were promoted in the 1960s, the capital-intensive HCIs required much more investment in capital, technology, and related infrastructure. In order to raise capital to invest in these large-scale industries, the government started the National Investment Fund (NIF) in 1973, which provided long-term, low-interest funding for companies. In effect, the NIF was a major source of financial support for the investment and development of HCIs (Cho and Kim 1995). The fund was operated by the Korea Development Bank in accordance with the nation's Five-Year Economic Plans (US International Trade Commission 1985).

This modernization effort indirectly propelled the growth of other sectors such as technical schools and related manufacturing industries. More importantly, the government established various job-training schools and technical colleges to overcome the shortage of semi-skilled labor that was required for building capital-intensive HCIs (Lee 2005; Kwon and Yi

2009). President Park also established government-run research institutes to support the import of foreign technology, thereby meeting the growing demand for technology of the HCIs. As a result, the number of government-funded research institutes increased from two in the 1960s to 10 in the 1970s (STEPI 2012). Unlike those established in the 1960s, the newly built research institutes were mostly specialized in specific industries, such as machinery, electronics, chemicals, and telecommunications.

As a result of the government's modernization efforts, Korea's industrial structure was upgraded from labor-intensive to capital-intensive industries. For instance, the ratio of value added by HCIs to GNP grew from 39% in 1971 to 55% in 1979. Furthermore, the HCIs' contribution to Korea's total exports increased substantially to 36% during the same period (Chang 2003b). Throughout this phase, the Park administration continued its export-promotion policies and promoted growth not only in size but also in quality. These government efforts were extremely effective in making Korean industries competitive in the global market (Jwa 2004).

The push for further economic growth extended to the enlightenment and engagement of the Korean people through the *Saemaul* movement. The previous decade's disproportionate focus on the manufacturing sector resulted in an increasing imbalance between urban and rural areas. In essence, the Saemaul movement was part of the government's efforts to reduce such imbalances. By cultivating the importance of diligence, self-help, and cooperation, the government aimed to implant a growth-oriented mindset to modernize the agricultural sector. However, as it did when supporting large corporations, the government was strict in providing financial support for the agricultural villages and did not support villages that were lacking diligence or self-reliance. This was highly effective in fostering healthy competition among the villages.

2.1.3 Stabilizing Stage

(1) President Chun Doo-hwan (1980–1988)

Despite the substantial growth of major HCI companies, the excessive investment in HCIs under the Park administration caused many side effects such as high inflation, overinvestment, and sector imbalance. Also, the Korean government had to deal with the repercussions of high oil prices from the two consecutive oil shocks of the 1970s. This led the IMF and World Bank to push the Korean government to decrease its market intervention and implement policies that could stabilize the economy.

The Korean government was aware of the problems caused by excessive growth-oriented policies and committed itself to stabilizing the domestic economy. In response to foreign pressure, the Chun administration shifted the focus of economic policies from growth acceleration to stabilization (Lee 2005). The stabilization policies dealt with two domains: price and employment. In order to stabilize price, the government used tightened fiscal and monetary policies and reduced the inflation rate to a single digit. This was a remarkable accomplishment considering that inflation remained in the double-digits throughout the 1970s. For employment rates to stabilize or grow, however, Korea had to maintain its rapid economic growth by continuing to increase exports.

As the global market had become hostile and grown to be more protective, Korea had to find a new competitive advantage in products that were more technology-intensive than before. The solution during the Chun administration was to optimize competition among Korean firms. Chun strictly carried out radical corporate restructuring policies—merging or abolishing less efficient companies through a governmental policy designed to promote systematic industry rationalization. In return, the companies that survived were given benefits in the form of tax reductions and financial support. In addition, unlike the previous industry-based support to cultivate certain designated strategic industries until the 1970s, the Chun government emphasized general support such as technology-related aid for all industries.

By the 1970s, Korea's R&D was mainly driven by government-owned research institutes. However, Chun devised policies that promoted private R&D to strengthen corporate competitiveness through tax reductions and various financial incentives. Due to Korean firms' large investments and strong government support, the private versus public expenditure on R&D increased from 48:52 in 1980 to 83:17 in 1989 (Korean Statistical Service Database 2015). With these efforts in technology development, the industrial structure shifted more toward technology-intensive sectors, resulting in the emergence of exports of more technologically advanced products such as ships, telecommunication equipment, and automobiles.

At the same time, as the government encountered the limits of a government-driven, central-planning economic system for continuous growth, the Chun administration promoted a new set of economic development policies that promoted market liberalization and privatization and began to focus more on qualitative over quantitative growth. Accordingly, the direct financial support to specific firms was substantially reduced relative to previous administrations. In addition, Chun privatized government-owned banks to establish a healthy financial market through a series of financial reforms including the deregulation of the interest rate. The government also set up long-term goals and procedures for further internationalization. For example, the administration established the Tariff Reform Committee in 1983, which took the responsibility of designing the step-by-step processes of import liberalization (Kim 2007).

(2) President Roh Tae-woo (1988–1993)

The success of the 1988 Seoul Olympics immediately after President Roh Tae-woo's inauguration raised the pride and morale of the Korean people, and this further propelled Korea's democratization and transition to a true market economy. The economic transition under the Roh administration was marked by heavy pressure from both inside and outside Korea to change. President Roh's domestic policies shifted the focus to democratization, diversification, and decentralization, while his foreign policy centered on accelerating the liberalization and globalization of Korea (Kwon and Yi 2009). During this period, the government's role was transformed from absolute control to soft regulation. Also, the government no longer selected specific industries or firms but focused on correcting earlier distortions and abuses of business–government ties.

The industry rationalization efforts during the previous Chun administration had essentially limited new firms' access to the market, which made the already-large chaebol even larger in terms of market share and sphere of influence. To neutralize the market stratification brought by Chun's policies, President Roh tried to invigorate free competition among all players in the market. In addition, the government enforced a more balanced and egalitarian approach to improving the welfare of Korea. In this light, President Roh increased the government's social overhead expenditures, which were largely neglected in the government budget of previous administrations. The government welfare budget continued to grow after President Roh (Koh 2008). However, Roh's labor-friendly policies, which were implemented to raise national welfare, resulted in low flexibility in the labor market.

For liberalization to enhance market efficiency and firm competitiveness, low interest loans were avoided and interest liberalization was promoted. In addition, the capital market was further liberalized. The stock market first opened in 1992 to foreigners and the government encouraged their participation. In the domestic financial market, the Roh administration relaxed the limitation on firms from entering non-banking financial sectors, such as insurance, securities, and investment trusts. This encouraged the chaebol's diversification and expansion of ownership in these sectors. This eventually made the internal procurement of capital possible. Hence, despite the initial objective of reducing the power of chaebol through various regulations, the chaebol's economic power was strengthened by exploiting the benefits of market liberalization.

On the other hand, as the government realized the growing importance of enhancing technology to transform Korea into an advanced economy, it made a strong commitment to cultivating human resources in the area of science and technology and enhancing related activities. During this period, the government established a distinctive national R&D system, which required the engagement of various participants. Under this system, public, private, and university research institutes were encouraged to cooperate to create synergies in R&D.

Overall, Roh's policies largely concentrated on promoting industrial competition through the implementation of global business standards, import liberalization, and the expansion of R&D investment in all industries. The Roh administration began under a favorable environment, which was often as the "three blessings or three low's".[4] However, some economic policies (i.e., limiting exports while increasing imports and promoting labor-friendly policies) worsened Korea's economic situation by deteriorating the trade balance, reducing the economic growth rate, and lowering the performance of firms in the global market. These problems were left as crucial tasks for the next administration.

2.1.4 Restructuring Stage

(1) President Kim Young-sam (1993–1998)

Although the economy was strengthened during the three military regimes of Park Chung-hee, Chun Doo-hwan, and Roh Tae-woo, this period was also marked by severe suppression of the media and violations of human rights. With persistent demands for reform by Korean citizens, the nation was finally able to progress toward the stage of democratization under new president Kim Young-sam. During this administration, there was even more active promotion of free trade and marketization. By joining the WTO in 1995 and the OECD the following year, Korea cemented its path toward liberalization and internationalization (Lee 2005; Kim 2007).

Although the Kim administration initially set a 100-day plan (February 22–June 30, 1993) that addressed core topics including privatization and the promotion of SMEs, the slow economic growth rate (3% average since

1992) became the primary concern of the government. The inefficient systems that had been accumulated over time began to surface during this period, and the government was pressured to ensure free participation and innovation within the market. As such, the government began referring to a "New Economy" (*shin kyeongjae*) in an attempt to break away from past customs and behaviors.

In order to resolve the problems (i.e., high cost and low efficiency) of the deteriorating competitiveness of Korean firms, the government particularly aimed to develop high technology industries. For this, the government decided to increase investments in higher education and research for basic science and technology to foster labor skills. However, the government's financial support was mostly concentrated on several key competitive university research institutes. The support to local universities and research institutes did not begin until the mid-1990s when the government realized that local research was necessary for local industrial development.

Financially, although there were a series of measures for liberalization, the pace of alleviation in government control did not accelerate until the early 1990s (Chang, Park, and Yoo 1998). However, during the Kim administration, the interest rate achieved nearly full liberalization through a step-by-step approach. Furthermore, the deregulation of the capital market made big strides, which was one of the major conditions for Korea to join the OECD. On top of this, restrictions on foreign activities in banking and non-banking sectors were greatly alleviated (Koh 2008).

However, the liberalization of the capital markets was more related to short-term foreign borrowing, which made the capital market unstable. Although there were many achievements during this administration, it lacked a proper monitoring system to regulate the fledgling financial sector, which was one of the major causes of the 1997 Asian Financial Crisis. As the Korean economy was hit hard by this crisis, the government was forced to turn to the IMF for economic relief. The resulting overhaul and restructuring of the Korean economy caused great social tension for years to come.

(2) President Kim Dae-jung (1998–2003)

The immediate task faced by President Kim Dae-jung was to recover from the economic crisis as quickly as possible, and the word "restructuring" resonated within the country throughout the five years of his term. Abiding by the strong recommendations of the IMF, the government implemented a series of reforms. At the macro-level, the government implemented strong currency regulations and tight budget controls. Government-led restructuring measures dismantled companies with insolvency problems and implemented international accounting standards. In the financial sector, policies were aimed to realign firms with best practices and establish proper safety nets. The banking sector was restructured through the liquidation and normalization of inefficient local banks in rural areas. Even larger commercial banks underwent heavy inspections and changes. Banks that were beyond fixing were forced to merge with more profitable banks, even with foreign ones. This showed the government's unflinching determination to pursue financial liberalization.

Perhaps the most radical change made during this period was the alleviation of restrictions on foreign direct investment (FDI) to improve the business environment. The government introduced a series of reforms that promoted FDI. For instance, in 1998, the government amended the Foreign Investment Promotion Act and established a one-stop service for expediting FDI. In the following year, in order to review FDI policies to ensure consistency, the government established the Committee on Foreign Direct Investment, which was comprised of various ministries and governmental organizations. The government also opened other business categories for further liberalization, including real estate rental and sales, and allowed for hostile M&As of Korean firms (Nicolas, Thomsen, and Bang 2013).

In addition to expanding deregulation and liberalization for quick recovery from the financial crisis, the administration continued to promote the technology industry. President Kim also proposed to transform Korea into an information society through a project called "Cyber Korea 21." This plan was to create a momentum to guide Korea into the knowledge and information era of the twenty-first century (Kim, Kelly, and Raja 2010). As a result of the value that the IT industry added, GDP increased from 8% in 1997 to 13% in 2000 (Lee, O'Keefe, and Yun 2003). This served as an important foothold for transforming Korea into the strong technology country that it is today.

Alongside these efforts, President Kim worked on providing equal opportunities for citizens through reforms in public education, health care, and the pension system. For instance, due to increasing unemployment from corporate restructuring, the government introduced training programs for re-employment in 1998. For job creation, the government adopted policies, such as support for establishing small and medium-sized ventures. Through the government's active response to the financial crisis, Korea achieved fast recovery and high growth during this period.

(3) President Roh Moo-hyun (2003–2008)

Although Korea had escaped the financial crisis quickly, the restructuring measures caused immense social tension and resulted in a more stratified structure for the Korean society. Since the beginning of his presidential campaign, President Roh Moo-hyun pledged to implement worker-friendly policies versus market-friendly measures. In order to remedy the income gap and increase the welfare of the *seomin* (common people), President Roh introduced worker-friendly policies that were aimed at increasing the elasticity of the labor market. In the beginning, President Roh's strategy turned out to be quite effective, but it also caused serious labor–management conflicts. In 2003, the loss of workdays due to walkouts by organized workers was 111 times greater than that of Japan, 37 times greater than that of Germany, and three times greater than that of the United Kingdom (*YTN News* 2004).

In the beginning of his presidency, Roh tried to nurture more balanced development and restrict the dominance of chaebol. While limiting the influence of large companies, Roh hoped to facilitate the growth of smaller firms. However, Roh's labor and people-friendly policies necessitated increased government spending. In order to raise additional funding required to solve the social problem of polarization, the Roh administration significantly increased taxes. This in turn led to a greater financial burden on citizens. The tax rate increased from 14.5% in 1970 to 20.2% in 2005 (MOSF 2012). Unfortunately, the financial pressure on Korean citizens was made even worse by the 2008 global recession. In the end, the worker-friendly policies of President Roh proved to be less successful in achieving their intended outcome, which was exacerbated by economic stagnation triggered by external causes.

The Roh administration, however, deserves much credit for establishing the free trade agreement (FTA) between Korea and the United States. While the agreement did not come into effect until 2012 under the Lee Myung-bak administration, President Roh's team was responsible for the initial negotiations that paved the way for its eventual ratification. Although the economic impact of the Korea–US FTA on both countries is still being examined, the agreement has significant implications for Korea in moving forward. For one, the United States is Korea's second largest export partner and fourth largest import partner, so the FTA has the potential to impact a tremendous number of products and consumers. By setting the wheels of the Korea–US FTA in motion, the Roh administration advanced Korea into the next stage of globalization and opened its markets further. With the successful ratification of the Korea–US FTA,

Korea actively pursued further FTAs with other large trading partners, including China.

2.1.5. Revitalizing Stage

(1) President Lee Myung-bak (2008–2013)

The Lee Myung-bak administration began under difficult conditions due to the global financial crisis in 2008. With the ongoing financial crisis around the world, the biggest task of the Lee government was to overcome the current crisis and vitalize the domestic market. Lee immediately initiated a series of policies to carry out market-friendly renovations and increased the flexibility of the labor market. The government actively committed to deregulation and creating a favorable environment for doing business. In contrast with the preceding administrations, President Lee amended the labor laws in accordance with international standards, which aimed to facilitate healthy labor–management relationships and regulate labor strikes.

To create Korea's future growth engine, Lee showed a strong commitment to green growth and technology by launching the Global Green Growth Institute in 2010. This institute later rose in significance when it became a treaty-based international organization, and it is expected to continue its role as an international platform for sharing green development models, especially with developing countries. Lee also focused on balancing regional and social disparities. At the beginning of his term, Lee introduced the Metropolis Economic Bloc, which aimed to develop Seoul and other regions in harmony and balance.

Furthermore, in order to foster the co-development of conglomerates and SMEs, the Lee administration established the Commission on Shared Growth for Large and Small Companies. The government also engaged in more trade agreements with other countries and regions, thus increasing the benefits of free trade. In order to further promote internationalization, the government amended the Foreign Investment Promotion Act in 2010 to alleviate restrictions on foreigners and to encourage more investments from abroad. This series of policy measures served as the basis for Korea's quick recovery from the global financial crisis. Korea's great achievement was highly praised as a "textbook recovery" (Yim 2011).

With all these efforts, Korea saw a significant rise in its international status under the Lee Myung-bak administration. President Lee was particularly outgoing, attending numerous state visits and summits during his term. In large part due to President Lee's incessant diplomacy, the

2010 G-20 Summit was held in Seoul. This was historic for Korea as it was the first non-G8 member to host the forum. This proves the international acknowledgment of Korea's expanding role in the global community. Furthermore, Korea joined the Development Assistance Committee of the OECD and significantly increased its development aid activities. As Korea continued to rise as a major player, President Lee put a special focus on engaging in proper activities to secure Korea's place in global affairs.

(2) President Park Geun-hye (2013–2018)

Korea was one of the countries that quickly escaped the 2008 global recession. However, domestic situations were still dire because of the prolonged exposure to the stagnated global market. Private spending reduced due to relatively low income and asset growth. Consumption also slowed due to low consumer confidence, thereby worsening the overall economic cycle within the country. The low growth phase of Korea triggered by low consumption and employment was revealed as more of a structural problem.

In addition, the past growth strategy which focused on manufacturing final products caused weak competitiveness in the upstream parts and components sector. This meant there was an increase in imports of more advanced components and materials, while the manufacturing industry upgraded its final products. On the other hand, with increasing global competition, many manufacturing firms had to transfer their manufacturing plants abroad to reduce production costs, thereby making the domestic employment situation worse. This situation is referred to as "growth without employment," as Korea's manufacturing sector showed strong growth over the past 20 years while employment in the industry declined (Bae 2014). The growing gap between conglomerates and SMEs also continued to widen during this period.[5]

To address the problems of decelerating and unbalanced growth, the Park administration defined its goals on two agendas: a "creative economy" for new growth strategies and "economic democracy" for better income equality. This was elaborated further in President Park's address to the National Economic Advisory Council in early 2014. In her speech, Park unveiled her "Three-Year Plan for Economic Innovation," by focusing on three areas: strong economic fundamentals, dynamic innovation, and balance between domestic demand and exports. Park hoped to demonstrate strong fundamental principles by reforming the public sector and increasing institutional transparency. To achieve dynamic innovation,

Park planned to establish "innovation centers" in Korea's 17 major cities and allocated a large amount of funding for start-ups and entrepreneurs. In addition, Park planned to spend approximately 5% of Korea's GDP on R&D by 2017 (4.03% in 2011) as an investment for enhancing Korea's business competitiveness (*Business Korea* 2013). To reduce the overdependence on the international market, Park tried to expand the domestic market through greater deregulation of domestic investment and demand.

Although the actual implementation and efficacy of Park Geun-hye's policies are still in process, it is clear that her approach is different from the policies of the previous administration under Lee Myung-bak. There is a greater level of emphasis on job creation by building an innovative economy, and a balanced society through economic democracy. However, as Korea continues to face new challenges such as an unbalanced industrial structure, deepening social stratification, and aging population, the government needs to adopt more comprehensive and systematic policies and utilize resources more productively to provide appropriate solutions for the future.

2.2 IMPLICATIONS FOR GOVERNMENT POLICIES: TURNING DISADVANTAGES INTO ADVANTAGES

The general policies of each Korean administration since the 1960s are summarized in table 2.1. The table shows how Korean presidents carried out different policies according to their situations. Most of these efforts were geared toward overcoming disadvantages and solving problems while creating new competitive advantages to enable sustainable growth. The governments did so by first setting economic goals, then identifying and resolving weaknesses, and ultimately creating new strengths. Once a particular target was achieved, the government moved on to the next development challenge and repeated the process of setting targets, overcoming weaknesses, and creating strengths. By repeating these steps, the government created a virtuous circle of economic growth that enabled Korea to continuously enhance its national competitiveness, thereby transforming it from a developing to an advanced country.

Although many scholars criticized the governments' interventionist policies for economic development, Korea's government policies demonstrated high effectiveness particularly in its early development stage. The success of government policies does not lie in the intervention itself, but in the enhancement of business efficiency. For example, the government did not support all exporting firms in the 1960s, but only those which showed

Table 2.1 KOREA'S ECONOMIC POLICIES BY PRESIDENTS

Economic Goals	Solving Problems	Creating Advantages	New Problems
Park Chung-hee (1) (1963–1971) Import substitution Export promotion	Foreign borrowing Low interest and tax	Growth of chaebol Learning from abroad	Trade deficit Limited growth with light industry
Park Chung-hee (2) (1972–1979) Export promotion Heavy & Chemical Industry	Investment with scale economies *Saemaul* movement	Vocational schools Government-run research facilities	High inflation Overlapping investments
Chun Doo-hwan (1980–1988) Stable growth Deregulation	Tight monetary and financial policy Restructuring the private sector	Private R&D investment Market liberalization and privatization	Increased power of chaebol Income gap
Roh Tae-woo (1988–1993) Liberalization Growth promotion	Tighter control on chaebol Welfare policy	Import liberalization Expanding R&D in all industries	Weak competitive-ness in global market Weak financial sector
Kim Young-sam (1993–1998) Internationalization Deregulation	Joined WTO and OECD Financial reform	Developing high-technology Liberalizing capital market	Weak financial infrastructure Financial crisis
Kim Dae-jung (1998–2003) Overcoming financial crisis Economic restructuring	Financial reform FDI promotion	High-tech industry Knowledge-based economy	Unbalanced growth Social inequality
Roh Moo-hyun (2003–2008) Social equity Democratization	Labor-friendly policy Anti-authoritarianism	Balanced growth Initiation of FTAs	Rigid labor market Economic stagnation
Lee Myung-bak (2008–2013) Market stimulation Internationalization	Flexible labor market Market-friendly policy	Promotion of FTAs Green industry	Slow economic growth Social welfare
Park Geun-hye (2013–2018) Job creation Balanced society	Public sector reform Restoring principles	Creative economy Economic democracy	Slow domestic employment Social rigidity

superior performance. Thus, this selective support policy facilitated competition and firms' operational efficiencies. Furthermore, the government gradually loosened its control over all economic sectors, which provided more opportunities for firms to utilize competitive resources from across the globe and create new competitive advantages.[6] Moreover, the administrations continuously pursued new policies to promote national growth, such as the information-based society (Kim Young-sam and Kim Dae-jung), the green industry (Lee Myung-bak), and the creative economy (Park Geun-hye).

Korea's development strategy is rather unique and different from traditional economic theories. Traditional theories primarily explain economic development through comparative advantages that are innate to a country, implying that a nation cannot create competitiveness in certain fields where it does not have inherent advantages. By contrast, Korea has demonstrated that a country can achieve economic development by continuously overcoming inborn disadvantages and creating new advantages. Chapters 1 and 2 reviewed key topics that commonly appear in discussions on Korea's rapid economic growth. Human and capital resources and the high productivity from efficiently utilizing those resources were developed under successful government policies. However, there is another group that played a critical role in catalyzing Korea's growth—the leaders of chaebol. This will be discussed in the next chapter.

CHAPTER 3

Korean Business Leadership for Corporate Growth

The role of executive leadership in corporate success is well noted. Drucker (1988) described leadership as the irreplaceable core of organizational business, while Collins (2001) claimed that three out of four companies falter due to unstable leadership. The role of leadership, as an advanced human factor, is particularly important for companies in less developed countries. This is because a nation or company in the early stage of economic development does not have other advanced factors that generate significant competitiveness. For these nations and companies, the most important factor starts from effective leadership on how to mobilize limited resources in an efficient manner to enhance competitiveness (Cho and Moon 2013a). This was evident in Korea's case. The early founders of Korean companies displayed spectacular vision and decision-making to lead their companies.

The existing theories of leadership emphasize the importance of either personal characteristics (e.g., trait theory) or influences of the external environment (e.g., situational and contingency theory). However, these theories do not provide a comprehensive picture of leadership because they are limited to less controllable factors. To improve the understanding of leadership, this chapter will introduce four new traits that can be acquired and improved through individual efforts. This chapter further examines the leadership qualities of three Korean entrepreneurs—Park Tae-jun, Lee Byung-chul, and Chung Ju-yung, the founders of POSCO, Samsung, and Hyundai, respectively.[1] For each case study, this chapter will discuss how the company overcame its disadvantages and created new advantages due to the specific leadership qualities of each CEO. Although these three leaders had widely different leadership styles and personalities, they possessed common attributes that are crucial for understanding the rapid growth and success of Korean companies.

3.1 THE FOUNDER OF POSCO: PARK TAE-JUN

Park Tae-jun was born in 1927 in Yangsan, a fishing village in the southern Kyungsang province. At the age of six, he joined his father in Japan and remained there until the end of World War II. Upon his return to Korea, Park Tae-jun entered the Korean Military Academy, where he met Park Chung-hee who was stationed there as a company commander. Park Tae-jun's encounter with the future president was a fateful one as Park Chung-hee had a direct influence on Park Tae-jun's illustrious career. When Park Chung-hee took power in 1961, he promptly appointed Park Tae-jun as his chief of staff and economic advisor. Later in 1968, Park Chung-hee was convinced that Korea needed to be self-sufficient in steel, and called upon Park Tae-jun to lead the newly formed Pohang Iron and Steel Company (later renamed POSCO).

Park Tae-jun maintained his relationship with President Park, and this benefited POSCO in many ways. In return, POSCO came under heavy pressure to perform well, and Park Tae-jun fully accepted this responsibility. He realized the need for early government support and was aware of the significance of the start-up capital for POSCO. The role of the Park Chung-hee administration in POSCO's founding was an important attribute to POSCO's success. However, the close ties and strong financial assistance from the government cannot fully explain POSCO's success during its early stage of growth. It is important to examine the role of the founder's strategic leadership, which directly contributed to the creation of firm-specific advantages.

3.1.1 The IBRD Report: Doubts on Korea's Steel Industry

When POSCO was founded, Korea lacked significant infrastructure and was mainly dependent on agriculture and unskilled labor. Due to Korea's poor domestic conditions, its immediate priority was to meet the shortage of food and shelter for its citizens. In the midst of this situation, President Park Chung-hee recognized the importance of the steel industry and believed that a successful entry into steel would lead to the growth of other related industries and eventually the entire Korean economy.

In order to pursue President Park's vision, the Korean government sought financing for an iron and steel mill from the International Bank for Reconstruction and Development (IBRD). The IBRD, however, was skeptical of Korea's steel industry prospects and rejected the request after a thorough evaluation. In the 1968 report titled "Korea—Current Economic Position and Prospects," the IBRD claimed that it was too early for Korea to enter the capital and technology-intensive steel industry and advised it to first develop labor-intensive industries (IBRD 1968). In March of the following year, the IBRD maintained this view at the third general assembly of the International Economic Consultative Organization. It released a new edition of the "Korea—Current Economic Position and Prospects," which reiterated the opinions of the previous year's report while adding that higher production costs in steel would offset Korea's advantage of cheap labor and diminish its global competitiveness (IBRD 1969). Other national governments such as Germany also expressed doubts regarding Korea's ability to succeed in the steel industry and declined to provide any loans for Korea.

Despite the lack of assistance from the international community, Korea pressed on with its steel ambitions. President Park Chung-hee conducted negotiations with politicians and businessmen to reallocate approximately $100 million of Japanese war reparations earmarked for agricultural development to build infrastructure for the steel industry. The government also convinced Japan to grant them aid and needed steel technology. This action marked Korea's entry into the steel industry, and with the government's support, POSCO successfully completed the construction of its first steel plant on July 3, 1973. While skeptics predicted a steep financial deficit for a minimum of three years, POSCO became profitable after six months. POSCO went on to shock the world when it surpassed the annual steel production volume of Brazil in the 1980s, an IBRD favorite for steel investment returns. With this achievement, POSCO exceeded the expectations of all steel industry experts and refuted the analyses and policy recommendations of the IBRD.

In April 1986, Park Tae-jun met Dr. Jaffe, the author of the IBRD report, at a convention for the International Iron and Steel Institute. When Park Tae-jun asked Dr. Jaffe whether he still believed his report was correct, Jaffe stood by his original analysis and conclusion. However, he added that the Koreans performed "beyond common sense," thereby making the report appear inaccurate. Dr. Jaffe's analysis was technically sound according to the conventional economic theory of comparative advantage, which dictates development of industries with obvious factor advantages.

However, this approach is incomplete because it assumes that a nation's specialty and ultimate potential are already determined based on its factor conditions. As Park Tae-jun demonstrated, a strong leader with specific qualities can drive a company to outperform these expectations.

3.1.2 Park Tae-jun's Leadership for POSCO's Success

Park Tae-jun was known for prioritizing "speedy operations." Under his direction, the constructions of POSCO in the early years were completed well ahead of schedule which not only saved time but millions of dollars (Seo 2011). This was even more extraordinary considering that the construction site was formerly a barren sand field that lacked any related and supporting infrastructure. Moreover, in his pursuit of speed, Park never sacrificed precision. Park was unyielding in his strict and methodical standards for steel plant construction and had no tolerance for haphazard work. In one particular anecdote, Park discovered a major structural flaw while the construction of the first steel plant was well underway. Park immediately halted construction, reproached the person in charge, and restarted the entire construction process after dismantling the half-completed concrete foundation. As a further testament to his commitment to doing things the right way, Park Tae-jun consistently upheld transparent business practices in the midst of widespread corruption in Korea during those times.

Despite exceeding all expectations, Park was not blinded by his early success. He was quick to recognize areas for improvement, and began to learn from existing steel leaders in the United States and Japan. Therefore, the company could acquire the knowledge and skills to design plants more efficiently. Notably, Park introduced the Project Evaluation and Review Technique (PERT), which he learned from his training in the United States while he was in the military academy. At the same time, Park implemented overseas training programs so that employees could learn foreign technology first-hand. Under orders from Park, technicians learned every detail of Japan's steel technology and transferred this knowledge smoothly to POSCO's domestic employees. As a latecomer in the industry, Park Tae-jun understood the importance of learning from established leaders to meet global standards.

Park Tae-jun was also skilled at creating synergies among various business elements. In an effort to secure stable resources for continuous growth, he successfully guided POSCO's entry into the energy industry. Park Tae-jun was also aware of Korea's energy insecurity and the volatility of the global energy market (Oliver and Hume 2012). To develop energy capabilities abroad, he established affiliate companies in multiple locations, including Australia, India, and North America. At the same time, by continuing POSCO's steel production activities within those countries, Park was able to establish cooperative ties that helped the company secure resources for steel production.

Park Tae-jun was a firm believer in the value of human capital. He said, "You can import coal and machines, but you cannot import talent." Since he also believed that recruiting was a critical element for success, Park implemented top welfare programs for POSCO employees. Under CEO Park's direction, POSCO constructed a top quality residential complex for steel workers and provided higher wages relative to other companies. He also offered many other incentives such as paid training programs in foreign countries. When Takeda Yutaka, the former CEO of Nippon Steel, met the board members of POSCO in Japan in 1960, he was impressed by the passion and diligence of POSCO's employees. He went on to exclaim, "I am surprised at the ability of CEO Park to foresee the success of Korea's steel industry and precisely pick the best people."

CEO Park was also well known for his diligence and dedication. Park believed that the best way to lift his employees' total commitment to work was for him to set a good example. Park spent most of his time on site with the workers while the first steel plant was being completed. He promptly abandoned all leisure activities and hobbies to focus on the plant construction. Park's diligence had a marked impact on all POSCO employees, who were motivated to follow the footsteps of their CEO.

Finally, Park Tae-jun was strong-willed, action-oriented, and determined. While skeptics expressed their doubts while touring the deserted sandy plains of the first production site, Park Tae-jun showed stronger determination to complete his mission. With the nation's hope for Korea's restoration on his shoulders, Park felt that he must succeed. CEO Park's patriotic motivation is well reflected in his famous quote: "We must possess dignity and feel a sense of duty in being part of a long-cherished business project for our nation. This project was funded by the blood of our ancestors. If we fail in building this plant, this will be a great sin to our national history and we will not be forgiven. If we fail, we must turn to our right and drown ourselves in the Young-il Gulf [of the East Sea]."

Since the construction of the first steel plant, POSCO has grown to become one of the top steel producers in the world. According to World Steel Dynamics, since 2010 POSCO has ranked the highest for five consecutive years, out of more than 30 world steel makers (Park 2014). POSCO's success story may make it easy to forget the level of skepticism that the company faced in the beginning. Park Tae-jun's strong leadership was the key in withstanding outside criticism and guiding POSCO forward in line with his own leadership qualities. The next section will discuss how Lee Byung-chul similarly guided Samsung through its early difficulties.

3.2 THE FOUNDER OF SAMSUNG: LEE BYUNG-CHUL

Lee Byung-chul was born in 1910 to a wealthy landlord in Uiryeong, an agricultural village in the southern province. After completing high school in Korea, he moved to Tokyo to study at Waseda University. Japan, like much of the world, was experiencing an economic depression at the time. Lee was a frequent participator in protests against the government and was incarcerated on one occasion. Shortly after this incident, he was taken with beriberi, a nutritional disease, and returned to Korea before completing his university degree. Upon his return, Lee inherited land that was worth 300 sacks of rice. He used this asset to open his first rice mill near his family home in Masan. When Lee realized the inadequacy of transportation facilities in Korea, he entered the freight industry. With bank loans and profits from his businesses, Lee purchased additional land and enjoyed a period of relative prosperity. However, with the outbreak of the Sino-Japanese War in 1937, bank loans discontinued and the market price of land plummeted. Lee had to cease all of his business transactions and close his stores.

Lee later recounted several key lessons that he learned from this experience: (1) be aware of both domestic and international political conditions, (2) know your limits, (3) avoid overly speculative ventures, and (4) follow your intuitions but have a backup plan. After his early failures, Lee went on to oversee Samsung's success in distribution, sugar refining, textiles, and electronics. Many attribute Lee's fortune to his wealthy background and education, but these facts alone do not explain the entire story. Much like Park Tae-jun, Lee possessed key qualities of leadership that allowed him to succeed as evidenced by his leadership of Samsung into semiconductors.

3.2.1 The Mitsubishi Report: Pessimism on Korea's Semiconductors

Samsung initially focused on labor-intensive goods such as TVs, radios, and other home appliances until the mid-1970s. In 1974, Samsung entered the semiconductor industry by acquiring Hankook Semiconductor and creating a semiconductor division within Samsung. This was a completely new venture for Samsung, which soon recognized the enormous growth potential of the semiconductor industry. In 1983, Lee Byung-chul gave his famous "Tokyo Declaration" and announced his commitment to building Samsung into a global leader of semiconductors.

Back then, advanced countries such as the United States and Japan were firmly entrenched as global leaders of the semiconductor industry. Lee's decision to enter the already competitive industry seemed unpromising at best, and most experts from both inside and outside Korea predicted Samsung's imminent bankruptcy. The negative forecasts were justified given Samsung's lack of original or core technologies relative to major multinational firms. Accordingly, the Mitsubishi Research Center published an internal report in 1983 titled "Five Reasons Why Samsung Cannot Succeed in the Semiconductor Industry," referring to a small domestic market, weak supporting industries, poor social infrastructure, small corporate size, and low technological capabilities (Hong 2011).

Despite such criticism, Lee continued to invest in the semiconductor industry, dispatching a group of employees to the United States for training through a consortium with Micron Technology. However, Samsung faced many obstacles with Micron—the technologies being shared were near obsolete, and the United States did not welcome the Korean technicians. As a result, Lee turned to Japan for help. Fortunately, the Japanese companies were more amicable and provided a smoother transfer of technology to Samsung. One of the most significant gains was the state-of-the-art technique of Very Large Scale Integration (VLSI) process that Samsung learned from Sharp Electronics. After overcoming a series of difficulties, Samsung defied all odds and succeeded in building its first production plant in 1984. Since then, Samsung has managed to become a global leader in the semiconductor industry by continuing to excel in product development and innovation. Despite its humble beginnings, Samsung boasts top market shares in the industry today.

Much like the IBRD assessment of Korea's steel industry, the arguments put forth by Mitsubishi and other critics were not entirely wrong. Korea's economy and Samsung's corporate situation were relatively feeble and limited. From the traditional economic perspective, Korea possessed virtually no advantages in capital, technology, market size, and supporting industries that could even hint at a small chance of success. However, similar to how POSCO proved Dr. Jaffe wrong, the conclusions of the report were overturned by Samsung's extraordinary performance. Both Mitsubishi and the IBRD failed to understand the potential of Korean business leaders and their way of doing business. By not succumbing to the inadequate business environment and continuing to create advantages, Lee Byung-chul was able to guide Samsung's successful entry into the semiconductor industry. Overall, the company's eventual dominance in the industry propelled Samsung to become a global leader today.

3.2.2 Lee Byung-chul's Leadership for Samsung's Success

In virtually all of his business decisions, Lee Byung-chul displayed speed and decisiveness. Much of his success is attributed to his early entry into certain industries. After experiencing his first failure with the rice mill closure, Lee Byung-chul opened a trucking business in Daegu called Samsung Trading Company. During those times, Daegu was a major hub of traffic routes in Korea, and Lee immediately moved to take advantage of this strategic location before others. Then, after the end of the Korean War in 1953, Lee established the sugar production company Cheil Jedang (widely known as CJ). The demand for sugar (as well as other basic food items) was immense in the war-torn economy, and Lee was quick to recognize the potential market and start the business.

Lee was also extremely precise about starting a new business plan. While most merchants concentrated on immediate returns and short-term goals at that time, Lee had long-term plans for his business. As Japanese policy on rice during the colonial period grew increasingly exploitative, he opened a noodle factory to alleviate food shortages. The business became a huge success in no small part due to Lee's focus on precise planning. He conducted thorough research of consumers' tastes and market behavior, which allowed him to produce noodles that were more attractive than other brands. Lee also traveled through cities such as Pyongyang, Shinuiju, Wonsan, and Heungnam in Korea, and Manchuria and Beijing in China in search of products to sell. His venture into China was unusual given that most traders and businessmen at the time limited their business activities to their home country. Lee, however, did not hesitate in being the first to expand his business scope outward, and after gaining a deep understanding of prevailing market conditions, he successfully sold apples and fish in Korea, Manchuria, and Japan.

Lee Byung-chul was also a good learner. He made it a point to study other industry leaders to identify trends and build new strengths. In his later days, Lee developed a routine of visiting Tokyo at the start of each year to design new business plans. With his grasp of the Japanese language and culture, Lee was able to analyze Japanese media reports and commentaries on economic trends. After carefully digesting the Japanese experts' analyses of the past year and forecast for the future, he met with reporters, experts, and businessmen in related fields to acquire in-depth information. Whenever Lee thought a particular issue was especially important, he ordered his team in Korea to validate the information and construct specific business plans.

Lee did not cling to one specific target for learning superior technology and advanced practices. He excelled at combining his business intellect with outside knowledge and experience. An important lesson he learned through his observations was to conduct simultaneous research on the Japanese and American markets. Lee noted that successful business ventures in the United States could still fail in Korea, but businesses that succeeded in both the United States and Japan had a much higher chance of success. By combining the best practices of American and Japanese companies, Samsung was able to quickly catch up and even surpass the industry leaders from the United States and Japan.

Lee Byung-chul also displayed tremendous dedication to his business. In Lee's *Hoam Autobiography*, he talked about how he discovered the value of sustainable business during a conversation with a barber in Akasaka, Japan. Lee was deeply impressed that the barbershop was passed down for three generations, with the expectation that the barber's son would continue the family legacy. Intrigued by the fact that a small barbershop could continue business for so long, Lee began to think about the future of his own company, Samsung. He quickly concluded that sustainability in business required a continuous commitment to the future. However, unlike the barbershop business, his business needed a longer term vision and larger investments to survive and prosper for generations. With this in mind, Lee chose semiconductors for its future business and continued to invest in the sector despite continuous deficits for 13 years.

Lee also realized the importance of dedicated employees for the company. This is why Lee took an unusually heavy hands-on approach to recruiting. As a firm believer in the importance of human resources, Lee personally interviewed all new hires to ensure that each member of Samsung's workforce personified his own dedication to the company. One of his favorite sayings is, "Do not hire a person if there are doubts, and do not doubt a person once hired." Lee's faith in his employees came from one particular experience he would never forget.

When Lee decided to leave Daegu for Seoul early in his career, he entrusted his brewery and orchard to a man named Lee Chang-eup. After Lee lost all of his Seoul facilities during the Korean War and retreated back to Daegu, he went through a period of grief and hopelessness like many of his compatriots. However, during this most difficult moment,

Lee unexpectedly received $2.3 million from Lee Chang-eup, who had been saving the profits earned from the brewery and orchard entrusted to him. Lee used this money as the initial investment for building Samsung Corporation in Busan. Due to his life-saving experience with Lee Chang-eup, Lee Byung-chul would build all of his future business relationships in the same manner.

There is another interesting anecdote regarding Lee's management of human resources. After the April 19 Revolution and the establishment of the Second Republic in 1960, the government attempted to purge corruption and quell the unrest from the previously rigged elections. Alongside other *chaebol* groups, Samsung was accused of corporate tax evasion, and the prosecution summoned Lee and other executives for questioning. However, the prosecutors became frustrated as all of Samsung executives admitted that they were guilty. When it was finally Lee's turn to answer, he calmly stated that there was no need to investigate the other executives because everyone was following his orders; he claimed that other members were innocent and he took sole responsibility for the crime. After the proceedings, the prosecution revealed to the media that Samsung was the only company where the executives admitted guilt and did not pass the responsibility to others. The lead prosecutor later spoke in private that he was impressed by Lee's ability to obtain such loyalty and commitment from his people.

When Samsung made its first foray into semiconductors, the public disparaged Lee Byung-chul as a megalomaniac, and experts across the world predicted Samsung's imminent demise. However, Lee silenced all critics when Samsung quickly emerged as a new leading player in the semiconductor industry. In 1982, Samsung's total revenue was approximately $6 billion, which was only one-fourth the revenue of Phillips, the largest electronics company at the time (Samsung Electronics 2010). However, Samsung's revenue more than doubled by 1995, and has grown rapidly since. This was due to the vision and strong goal-oriented mindset laid down by Lee Byung-chul.

3.3 THE FOUNDER OF HYUNDAI: CHUNG JU-YUNG

Chung Ju-yung was born in 1915 to a family of peasant farmers. He had a rather insecure childhood, running away from home four times to escape his life of poverty. In the young Chung Ju-yung's mind, a farmer's life was grueling and did not pay enough to feed a family. Chung began working in many different jobs from an early age to change his destiny. Eventually, Chung found work at a rice store. His diligence, attention to customers, and good business sense paid off when he inherited the store along with all of its customers and suppliers.

Throughout his career, Chung successfully branched out into many other industries. He opened an auto repair shop, in anticipation of increasing demand in the auto market, and entered into construction after witnessing large profits in the industry. In addition, after observing the mass transportation of construction materials, fuel, and wartime supplies, Chung built a successful shipbuilding industry. Later, Chung started an auto manufacturing business when he foresaw Korea's transition into personal vehicles with rising income, and he established Hyundai Semiconductor after witnessing Samsung Electronics' success. Hyundai's triumph was mainly due to Chung's accurate instincts and strong business intuition. This is especially visible in Chung's navigation of Hyundai into the automobile industry. However, there is more to Chung's leadership than his innate characteristics.

3.3.1 The US Consumer Report: Low Evaluation on Korean Cars

In 1967, Chung Ju-yung started Hyundai Motor Company despite insufficient capital, technology, and relevant experiences. With the technological cooperation from Ford Motors, Hyundai produced its first car, the Cortina, using the specifications of a Ford model with the same name. However, the Cortina had many problems as it was originally designed for the well-paved roads of the United States. Unlike American roads, the roads in Korea at that time were mostly rough and unpaved, causing Cortina to undergo frequent damages and breakdowns. As such, Hyundai had to stop manufacturing the Cortina in 1971. Hyundai went on to introduce its second model, the Pony, in 1974. This was Korea's first domestically produced car, with the majority of the technology belonging to Hyundai. With the successful production of the Pony, Korea emerged as the sixteenth country in the world to have an independent auto industry (Kim 2014). Chung wasted no time in utilizing this breakthrough, and in 1976 Hyundai began exporting Korean vehicles, first to Ecuador, then to the Middle East, and eventually worldwide.

However, problems surfaced in 1986 when Hyundai began selling a model called the Excel in the US market. The Excel fell far behind its competitors in all criteria other than price. In the early 1990s, the Excel repeatedly ranked at the bottom of a number of consumer surveys, including *Consumer Reports*. The report also claimed that the Excel's poor outing in the United States was foretelling Hyundai's future success in other countries. Even worse, Hyundai became a popular mockery due to its poor quality, greatly degrading the corporate image of Hyundai in America.

Despite the failure and humiliation Hyundai faced early on, Chung Ju-yung remained undeterred. As one of Chung's last directives before relinquishing leadership of the company, Hyundai had initiated drastic quality improvement measures to ensure that the upcoming medium-class Sonata succeeded in the American market. Following the leadership of his father, Chung Mong-koo complemented this with an aggressive 100,000-mile/ 10-year powertrain warranty to build consumers' confidence in Hyundai's quality. This was an unprecedented marketing strategy during a time when top automakers from Europe, America, and Japan only offered up to 50,000-mile/5-year warranties. Chung's quality initiative ultimately proved to be successful for Sonata.

However, Hyundai did not stop there. It never ceased the quality improvement process, and the designs for Hyundai cars were continually enhanced over time. Consumer journals that had previously given Hyundai negative reviews re-evaluated the company's competitiveness, and Hyundai began to gain positive recognition. As consumers began to associate Hyundai cars with quality and value, Hyundai further improved its market positioning. Recently, Hyundai has expanded its lineup with the introduction of upmarket models such as the Equus and Genesis, and their superior performance and top safety ratings are making headway among sophisticated buyers in the United States and Europe.

Currently in 2016, Hyundai is the fifth largest auto producer in the world, and it continues to increase its share in existing markets. In addition, Hyundai is attaining significant market share in emerging economies such as India, Russia, and China. An automotive specialist recently praised Hyundai in a column in the *Washington Post*, citing Hyundai's success as an important lesson for America's unproductive politicians. He stated, "Our less-than-productive supposed leaders could learn several important lessons—Hyundai learned quickly from its mistakes, did not waste a crisis, wasted absolutely no time in finger-pointing, and kept its vow to do better" (Brown 2012). As a leader, Chung Ju-yung instilled these positive values into Hyundai, which continue to pave the way for Hyundai's success in the future.

3.3.2 Chung Ju-yung's Leadership for Hyundai's Success

Chung Ju-yung is well known as a man of action. When accused by his subordinates of asking for the impossible, he always retorted, "Have you tried?" This quote reflects Chung's ever positive and action-driven attitude and has become somewhat of a motto throughout Hyundai. In the winter of 1953, Korea hosted a memorial event for countries that participated in the Korean War, and Chung was asked to construct a grassplot for visiting delegates at the UN military cemetery in Busan. It was winter and attaining fresh grass was almost impossible, but Chung surprised everyone by purchasing a barley field near the Nakdong River and transplanting it to the site.

Like the other two successful founders, Chung Ju-yung moved quickly in business. By observing the changing needs of consumers, he gained valuable insight into the market demands of postwar Korea and quickly occupied desirable markets before others. In the 1970s, once the basic infrastructure of Korea was relatively well established, there was a demand for further development in heavy and chemical industries. In response, Hyundai strategically entered the shipbuilding industry. In the 1980s, Hyundai responded to changes in the market by diversifying and expanding its business to securities and other financial sectors.

Throughout the history of its operations, Hyundai has always displayed such proactive responses to dynamic market conditions. Once Hyundai experienced early success in Canada, Chung quickly expanded Hyundai's sale of low-cost automobiles throughout North America. In another instance, Chung pioneered Hyundai's entry into the Middle East market immediately following the 1970s oil shocks in order to capture an early position in the foreign market, which was crucial in its future business. Chung followed the experiences of successful Japanese business ventures during the Korean and Vietnam Wars because he understood the importance of fast market penetration in the face of special circumstances such as wars and economic shocks. The resulting successes highlighted Chung's insightfulness and "speedy" responses to the changing demands of the Korean and foreign markets.

Chung also prioritized precision as well as speed in actual production and services, and he especially emphasized the importance of upholding delivery schedules. Chung's early auto repair facilities always finished scheduled maintenances on time, no matter how many cars were in line for repair. Due to Chung's reputation for punctuality, Hyundai Construction was able to rise above intense competition and secure contracts for numerous projects including the Patani Naratiwat Freeway in Thailand, Kamlanman US military complex in Vietnam, and Asuri Ship Repair Center in Bahrain. This credibility was to become Chung's defining trait in business. In his interview with the *Seoul Economy Daily* in June 1976, Chung said, "In long-term business, credibility is the most important asset. It is very difficult to earn credibility and it takes a tremendous amount of time. What is more difficult is to maintain credibility or trust once you have earned it. While it is hard to maintain trust, it can be easily lost. Being a trusted company is having the trust of people. It is my firm belief that no one should do anything that acts against trust."

Another key quality of Chung Ju-yung was his ability to benchmark established leaders. Whereas founders of POSCO and Samsung relied more on Japanese expertise in steel and electronics, Chung Ju-yung leaned more toward American standards. This was largely due to Chung's frequent contacts with Americans early in his career. Chung's younger brother, Chung In-yung, spoke English and was on good terms with the US Army personnel, and he utilized his brother's contacts to secure many projects such as the airstrip of the Osan military base and the dock at Incheon Port (the reconstruction of the first Incheon dock was the largest construction project in the history of Korea). Through these dealings, Chung was able to witness the strict and high standards of the US military. Unlike Korea, the US military had detailed specifications for everything from tool sizes to repair processes, which were documented in handbooks and manuals. The efficiency and standardization of US military activities left a deep impression on Chung, and this influenced his management style for years to come.

Among many stories of Chung's dealings with the US military, there was one incident in 1952 when President-elect Dwight Eisenhower visited Korea. An issue arose because there were no suitable hotels for Eisenhower and his entourage for this ceremonious occasion. As a solution, the US forces decided to set up a temporary residence in Unhyeongung, one of the old palaces in Korea. However, *Unhyeongung*, like most antiquated buildings, lacked the comfort of modern toilets and heating systems. When the US delegation asked Chung to solve this problem, Chung searched frantically for Western toilets and amenities and built a modern-style bathroom and heating system on site in an amazingly short period.

This is just one of many examples that highlight Chung's skill in bringing in outside resources to come up with creative solutions. Chung displayed this ability again when constructing a water control system at the Sosan tide embankment in 1984. Construction was almost impossible due to the strong current. In order to solve the problem, Chung sank a 322-meter, 230,000-ton tanker to the bottom of the sea, which scattered the troublesome current and allowed construction to proceed (Jung and Woo 2013). Chung's creative solution would not have been possible without his prior experiences in the shipbuilding business. Hence, the synergistic combination of various experiences can be an important source of competitive advantage for leaders.

In another famous example, Chung secured a $931 million contract for the Jubail industrial harbor project, which was referred to as the largest construction of the twentieth century at the time (Lee 2008). The port required the installation of massive 10-story-tall steel jackets in addition to thousands of tons of steel and concrete materials. Because Hyundai Construction had set an unrealistically low bidding price in a desperate attempt to secure the contract, Chung faced seemingly insurmountable cost and time restrictions. His solution was to utilize the pre-existing industrial complex in Ulsan to build the jackets rather than constructing them on site, which would have resulted in massive overhead costs. The completed jackets and materials were then shipped from Korea to Saudi Arabia without insurance to save additional costs. The employees and top management teams balked at the idea, many of them denouncing it as madness. To this, Chung replied with his trademark phrase, "Have you tried?" Chung's seemingly impossible plan succeeded in the end, and the Jubail industrial harbor project was added to Hyundai's long list of landmark achievements.

As was the case with Park Tae-jun and Lee Byung-chul, Chung Juyung's achievements were only possible due to his unwavering dedication. Like Park and Lee, Chung carried the weight of his country's development on his shoulders, and as such, did not view failure as an option. He never backed down from a challenge, and when others only saw failure and impossibility, Chung saw opportunity for growth. His confidence, however, was not a fantasy as Chung always backed it up with results. While soliciting orders for ships from foreigners, Chung was asked where his shipyard was, to which he replied, "If you buy a ship, I'll build one with the money." Chung delivered on his promise—he completed the ship order on time, and the resulting Mipo Shipyard in Ulsan went on to become the biggest in the world.

Chung also displayed tremendous diligence throughout his entire career. Even in his eighties, Chung maintained a strict schedule, waking up at 5:30 every morning and walking two kilometers to work. Chung always claimed that he was never tired because he genuinely enjoyed working. This quality continued with his employees. Chung was a very demanding boss, who was not without his share of conflicts. However, Chung always found a way to rally his workers toward a common goal and complete projects on time. Chung's employees would never have labored so hard for the company if their leader did not do the same. Chung led Hyundai by example, and his thorough embodiment of leadership qualities has carried on with the company to this day.

3.4 COMPETITIVE ADVANTAGES OF KOREAN BUSINESS LEADERS IN PERSPECTIVE

The success of these three companies cannot be completely explained by conventional economic theories on competitiveness, as was the case with the role of government in Korea's economic growth, explained in chapter 2. None of these companies started off with significant advantages, but they succeeded in creating new advantages with limited capabilities. POSCO, Samsung, and Hyundai were able to venture into uncharted territories and take new routes beyond the ones prescribed by existing theories through the strong leadership of their respective founders.[2] Park Tae-jun, Lee Byung-chul, and Chung Ju-yung challenged experts' expectations and succeeded in spite of obvious disadvantages because they demonstrated specific traits as business leaders. Some of these traits in their way of doing business were common to all three founders and are worth examining in detail.

First, all three leaders were quick and accurate in their business decisions on how they ran their companies. Park Tae-jun managed to inspire his workers to complete construction projects at an unprecedented rate, Lee Byung-chul quickly penetrated opportune markets without hesitation, and Chung Ju-yung showed an undying commitment to meeting delivery schedules on time. What is more impressive is that all three leaders managed to demonstrate speed without sacrificing quality. For example, shortcuts were not allowed under Park Tae-jun. He had no issues restarting a faulty process, no matter how laborious. Similarly, Lee Byung-chul and Chung Ju-yung were dedicated to continuously improving their products and transforming Samsung and Hyundai from cheap mass-producers to high-quality brands.

Another common attribute is a commitment to learning for continuous improvement and upgrading of the firm's advantages. From their humble beginnings to later prominence, Park, Lee, and Chung maintained an open mind and sought to acquire knowledge and technology from world-class leaders. Lee Byung-chul engaged in learning most of the early technology from the more experienced Japanese and Western firms. Even after Samsung accumulated significant market share, Lee never stopped visiting Japan and other countries to consult with foreign industries and media experts. In the same vein, Park and Chung engaged heavily in foreign training programs and consultancies. Since all three companies were latecomers to their respective industries, they had much to gain from the experiences of their predecessors, and all three CEOs actively pursued learning to this end.

A third trait is the successful handling of diverse business activities. Park, Lee, and Chung all ventured into multiple business areas and demonstrated an ability to create synergies among them. When Park decided to enter into the energy industry in foreign countries, he also continued POSCO's steel production to supply the necessary materials for the construction of facilities. Lee was able to expand Samsung into a massive conglomerate by funding strategic businesses (e.g., semiconductor) with profits made from other cash-cow divisions, aiming to achieve sustainable growth. Chung also demonstrated this ability when he made creative use of a ship to divert water currents for a dam project.

The fourth and final leadership quality is dedication. All three leaders were against insurmountable odds and faced challenges through much of their early careers. However, they had a clear vision for the future of their companies and remained committed to realizing their ambitious goals. Park Tae-jun persisted in transforming an inhospitable area into his first steel plant; Lee Byung-chul made his audacious Tokyo Declaration to predict Samsung's future as a global leader in electronics; and Chung Ju-yung never relinquished his goal to transform Hyundai into a quality automobile brand. In all three cases, the leaders had clear and definitive objectives. They then worked tirelessly to realize their goals and inspired their employees to do the same. In addition, the dedication of all three leaders was accompanied by strong patriotism. They dedicated tremendous time and effort into their respective businesses at the cost of their personal interests. Although this patriotism was underappreciated and often neglected by Western scholars, it indeed played an important role for starting a business in the initial stage of Korea's economic development.

These four traits, commonly held by Park Tae-jun, Lee Byung-chul, and Chung Ju-yung, were defining factors in POSCO, Samsung, and Hyundai's success. With great challenges ahead of them, these three Korean business leaders showed how their leadership qualities could turn a crisis into an opportunity for corporate growth. Moreover, these leadership traits can all be cultivated through education and training, thereby making them applicable to other individuals. Although these case studies can provide useful lessons for other business leaders, their relevance extends beyond the firm level to all aspects of domestic and international competition. The next chapter will formally define these factors under a comprehensive model and apply them to the success of Korea's economy.

PART II
The ABCD Model

A New Framework for Explaining Korea's Economic Success

In September 2011, the Brazilian magazine *Negócios* published an interesting article titled "Not India or China, but how about imitating Korea?" (Fortes 2011). This was the feature story of an issue that had a humorous illustration of a Korean man on the cover. The subtitle read, "Revealing the secrets of Korea and its business that achieved rapid development by *'Pali Pali'* (meaning quickly quickly) and copying others." This reflects the popular view that Korea's speed and imitation are its two engines for success.

The 26-page article included many graphs and statistics that illustrated these two characteristics of Korea. It began by recounting the rapid reconstruction of the Cheonggye Stream to emphasize the speed at which the Korean government moved. Then, it described the success of large Korean firms such as Samsung that have long imitated their more established global counterparts while incrementally advancing elements of design through the help of foreign experts and by establishing their own design centers in major cities such as Milan, London, Paris, and New York. Although these two factors certainly played a part in Korea's rapid growth, they alone cannot account for Korea's continued success over the past several decades. There are other key factors that are required for such success in addition to those mentioned in the Brazilian article. To understand Korea's remarkable half century of growth and fully explain the secrets behind Korea's success, the ABCD model will be introduced in this chapter.

Part II consists of three chapters. Chapter 4 introduces the four factors and eight subfactors of the ABCD model through examples and case studies. Chapter 5 dives into the theories that support the ABCD model. The final section, chapter 6, explains how three of Korea's most successful firms—POSCO, Samsung, and Hyundai—achieved rapid corporate growth and became global leaders by applying the ABCD model.

CHAPTER 4

The ABCD Model

The Success Factors of Korea's Economic Growth

This chapter introduces the ABCD model to explain the Korean strategy, or K-strategy, for economic growth. It is composed of four factors—agility, benchmarking, convergence, and dedication.[1] Each of these factors is further divided into two subfactors. While these factors are common to many successful Korean firms, they have not been well identified or clearly organized in the existing academic literature. As in *Negócios*, earlier scholars and experts have only uncovered a subset of factors that have contributed to Korea's rapid growth. This chapter utilizes examples across business, sports, and entertainment in order to facilitate the understanding of the ABCD model.

4.1 AGILITY: SPEED COMBINED WITH PRECISION FOR INCREASING PRODUCTIVITY

Foreigners who come to Korea frequently encounter its Pali Pali culture, which highlights Koreans' knack for speed. Some notable examples include: (1) As soon as Koreans insert a coin into the coffee vending machine, their hand is already in the delivery compartment waiting for their coffee, (2) Koreans incessantly push the close button inside the elevator until the door closes, and (3) Koreans close and reopen the website browser if it does not load within three seconds.

The *New York Times* discussed Koreans' obsession over speed in an article titled "Connected, Yes. Competitive, Maybe" on September 29, 2011

(Choe 2011). According to this article, Koreans generally decide what to order at a restaurant based on what comes out the fastest; are already standing and waiting in the aisle before an airplane comes to a complete stop; and have quick-service deliverymen on motorcycles who defy the laws of traffic and get to their destination by weaving through traffic. While humorous, this is a pretty accurate depiction of Koreans and their sense of urgency. However, there is more to Korea than an obsession over speed. Koreans are also precise in what they do, and the combination of these two characteristics has played a significant role in propelling Korea into an economic powerhouse.

Many western scholars tend to overlook the role of precision and only focus on speed when evaluating Korea's competitiveness. Although Korea did not possess abundant resources and was dependent on imports for certain technologies at times, Korea was able to surpass the countries from which it imported technologies. Korea achieved this through high speed and a certain level of precision. In fact, it is crucial to understand that advanced technology in itself is not indicative of success. Although advanced technology offers many benefits, on some occasions, it may be too advanced for certain consumers who prefer user-friendliness and compatibility. On the other hand, a prudent combination of speed and precision—or *agility*—can create significant value for consumers, which can lead to exceptional success as demonstrated by Korea.

4.1.1 Speed

Speed has undeniably played a crucial role in the development of Korea. At the national level, Korea's economic growth in the 1960s and 1970s would not have been possible if President Park Chung-hee did not implement speed-oriented industrialization policies. At the corporate level, the founders of major conglomerates achieved global recognition and widespread customer satisfaction through their abilities to provide quality-products at shortened production times.

This intangible asset, speed, is overlooked in traditional economic theories on comparative advantage. According to the traditional paradigm, it would be impossible for a country like Korea with virtually no natural resources to achieve its present level of economic growth, and even if it did, its limited resources would impair its ability to shift to other industries. Traditional theories claim that nations that have petroleum should develop petroleum-related industries and nations with large pools of labor should develop labor-intensive manufacturing industries. However,

Korea's achievement across high-tech and heavy-duty industries contradicts this conventional perspective.

Korea's economic development was fueled by *created assets*—resources that are not innate to its land. Korea created its own competitive sources, and the first of these was speed. With imported resources and acquired technologies, Korean people worked harder and faster to make up for its lack of natural resources. Koreans dedicated themselves enthusiastically to catering to the demands of the global market once they saw that there were opportunities for success. They willingly accepted this challenge and succeeded under pressure by working hard in hopes of prosperity. This occurred during the nation's growth plans from the 1960s to 1970s, where the government pressured and motivated Korean citizens to meet ambitious goals for prosperity. The Korean people have persisted in these efforts ever since, and this strong mindset allowed Korean companies to achieve the prosperity that they enjoy today.

The true essence of business does not lie in defeating competitors but rather in creating value for consumers. A company must focus on continuously creating competitive products through careful examination of consumer needs. If a company is blindsided by its internal competitive strategy and neglects the changes of the business paradigm, it will eventually lag behind new players in the field. The CEO of Sony Corporation once said, "The ultimate goal of Sony is to make its state-of-the-art technology obsolete." Sony was already a top global company at the time of this bold statement. However, Sony's pace of innovation gradually declined and eventually other firms such as Samsung Electronics caught up to its technology standards (Moon and Lee 2004). Although Sony continuously pursued changes for sustainable growth, it has struggled since 2009 due to its inability to adapt to the fast-changing environment.

Nokia, once the world's largest mobile phone producer, also experienced a sharp decline in its stock price for similar reasons. Nokia made the fatal mistake of only focusing on the advancement of its technology without keeping abreast of the rapidly changing mobile phone landscape and consumer demand. It simply assumed that its highly advanced technology would maintain its dominance. Nokia soon had to forfeit all of its major assets to Microsoft, including its symbolic 20-year-old Symbian operating system, and ultimately sold the whole company to Microsoft in 2013. Regarding this, Choe (2012) reported that leading companies such as Nokia, Motorola, and BlackBerry failed to respond quickly to the smartphone boom led by Apple, leading to substantial declines in their market share in the mobile phone industry.

On the other hand, the British newspaper the *Guardian* published an article (Barkham 2012) titled "Samsung: Olympic Smartphone Firm Aims for Big Global Wins." In this feature story, the author analyzed Samsung Electronics' victory over Apple in the smartphone market and attributed Samsung's success to speed. In particular, the *Guardian* highlighted Samsung's rapid response to market changes, which demonstrated the company's alertness or crisis consciousness—a widely used term within Samsung. The *Guardian* also mentioned the two popular mottos of CEO Lee Kun-hee: "Change everything except your wife and children" and "the real strength of Samsung is speed." Samsung's crisis-driven motivation and prioritization of speed are well illustrated in this article.

Korea's speed is not unique to a single firm—it can also be seen at the industry level. A good example is Korea's *Dongdaemun* (DDM) fashion town, an apparel district in Seoul established by war refugees in the 1960s. While DDM experienced enormous growth throughout the 1990s, it faced new competition with the influx of cheap foreign apparel after the 1997 Asian Financial Crisis. To overcome this newfound competition, DDM pursued a new strategy that eventually enabled it to become one of the most successful cases of Korean business.

DDM's solution was to build a unified zone spanning one-mile that incorporated all facets of the fashion industry. This zone served as a one-stop station for everything from design and production to sales of fashion items. This cluster had the fastest and most efficient distribution channel among all competitors. DDM eventually grew into one of the world's largest fashion markets and further drove the boom of the fashion and cosmetics industry within the country. Several studies (e.g., Jin and Moon 2006) compared the competitiveness of the DDM district to similar markets in other Asian countries and concluded that DDM demonstrated higher competitiveness in speedy design, production, and delivery. To this day, DDM is quick to learn the hot items from popular luxury brands and rapidly distribute these items to the market.

In addition to the firm and industry levels, the advantage of speed can be found at the national level of Korea. Internet speed can be a representative variable for evaluating the speed of a country because it involves almost all sectors of a country. The speed of Internet access affects the efficiency of people's lives and businesses. Korea is famous for its fast Internet speed, even in comparison to advanced countries. According to the Akamai's State of the Internet Report, Korea's global average connection speed (23.6 Mbps) was the highest among 194 countries during the first quarter of 2014. Korea's connection speed is almost two times that of the average of the top 10 countries (13.3 Mbps), and it is significantly higher than the next fastest country, Japan, which is at 9 Mbps. Despite its already advanced Internet connectivity, Korea continues to show improvement—its 23.6 Mbps in Q1 2014 showed 12% sequential growth over the prior quarter (Akamai Technologies 2014).

4.1.2 Precision

Despite speed's many obvious benefits, speed without precision poses risks. Prime examples are the collapse of the Sungsoo Bridge and Sampoong Department Store in Korea during the 1990s due to shoddy construction. The importance of precision in business activities cannot be overstated. Many accidents that occur in the business field are due to imprecision, and defective products are largely the result of imperfections in the manufacturing process. If precision is sacrificed for speed in the manufacturing process, companies will ultimately incur great losses due to product recalls, realignment of value chain activities, and dissatisfied customers. What is more costly is the need for companies to win back consumers' trust. In a well-known example, Toyota was forced to recall approximately 19 million vehicles globally between late 2009 and early 2011 due to a quality control problem (Klayman 2014). This was nearly two times the volume of Toyota's annual production, which caused Toyota to incur a massive financial loss and experience a significant blow to its reputation. For all these reasons, precision is a necessary component for success in addition to speed.

The importance of precision is amplified for countries that wish to become an advanced nation. In a truly advanced country, fraudulent construction projects are unimaginable, defective products are unlikely, and corruption is rare. Corruption, in fact, often occurs due to the lack of a precise regulatory system that can ensure appropriate behavior in business or politics. Evidence can be easily found in many national competitiveness reports and other relevant research. Misconduct and imprecision potentially leads to large costs, which hinder economic progress. One of the reasons that a country such as Singapore, which possesses limited natural and human resources, was able to achieve such rapid economic growth is because it established a social environment that valued transparency and precision at the level of advanced countries.

The development of Korea's Pali Pali culture has been accompanied by precision to some extent. The Korean Customer Satisfaction Index (KCSI)[2] was first developed in 1992 by the Korean Management Associate Consultants to measure customer satisfaction with the products and services provided by various Korean industries. Contrary to quantitative growth indicators such as GDP, the KCSI index measures the economy's qualitative growth. Over the past 22 years, KCSI scores for the manufacturing and service industries increased by approximately 50% and 100%, respectively. The dramatic improvement in KCSI scores implies parallel improvements in the precision and quality of Korean products and services.

I once asked an industry expert how Korea was able to achieve global leadership in shipbuilding despite Japan's higher technological capacity and China's lower manufacturing costs. His explanation was simple—Japan's *monozukuri* (artisanship) consumes too much time and lacks the flexibility to address varying customer needs. China, on the other hand, lacks sufficient precision for quality shipbuilding even though they have cheap labor. Korean companies, however, have both—they can build ships faster than their competitors with relatively high precision. In short, Korea's shipbuilding industry achieved competitiveness because of its combination of speed and precision.

The importance of speed and precision is not limited to business and can also be applied to sports and culture. For instance, the Korean national team displayed remarkable results during the 2012 London Summer Olympics. Among many other sports that require speed and precision, fencing especially requires these two traits. As one can imagine, accurately attacking the opponent with a slender rapier is an extremely difficult task. For many years, European fencers have dominated this sport with their superior physical attributes and experience. However, in the 2012 Olympics, the Korean fencing team achieved remarkable success by overcoming their relatively inferior physical attributes with fast footwork (i.e., speed). Of course, if the Korean fencers also did not possess the precision required for fencing, they would not have achieved the good results.

The importance of agility is not only applicable to developing countries but also developed countries. When I was in Paris a few years ago, I had a chance to visit the Château de Versailles. However, I came across a vast crowd and a long line for entry. After waiting in the cold for some time, I was finally able to enter the ticket office and noticed the reason for the long wait; there was only one ticket booth manned by two employees. What was worse, only one employee processed the tickets while the other handled phone calls (the automated ticket vendors were also out of service). Speed and precision were nowhere to be found throughout the tour.

Given that France is an advanced nation, such problems stemming from a lack of agility will not surface immediately. However, if slowness and inefficiencies continue in business areas, France will soon encounter serious economic problems. Today's economic issues in Europe and other countries should not only be addressed through macroeconomic policies such as government financing and monetary circulation but also through a more fundamental approach to improve productivity in the business field.

4.2 BENCHMARKING: LEARNING THE BEST PRACTICES FOR EFFICIENT CATCH-UP

In 2012, Apple filed a lawsuit against Samsung claiming that Samsung infringed on its patents with its smartphones. This led to numerous trials in which Apple won its claim and was awarded substantial compensation.[3] Many business critics interpreted the verdict as a major loss for Samsung Electronics, arguing that the iPhone market was an established business where Samsung could only hope to compete by imitating Apple. This sentiment was echoed in the *New York Times'* 2012 article titled, "After Verdict, Assessing the Samsung Strategy in South Korea." This article quoted another Korean newspaper which stated that "copying and clever upgrading are no longer viable," further highlighting that "Samsung must reinvent itself as a first-mover, if it hopes to beat the competition despite the huge risks involved in acting as a pioneer" (Choe 2012).

However, one must carefully consider whether it is always best to invent new products. A careful review of history shows that being the first mover may not always be the best strategy in all contexts. To be clear, this is not to say that firms should avoid innovation and opportunities to become the first mover. However, the fact that firms sometimes gain more competitiveness through effective benchmarking instead of innovation should not be understated (Moon 2010b). Also, there is a high probability for first movers to encounter high costs and uncertainty in developing new technologies, and this is why being the first mover may not always be the best strategy for all types of firms and industries.

In an efficient market system with fluid technology transfer, it is often cheaper to adopt existing technologies than to develop them independently. At the industry level, when a competitive firm develops a technology and transfers it to followers, the total amount of investment made by these firms will be less than the total investment made by each firm that tries to develop its own technology. This raises the efficiency in resource allocation for the industry as a whole. Also, from the firm's perspective, attaining existing resources and technologies in the market is generally more efficient than developing everything internally. Logical business behavior involves reducing costs and risks as much as possible, and this is why firms often need and prefer benchmarking incumbent technologies and utilizing existing resources.

However, benchmarking encompasses more than simply learning or imitating—it is not synonymous with being a "copycat." The public tends to praise and appreciate revolutionary innovations and changes but disregards the efforts of countless players who implement incremental changes. Many do not even consider such minor improvements as a strategy (Porter 1996). Yet, these incremental improvements are what drive market and industry development on many occasions. Groundbreaking innovations do not occur frequently. Therefore, benchmarking becomes much more important as firms need to constantly learn from others to deal with rapidly changing business environments.

Going back to the Apple–Samsung lawsuit, should Samsung continue its imitation strategy despite its loss to Apple in the US courts? The answer is both yes and no. For a new product to be widely accepted, there must be an incremental improvement ("alpha") that represents a meaningful contribution to the market. Some media praised Samsung's benchmarking strategy and described Samsung as a company that provided a better product beyond imitating other companies. When the jury compared the products of Samsung and Apple, they acknowledged Samsung's addition of "alpha" to Apple's product (i.e., Samsung's product = Apple's product + alpha). However, they judged the "alpha" to be negligible and did not find significant distinctions between Samsung and Apple's smartphone models. Of course, social and political factors may have affected the decision, but only endogenous variables directly related to this case will be considered here.

4.2.1 Learning

One can either learn from past experiences or by observing others. When comparing the two options, the former may require a lot of trials and errors, and often times, the latter can serve as a shortcut to learning advanced knowledge, which is often referred to as imitation. The word "imitation" is frequently used by foreigners when describing Korea, but what they are actually referring to is "counterfeiting." Imitation and counterfeiting may seem similar but are quite different. A counterfeit does not replicate the original product but only forges its external appearance. For example, a counterfeiter may be able to mimic the design of a Chanel purse, but he (she) is unable to replicate Chanel's exquisite production process.

This example illustrates the idea that a unique and exquisite quality of an authentic product cannot be reproduced or superseded by a counterfeit. Korea was once infamous for its mass production of counterfeit products, and it was accordingly viewed as a country with low protection of intellectual property rights (IPR). Counterfeiting involves the embezzlement of technologies, designs, or unique ideas and is a violation of IPR regulations, which should be treated as a criminal act. Therefore, a well-regulated society will eliminate the presence of counterfeit products.

Imitation, on the other hand, is different from counterfeiting and has played an important role in human advancement over time. While counterfeiting only involves mimicking the surface features, imitation refers to emulating all features and aspects of a product. Some of the greatest figures in history attribute their success to imitation, which is in essence, learning. The renowned artist Pablo Picasso once said, "Good artists copy, great artists steal." This catchy phrase was reiterated by Steve Jobs who proudly proclaimed, "We have always been shameless about stealing great ideas." An interesting fact is that these two great creative minds picked up their ideas from the British poet T. S. Elliot, who once said, "Immature poets imitate; mature poets steal." Henry Ford also once said, "I invented nothing new. I simply assembled the discoveries of other men," when talking about his successful automotive business. In the end, all of these thoughts can be traced back to Isaac Newton's famous quote, "If I have seen further, it is by standing on the shoulders of giants."

It is worth mentioning that although Apple sued Samsung in 2012, Apple has a history with Microsoft over a similar issue. In 1994, Steve Jobs invited Bill Gates to his conference room to resolve a conflict over design theft. As expected, he angrily accused Bill Gates of deceit and malpractice. After Steve Jobs's rant, Bill Gates simply replied in his usual husky voice, "Well, Steve, I think there's more than one way of looking at it. I think it's more like we both had this rich neighbor named Xerox and I broke into his house to steal the TV set only to find that you had already stolen it." Bill Gates's allegory is fairly accurate as Microsoft copied the graphic functions of Apple's computers, which was based on Xerox's original graphics. To the foundation provided by Xerox, Apple and Microsoft added their respective unique functions and launched the Macintosh and Windows operating system (OS), respectively. Microsoft eventually went on to bundle its OS with Internet Explorer and the Office suite. Thereafter, Microsoft's strategy emerged as the best practice in the field that set the global standard.

Why do these great people and companies imitate others? The answer is simple—when a person, company, or nation tries to rise from scratch, there are many barriers, costs, and risks. They generally lack the capacity, human resources, and information to make good decisions. In the initial stages of development, it is extremely difficult to control related fields and construct successful long-term strategies. In this precarious situation, learning by imitating others is the most efficient way to grow. In the case of Korea, the government and businesses neither had the experience nor infrastructure to independently develop after the war. Domestic capacity was extremely frail and lacking. As a solution, Korea learned from the experiences of Japan, which had undergone radical changes during its shift to capitalism and democracy. Also, since Korea did not know which products would sell in markets, imitating the products of global leading companies was certainly a logical step. Korea did not possess the capital or advanced technology to develop multiple competitive sectors at once. As a result, the Korean government had to select and concentrate on a few strategic industries and firms to implement the industrial development plans. This led to the rise of *chaebol*, which demonstrated top performance and increased the nation's wealth.

Chaebol, on the other hand, had to quickly master advanced technology, render mass production, and increase sales in order to reinvest in other areas. The easiest and most effective way to do this was through imitation, or more precisely, learning from other successful companies. Samsung benchmarked Apple in the smartphone industry and imitated Japanese electronics firms such as Sharp and eventually outgrew the Japanese companies that used to license their technology to Samsung and train its employees. Hyundai Motor grew by learning Ford's models and manufacturing system while studying the operation systems and engine technologies of Mitsubishi before rising as the fifth largest automaker in the world (Statista 2015).

Following Korea and other Asian NIEs, Vietnam emerged as one of the fastest growing economies in the world. However, many still worry about Vietnam's economic instability. Similar to Korea in the 1960s, the Vietnamese government gave huge loans to public companies to facilitate business diversification. To this end, Vietnamese companies expanded their businesses by imitating the diversification strategy of the Korean chaebol, but are now experiencing huge financial risks. Unfortunately, the Vietnamese companies failed to accurately learn the Korean chaebol's strategies and ended up being simple followers. If the Vietnamese companies had thoroughly studied the positive and negative experiences of the Korean chaebol and properly learned their strategies, they would have experienced much less financial difficulties.

One way to analyze learning at the national level is to look at the level of imported technologies. In 2011, Korea's technology imports amounted to $9.9 billion, ranking tenth among OECD countries. This was approximately one-seventh of the United States' and one-fifth of Germany's. On the other hand, Korea's technology exports amounted to $4 billion, indicating a technology trade deficit against other advanced countries that had high technological capacities. However, as shown in table 4.1, countries with high rankings in technology exports also had a high ranking in technology imports. This implies that advanced countries that produce high levels of technology also utilize technologies developed in other countries instead of developing all technologies internally.

There is a similar pattern when looking at Korea's technology trade at the industry level. Industries that have the highest technology exports (i.e., electronics, machinery, and information and communication) also have the most imports (see table 4.2). This shows how industries attempt to develop core technologies while simultaneously importing additional external technologies. Going back to the earlier example, Korean companies stand apart from Vietnamese companies because companies such as Samsung and Hyundai did not blindly follow the industry leaders such as Apple, Sony, Mitsubishi, and Toyota. Samsung and Hyundai did not merely import technologies from

Table 4.1 TECHNOLOGY EXPORTS AND IMPORTS BY MAJOR OECD COUNTRIES (2012) (UNIT: BILLION $)

Rank	Country	Export	Rank	Country	Import
1	United States	113.06	1	United States	77.29
2	Germany	61.11	2	Germany	53.08
3	United Kingdom	49.17	3	Ireland	44.58
4	Ireland	40.88	4	Netherlands	29.43
5	Netherlands	39.99	5	United Kingdom	27.22
6	Japan	29.89	6	Switzerland	24.40
7	Switzerland	21.09	7	Italy	18.50
8	Sweden	20.92	8	Sweden	11.55
9	Italy	13.78	9	Belgium	10.54
10	Belgium	12.61	10	Korea	9.90
11	Finland	10.75	11	Spain	9.02
12	Spain	9.87	12	Australia	8.58
13	Israel	9.45	13	Finland	8.01
...	...	...	14	Denmark	7.13
19	Korea	4.03	15	Poland	6.04

Source: Ministry of Science, ICT, and Future Planning of Korea (2013).

Table 4.2 KOREA'S TECHNOLOGY EXPORTS AND IMPORTS BY INDUSTRY (2012) (UNIT: MILLION $)

	Export		Import	
Industry	Value	%	Value	%
Electric and electronics	2,029.3	38.2	6,496.2	58.8
Machinery	1,029.5	19.4	1,249.9	11.3
Information and communication	957.5	18.0	1,180.7	10.7
Construction	947.2	17.8	366.8	3.3
Chemistry	104.7	2.0	485.8	4.4
Materials	12.9	0.2	227.4	2.1
Forestry and fishery	111.1	2.1	117.3	1.1
Textile	4.9	0.1	93.1	0.8
Others	113.7	2.1	834.8	7.6
Total	5,310.8	100.0	11,052.0	100.0

Source: Ministry of Science, ICT, and Future Planning of Korea (2013).

abroad, but further improved them before exporting the final products embodied with enhanced technologies. This incrementally added value is what allowed Korean companies to surpass incumbent leaders and become leading players in their respective industries. The next important step for the companies of Vietnam and other developing countries is to learn how Korean companies (or Korea in general) were more than copycats. For this, a good understanding of best practices must take place.

4.2.2 Best Practice

The reason companies such as Microsoft, Samsung, and Hyundai are not deemed as "copycats" is because they produced their own set of best practices. In other words, while these companies initially copied others, they also incrementally added their own unique elements to the existing best practices. This is what I call the "benchmarking + alpha" strategy (Moon 2010b). A counterfeit can never surpass the authentic product. However, a well-imitated product with unique quality improvements can eventually transcend the original benchmark. By 2013, Korea ranked sixth in terms of the number of patents granted by the US Patent and Trademark Office over the past 50 years, which is well ahead of other advanced countries (Statistics from US Patent and Trademark Office). This shows that Korean companies generated a large amount of technology advancements and innovation after going through their learning phase.

Samsung has invested heavily in the semiconductor business since 1987. Ever since, the company has experienced significant milestones, including the development of the world's first 64MB DRAM in 1992 and the global top production of flash memory in 2003. Samsung has surpassed the majority of its Japanese and American rivals in technology and market share, and is a close number two just next to Intel in semiconductor production today. According to the Semiconductor Value Chain Service by IHS, Samsung Electronics was expected to earn approximately 10% of total global semiconductor revenue (*IHS Technology* 2014).

Until the early 1990s, Hyundai had used Mitsubishi's engines in its cars. This is because Mitsubishi offered a 50% reduction in royalty fees if Hyundai shut down its research program to develop its own engine in the mid-1980s. Although Hyundai was initially attracted by this offer, the company's executives ultimately concluded that Hyundai should have its own engine. Over the next few years, Hyundai developed a series of engines—the Beta (1995), Upsilon (1997), Delta (1998), and Omega (1999), establishing its own line-up of engines for passenger cars. In 2001, Hyundai revealed the Beta 2 engine, which was used for the new Avante and Tuscani car models. Upon acquiring Kia Motors, Hyundai exclusively developed the Theta engine (2004) for medium-sized passenger cars. After 13 years of development efforts, Hyundai now exports engines to its earlier licensor, Mitsubishi.

In addition, Hyundai formed the Global Engine Alliance with Chrysler and Mitsubishi in 2002 and received royalty fees. With this venture, Hyundai developed the Theta engine, which was declared as one of Ward's 10 Best Engines in October 2005. Hyundai's Tau engine for large vehicles also made the list for three consecutive years, which was later joined by the Gamma GDi engine in 2011 (*Chosun Daily* 2012). Although Hyundai started off by importing engines, it continuously worked on improving its own product to be competitive with the global standard. By doing so, Hyundai was eventually able to establish a new global standard.

In the Olympic sports of archery and *Taekwondo*, Korea currently maintains the best practice, which is why foreign teams recruit Korean coaches. Many people say that Koreans excel in archery because they are the descendants of the *Dong-yi* tribe, who were known for their mastery of the bow and arrow. Whether this statement is true or not, the Korean archery team has continued to rank among the world's best. They had a successful showing in the 2012 London Olympics, winning numerous individual and team medals and rebutting *USA Today*'s prediction that the Korean national team would not win many medals because other countries also had Korean coaches (Kang 2012).

However, Korea no longer claims the top individual rankings in archery. The top male and female archers in the world are Brady Ellison of the United States and Deepika Kumari of India. Both of these archers were mentored by Korean coaches who introduced them to Korea's unique training methods. Ellison and Kumari successfully adapted to Korea's global-standard training methods and added their own individual skills to exceed the level of Korean players. In other words, after benchmarking the skill of Korean players, they superseded Koreans by improving the benchmarked skills with their own unique strengths.

It is nice to say, "Become a leader or a pioneer by facing challenges, taking risks, and being innovative." However, in the world of business, this motto is neither practical nor meaningful. If the current environment is ignored and only new things are pursued, there will be grave risks. This is why only a modicum of ventures succeed despite numerous attempts. Three-quarters of American start-ups do not return investors' capital; one-third lose all their money, and more than 95% fail to see the projected return on investment (Gage 2012). Even Microsoft, a large and competitive company, faced serious problems during its transition from Vista to XP. Much of it was due to its unawareness of existing products and excessive focus on becoming unique. The reason we teach history is not to depreciate the value of innovation, but to show that history, particularly the best historical practices, can serve as the basis of new creations. Before attempting to create something new, we need to first fully understand the fundamental wisdom from existing achievements. In essence, the core message of benchmarking is to adhere to the three I's: imitate (learn), improve, and innovate.

4.3 CONVERGENCE: MIXING SYNERGISTICALLY FOR CREATING NEW VALUE

Among many methods, exploiting and combining existing resources in a synergistic way is an efficient and less costly solution, which leads to the next key factor in Korea's economic success—"convergence." This is well illustrated by the famous Korean dish *bibimbap* (meaning "mixed rice"). Interestingly, one of the unique features of Korean cuisine is mixing—Koreans tend to love food that mixes diverse ingredients such as soup and Korean-style chowder. Among numerous Korean dishes, the most widely known is probably bibimbap, which is a good example for the next key factor—convergence.

As a dish that combines vegetables, meat, rice, and pepper paste, bibimbap is a perfect example of mixing to create synergies. Bibimbap is more than just a mixture of ingredients; there is additional value created from the synergies among the various ingredients. Bibimbap is popular because it allows people who dislike vegetables to consume them in a better tasting way. In this manner, bibimbap creates a synergistic effect for both taste and nutrition. Simply put, the competitiveness of bibimbap as a food item can be analyzed as follows. First, bibimbap includes many important nutritional ingredients such as rice, vegetables, and meat, so one can consume them in one dish simultaneously. Second, there is a wide range of tastes that can be created depending on the ingredients of choice, thereby increasing the diversity of choices. Third, the preparation and consumption of bibimbap is quick and efficient, served as a healthy alternative to fast food. As long as proper ingredients are used to avoid bad combinations that worsen the taste or nutrition, bibimbap is an excellent example of convergence.

In a business context, the holistic strategy can be applied to how firms diversify their products, portfolios, or businesses. Just as a good combination of certain ingredients is tastier and healthier, firms can become more competitive and profitable from the ideal business portfolio mix. Therefore, successful "convergence" strategy needs two elements, "mixing" and "synergy creation." *Mixing* allows the firm to exploit the advantages of various resources simultaneously, and *synergy creation* allows the firm to create additional value using the simple collection of separate components. Each one will then be discussed in more detail below.

4.3.1 Mixing

In recent years, conglomerates such as Samsung and LG located their design centers in big cities such as Milan, London, Paris, and New York to foster innovations in design and technology development. However, these centers were not built to only conduct design activities but to research the tastes and needs of the sophisticated consumers in the global market. Some Koreans argue that "unique, Korean-style products will be most successful in the world," reflecting their dedication to maintaining Korea's original values. However, this statement only pertains to things where Korea sets best practices or global standards, such as Taekwondo. If businesses only focus on adhering to Korean consumers, products risk rejection from foreign consumers. Therefore, we need to address both Korean and global tastes in order to outperform competitors (Moon 2005b).

The viral spread of *Hallyu* (K-pop in particular) is the fruit of the combination of Korean and global tastes. In the *New York Times*, an article titled "Bringing K-pop to the West" described K-pop as a fusion of synthetic music, visual art, flashy outfits, and voluptuous beauty added to purity (Choe and Russell 2012). The article also noted the frequent use of both Korean and English lyrics as a strategy to create melodies and choruses that are easy to remember. Also, the choreographies of these songs were designed with easy-to-follow and addictive motions, which attracted fans from all ages and cultures.

In addition to K-pop, the mixing strategy of bibimbap is apparent in Korea's national economic development process. Some scholars (Kuznets 1988; Amsden 1991; Amsden and Hikino 1994) argued that Korea's economic growth was possible due to direct government intervention and anti-market policies. Strangely enough, the World Bank (1993) and Ito and Krueger (1995) contended the opposite, stating that pro-market policies from the government spurred Korea's growth. The reason for these contradictory views is that scholars only focused on one aspect of development instead of employing a multi-spectrum analysis. It would be most accurate to say that Korea utilized a mix of various policies under the goal of fast industrialization. The government did regulate the economy in some ways, but pro-market policies and market autonomy were also granted when they seemed more effective. The government took on multiple and simultaneous positions by mixing the two disparate economic policies to find the most effective solution.

In developing countries, markets are often inefficient or dysfunctional; in this sense, the diversification of Korean companies is a remarkable case. Korean companies entered diverse markets, as long as they had potential for high profits during the early stages. A good example of this is Samsung's entry into the sugar, textile, semiconductors, and electronics industries. One reason Korean companies diversified into various industries is that demand greatly exceeded supply at the initial stage of economic development. Consumers from countries in early development rarely seek high-quality products with premium prices; they look for basic products that can fulfill their immediate needs for survival. Back in the 1960s, it was apparent that Korean firms should maximize their profits from these sources rather than focus solely on a single business. Although unrelated, these businesses were virtually profitable on a standalone basis.

Another reason is that Korean companies lacked capital during the developmental stage. Earlier studies (e.g., Teece 1983) rationalized the diversification strategy as a way to utilize excessive capital, but Korean companies had to engage in unrelated diversification to accumulate capital in the first place. Samsung, for example, gathered profits from the production of sugar and apparel and reinvested them into other industries such as electronics. Table 4.3 illustrates the shift in diversification of Samsung's business activities from the 1960s to 2012. In the 1970s, food and textiles accounted for over 50% of total sales. However, by 1987 this percentage dropped to approximately 8% as Samsung diversified into high-tech businesses such as semiconductors and telecommunications. With the breakup of Samsung due to the restructuring process following the 1997 Asian Financial Crisis, Samsung was reorganized to increase synergies among related sectors. In 2012, the majority of sales (almost 60%) were concentrated in electronics, effectively reversing the trend of previous decades in unrelated diversification.

It is important to note that although businesses were often unrelated at the initial stages, Korean companies focused on interweaving their business structure through cross-investment. Korean firms in preliminary stages tended to dive into unrelated industries due to a lack of capital, unsophisticated market demand conditions, and insufficient related industries domestically. However, as firms grew and the Korean economy improved over time, they began to focus more on synergy creation through related-industry diversification. This is because it becomes less likely for mature firms to create significant synergies and earn large profits across unrelated industries. Whether unrelated or related, synergy creation is necessary for firms to maintain sustainable growth and profitability.

4.3.2 Synergy Creation

Does mixing always lead to good performance? Children sometimes put toys in their food. I once saw a child making bibimbap by pouring milk into a bowl of rice and adding cereal, *kimchi*, and chocolate syrup. You can imagine how any parent would react in this case—the child was promptly stopped from eating his style of bibimbap. Although this is an extreme example for an illustrative purpose, it shows us the importance of harmony and balance when mixing different ingredients.

Businesses utilize mixing strategies in the form of related and unrelated industry diversification. Mixing diverse industries that do not create synergies resembles the undesirable bibimbap in the previous example, where there is no harmony among the ingredients. Industry diversification with high synergy creation, on the other hand, is more akin to the

Table 4.3 COMPOSITION OF SALES OF SAMSUNG GROUP

1965		1976		1987		1998		2012	
Food	48.0%	Textiles	28.0%	Wholesale and retail trade	35.0%	Wholesale and retail trade	35.0%	Electronics	58.1%
Textiles	40.0%	Food	25.0%	Finance (insurance)	30.2%	Finance (insurance)	24.4%	Finance	15.4%
Insurance	12.0%	Home appliance	24.0%	Home appliance	18.3%	Home appliance	19.9%	Wholesale and trade	5.8%
		Insurance	18.0%	Food and leisure	4.4%	Vehicles	6.3%	Chemical products	5.5%
		Paper	3.0%	Textile	3.7%	Semiconductor	6.0%	Transportation equipment	4.7%
		Construction	1.0%	Vehicles	3.3%	Textile	3.5%	Construction and technology	2.9%
				Construction	2.4%	Other services	1.6%	System integration and management	1.5%
				Semiconductor	0.8%	Food and leisure	1.1%	Retails	1.3%
				Paper	0.5%	Telecommunications	1.0%	Others	4.8%
				Machinery, iron, and steel	0.1%	Minerals	1.0%		
				Nonmetallic minerals	0.1%	Machinery, iron, and steel	0.4%		
				Telecommunications	0.1%	Paper	0.3%		
				Other services	0.1%				

Source: Chang (2003a) for 1965, 1976, 1987 and 1998 data. The data for 2012 are from Lee (2013).

ideal, tasty bibimbap that combines ingredients to synergize nutrition and taste.

From the early to intermediate phases of economic development, Korean companies engaged in a diversification strategy that created synergies from unrelated mixing. Korean-style diversification was judged as unrelated and unfair, with conglomerates manipulating the market with their enormous size and power and the "octopus-leg" type of diversification. However, when chaebol's diversification strategy is examined by looking at their resource utility, the level of synergies created from unrelated diversification was significant. The reclamation work at Seosan via the "Chung Ju-yung Way" highlights the synergy created from a diversified business portfolio. Also, Samsung's ability to overcome the recent global recession rested largely on its (unrelated as well as related) diversified businesses as they mutually supported each other. When one business was in trouble, the profits from another business compensated for its loss and vice versa. This, in fact, is the power of a well-designed business portfolio.

On the other hand, when there is improper mixing of a business portfolio, a company is most likely to face many obstacles. For instance, Sony failed in its venture into the software industry, which represented a bad combination of ingredients. Samsung Electronics and Sony were once firms that both focused on manufacturing hardware devices, but when Sony jumped into the music, movie, and video game industries, the two headed down different paths. Sony's new business plan led to financial trouble, while Samsung continued to thrive.

Let's look at some statistics on Samsung and Sony's business portfolio. In 2001, Sony had a similar business composition to Samsung, with electronics comprising the largest share of total company sales (68%) and operating income (85%) (Sony 2001). By 2013, the majority of sales had moved to the mobile phones and home entertainment divisions, but the operating income of these two segments was negative (Sony 2013). This implies that Sony's expansion into these new businesses resulted in negative synergies, thereby decreasing its competitive advantage. In contrast, Samsung Electronics' IT and mobile phones accounted for a significant portion of the 2012 sales at 49%, and they also comprised the largest share of total operating profit at 67% (Samsung Electronics 2013). Unlike Sony, Samsung's convergence across business sectors created positive synergies and profitable growth.

There are also cases of Korean firms failing due to poor diversification. A large Korean confectionery company, entered the construction industry in 1990 but this business division went bankrupt after experiencing a huge deficit in 1999. Making sweets and constructing buildings are clearly different and these two businesses lacked any shared resources or capabilities. When entering another industry, the potential for synergy creation among different fields is a critical factor to consider. Effective convergence through mixing and synergy creation is a vital driving force for competitiveness.

4.4 DEDICATION: DILIGENCE WITH GOAL ORIENTATION FOR A STRONG COMMITMENT

On July 7, 2012, a Korean newspaper covered an interesting story about an American CEO who had lived in Korea for 22 years. Titled "Diligence and Hard Work Are Embedded in Koreans' DNA," the article wittily compared the lifestyle and mentality of Americans and Koreans (*Dong-A Ilbo* 2012). The article began by praising Koreans for their diligence. According to the author, this defining Korean trait helped his company's Seoul office to create various security solutions and export them back to its American headquarters as well as other regional offices in more advanced markets. Also, the article narrated heroic tales of how the Korean government built the 1988 Olympic stadium from a sand field, quickly escaped the IMF crisis with a nationwide gold donation campaign, and successfully secured its bid for the 2018 Pyeongchang Winter Olympics.

The author's conviction of Koreans' diligence was strengthened during his recent visit to the United States. Although Americans worried about its stagnant economy, they did not seem to show due diligence and action. To illustrate this point, he recounted a trip to the Department of Motor Vehicles to renew his license. Although it was only four o'clock in the afternoon, many of the staff had already left for the day. What was worse, the manager on duty was on vacation, and the office asked him to come back the following week. In stark contrast to the United States, there are a multitude of 24-hour services in Korea that offer assistance regardless of time and place. Overall, the article highlights these distinctions between Korea and other countries and clearly depicts the role of diligence in Korea's economic development.

When the sources of economic development and firm competitiveness are observed, the focus tends to be on nonorganic resources such as technology. Technology undoubtedly plays a big role in the growth of firms and industries. Yet, what is more important is the productivity of the people who produce, exchange, and manage these technologies and resources. At the firm level, managers are the ones who decide which resources should be developed and where they are invested. Indeed, productivity continues to be closely tied to people despite the growth of automated manufacturing systems and advanced technologies, and for service-related industries, this becomes even more apparent. Studies of organizational behavior often tie employees' performance to their motivation, and to this end scholars have explored methods for motivating employees to work hard and be creative. In the same light, diligence and goal orientation of people are the two conditions that are crucial for growth.

4.4.1 Diligence

Many considered Jewish people as the most successful immigrants in the United States. Jews are generally considered highly diligent and hard-working, and this can be proven by their accumulation of wealth and influence across the world. Although their diligence was extraordinary and contributive, the Jews met their match when Koreans began to settle in the United States. When Jewish people first immigrated to the United States, they quickly found success in the grocery store business. They established a reputation for delivering fresh vegetables and quality products to customers. However, as Korean immigrants followed, they opened similar grocery stores, and posed threats to the Jewish owners. In addition to establishing stores in the same vicinity, Koreans opened their stores 30 minutes earlier than their Jewish counterparts. In response, Jewish owners began opening their shops an hour before the Koreans. This continued to escalate until the Korean owners began to open for 24 hours, forcing many Jewish shops to close.

The diligence characterized in the example above can be further highlighted by Korea's ascension into the OECD in the mid-1990s despite being one of the world's poorest countries only 30 years before. The average annual growth rate of Korea since the start of its development in the 1970s was approximately 7% (Bank of Korea 2015). Economies such as Taiwan, Singapore, and Hong Kong also experienced similar economic success, but the sizes of their economies were much smaller than that of Korea. Among countries with populations over 50 million, Korea's rapid growth stands alone.

According to World Bank (i.e., World Development Indicators) statistics, Korea's GDP per capita in 1961 was less than $100. In the same period, Ghana's was $190 and Argentina's $1,148.[4] In 2014, Korea's GDP per capita was $27,970 while Ghana's was $1,443 and Argentina's $12,569. Korea is currently aiming to reach a GDP per capita of $40,000 in the near future. Argentina started off as the fifth largest economy at the beginning of the twentieth century but eventually collapsed due to political strife and turmoil. Korea's economic growth, however, managed to survive despite political instability and economic crises.

Much of Korea's success is attributed to its people's diligence. According to OECD statistics, Korea has the second longest annual working hours among the OECD member countries, with Koreans working 366 hours more than the OECD average (see table 4.4). Although Korea is second to Mexico in terms of working hours, there are other statistics that tell a different story. For example, the OECD data includes paid vacation and legal holidays of which Mexico had 44 days while Korea only had 26, about 60% that of Mexico. This difference impacts the overall working hours due to different national policies and definitions. Other reasons include cultural and societal differences. For example, lunch breaks are much longer in Mexico than most other countries (including Korea), ranging from one hour for normal workers to three hours for executives. Third is the hidden cost of inefficiency. There are many obstacles to efficient work. For example, it takes weeks to open a checking account, and hours to wait for callers to Mexico's cellphone carriers (Booth 2011). Therefore, the actual hours of work in Korea would be more than Mexico when taking these considerations into account.

Korean's tremendous effort to recover from the 1997 Asian Financial Crisis received much attention from the Western press. The *Economist* in

Table 4.4 ANNUAL WORKING HOURS PER WORKER OF OECD COUNTRIES (2013)

Country	Hours	Country	Hours	Country	Hours
Mexico	2,237	Czech Rep.	1,772	Luxembourg	1,643
Korea	2,136	Slovak Rep.	1,770	Austria	1,623
Greece	2,037	New Zealand	1,760	Sweden	1,607
Chile	2,015	Italy	1,752	Switzerland	1,585
Russia	1,980	Japan	1,735	Belgium	1,570
Poland	1,918	Portugal	1,712	Slovenia	1,547
Hungary	1,883	Canada	1,706	France	1,489
Estonia	1,868	Iceland	1,704	Denmark	1,411
Israel	1,867	Australia	1,676	Norway	1,408
Turkey	1,832	United Kingdom	1,669	Germany	1,388
Ireland	1,815	Finland	1,666	Netherlands	1,380
United States	1,788	Spain	1,665	Average	1,770

Source: OECD (2013a).

an article published on July 4, 2007, titled "Ten Years On," introduced how Asian countries responded differently to the economic crisis. According to the article, Korea was the most diligent in implementing economic and financial reforms. It also added that Korea now holds the healthiest and most stable financial system in Asia. This evaluation was largely supported in late 2007, when Korea was less affected by the global financial crisis and recovered quickly compared to other countries. As these experiences show, diligence is deeply rooted in Koreans and acts as a vital force for sustainable growth in the economy.

4.4.2 Goal Orientation

Laziness cannot benefit an individual or a country; people consider commitment and diligence to be intrinsically positive qualities. However, when people work diligently under a tyrant or incompetent leader, the country cannot undergo positive national development. Similarly, the Japanese, who are often praised for their diligence and meticulousness, have not seen much national growth over the last couple of decades. What else, then, is needed to propel economic development?

The answer is the presence of proper goal orientation. Goal orientation is crucial as it channels people's diligence in the right direction. A good example of strong goal orientation is the motivation of Korean sports teams when they play against the country's perennial rival, Japan. According to the FIFA world rankings, Korea has usually ranked below Japan. However, in soccer matches against Japan, Korean players show a unique determination and eagerness to win. This strong goal orientation helped Korean soccer teams achieve a winning record against Japan in matches over the past 60 years.

Even scholars such as Ramírez and Rubio (2010) discussed the peculiar history and characteristics of the Korean people against Japan. According to their research that examined the cause of motivation of Koreans, they argued that every Korean's desire to defeat Japan served as the greatest driving force for Koreans. This analysis is true to some degree; however, there is a more general and important transition in the Korean society that reflects proper goal orientation. This is the *Saemaul* movement of the 1970s. Reflected in the lyrics of its theme song (refer to box 4.1), the Saemaul movement had a great impact not only on the country's physical improvement but also on shaping the mentality of the Korean society. Building new houses after destroying straw-thatched homes, building new towns through hard-work, increasing income, and making

Box 4.1: LYRICS OF THE *SAEMAUL* MOVEMENT SONG

Morning bell rang, morning has come, you and me wake up,
   let's cultivate a new village.
Break down a thatched cottage, widen the village road, make a blue hill,
   let's trim with care.
Help each other work with diligence, strive for higher income,
   let's make a rich village.
We are all together fighting and working, working and fighting,
   let's make a new country.
(Refrain) Comfortable *Saemaul*, let's make it by ourselves.

Source: Revised from KDI (2012).

the country strong and prosperous out of a devastated homeland that was war-stricken, were all initiated under nationwide efforts.

Another good example of goal orientation is the Korean Judo champion and Olympic gold medalist Kim Jae-bum. Kim faced huge disappointment when he came in second place in the 2008 Beijing Olympics. Determined that he would accept nothing less than a gold medal, Kim entered the 2012 London Olympics with a stronger mindset. Unfortunately, his physical condition in 2012 was at its worst as he received the lowest grade in Korea's national disability standard due to a dislocated shoulder and elbow.

Despite the odds against him, Kim overcame his inept physical condition to win the gold medal. After the match, he attributed the turnaround from the Beijing Games to a change in mentality. There is a Korean saying, "*Jook-Gi-Sal-Ki-Ro*" (life or death), which stresses an undying will to succeed in life. Kim described his mindset as such during the 2008 Beijing Olympics. However, in preparing for the 2012 London Olympics, he noted a newfound motto, "*Jook-Gi-Ro*" (to the death), which is a modification of the original Korean saying, implying even more determination. This may sound like mere play on words, but the subtle difference carries huge significance: both stress the importance of goal orientation, but the latter puts additional concentration on an unwavering dedication toward a specific goal.

"You can live only if you have the spirit of *to the death*" is a popular statement in Korea. This quote was perhaps most famously said by Admiral Yi Sun-shin during the Japanese invasion of Korea in 1592. During the early years of economic development in the 1960s and 1970s, Korean firms and the government also embodied this similar mindset of "to die if we fail." It was common during that time to see office buildings lit well into the night as employees worked tirelessly toward specific goals. Korea's present situation, however, is much different from 60 years ago. Now, Korea may not need to push its limits in order to survive or advance given its economic development. Nevertheless, it is still necessary for Koreans to embody a strong goal-oriented mindset to continue to reap the rewards of economic growth. Otherwise, the Korean people may experience their own version of Japan's lost decades.

4.5 THE ABCDs: A COMPREHENSIVE FRAMEWORK FOR ENHANCING COMPETITIVENESS

People refer to Korea's extraordinary success as "the Miracle on the Han River." However, if Korea's development is indeed a "miracle," then by definition there would be no insights or lessons for others to learn. When analyzing Korea's success, it is important to accurately assess the relevant factors of this seemingly miraculous phenomenon. Earlier scholars have attempted to analyze Korea's success for decades but have failed to construct a comprehensive explanation. Some Western scholars attributed Korea's success to Confucian work ethics, while others highlighted Korea's export-oriented policy.

The Brazilian magazine *Negócios* ascribed Korea's success to its speed and imitation abilities. Although these are all correct to a certain degree, they are also limited because they are only a subset of the whole picture, and making inferences based only on these factors may lead to misleading or dangerous conclusions. There are other pieces that are central to complete the entire puzzle. The hidden secrets of Korea's success are more comprehensive and interconnected than one might expect. This is the power of the ABCD model; it gives important implications to other countries due to its comprehensive and rigorous framework of analysis. Agility must be based on speed and precision. Benchmarking must be pursued through learning the best practice. Convergence is created from mixing the right resources to maximize synergies. And lastly, dedication requires diligence with a clear goal-oriented mindset.

The ABCDs of K-Strategy show how agility, benchmarking, convergence, and dedication supported and propelled Korea's economic growth. Nonetheless, if Korea wishes to develop further, each of the ABCDs must continue to be implemented and improved to a higher level. Korea moves quickly but still remains behind the precision level of some advanced countries; there are a number of Korean companies that engage in imitation without paying regard to what the best practice is; firms struggle to create synergies but often unsuccessfully synchronize unrelated and related diversification; and finally, some Koreans work diligently without proper goal orientation.

On top of its strategic implications for developing countries and firms, the ABCD model offers a message to already advanced countries and firms. Advanced countries (e.g., France) and leading firms (e.g., Sony, Nokia) can also maintain or enhance competiveness through the ABCDs, as demonstrated in this chapter. Therefore, in order to design constructive strategies to strengthen competitiveness, and reap the rewards of quick economic development, it is worthwhile to derive lessons from the Korean case. By enhancing the four factors and eight subfactors of the ABCD model and adapting them to their own environment, countries and firms can create sustainable competitiveness for years to come.

This chapter mainly aims to show the importance of the ABCDs in achieving competitiveness at both national and corporate levels based on extensive case studies. However, as a meaningful model should always be established under rigorous theoretical background, the next chapter will explain the theoretical aspects of the ABCD model to facilitate the understanding of the logic behind the model.

CHAPTER 5

The ABCD Model

Theoretical Foundation

The preceding chapter described how the four variables of the ABCD model contributed to Korea's economic success. This chapter will explain the theoretical foundation of the ABCD model. In order to show the need for a new model, chapter 5 begins with a review of important studies on Korea's economic success. Based on this literature review, the chapter continues by discussing some of the apparent problems of these studies and explains how the ABCD model can complement and advance existing studies. By reviewing the academic literature on the Korean economy at the national level and the sources of competitive advantages at the firm level, the usefulness of the ABCD model is explored and distinguished from other theories and models.

5.1 ECONOMIC PERSPECTIVES ON KOREA'S GROWTH

5.1.1 Important Studies on Korea's Success Factors

Over the last few decades, there have been numerous studies that tried to explain the rapid growth of the Korean economy. In this section, several prominent studies on this topic are highlighted to explore their explanatory variables before discussing some of the common shortfalls. The influential work of Amsden (1989) reviewed Korea's way of learning and how Korea adopted existing Western technologies rather than independently pursuing innovation. The work also emphasized the efficacy of the Korean government's interventionist policy through the optimal allocation of scarce resources. It also gave credit to large diversified business groups, the abundance of competent managers, and low-cost and well-educated labor.

On the other hand, Song (1997) attributed Korea's growth to the outward-, industry-, and growth-oriented strategy, and named this the "OIG-oriented" strategy. Song argued that Korea prioritized outward over inward looking, industry over resource or service, and growth over equity as the nation's development strategy. Another distinctive perspective was the positive influence of non-economic factors on economic growth. Song emphasized the role of the new Confucian ethics,[1] which was a combination of traditional Confucian ethics (e.g., family and collective orientation) and Western Christian ethics (e.g., pragmatism, economic goal orientation). In addition, he noted that Korea's urbanization and economic growth were propelled by proper land use, family-planning programs, private savings, and favorable consumption patterns.

Another notable study is the one conducted by the World Bank (1993), which examined the economic policies of the eight "High Performing Asian Economies." This study attributed the eight countries' superior performance to their efficient physical- and human-capital allocation measures. It also gave credit to each government's strong intervention-ist but market-friendly policies, which helped in promoting strong market competition, efficient resource allocation, and productivity growth. The study further distinguished these policies into three types—funda-mental, selective, and institutional.[2] In a similar vein, S. Cho (1994) also acknowledged that the primary source of Korea's condensed growth was due to government intervention and its seven five-year plans; however, he highlighted Korea's unbalanced growth strategy through massively sup-porting the *chaebol*.

Following this academic pursuit, Toussaint (2006) credited Korea's suc-cess to many factors, including strong state intervention and authoritar-ian planning; substantial technical and financial support from the United States; radical land reform; gradual transition from import substitution to export promotion; good education; and state control of the banking sec-tor, currency exchange, capital flows, and product prices. Whereas these studies commonly emphasized the government's role in Korea's national development, Chang (2003a) conducted a more business-focused approach by examining the internal operations of chaebol. He emphasized chaebol as the important source of Korea's rapid economic growth until the 1980s because they provided efficient ways for allocating limited resources in Korea's early and high-risk stage of economic development.

More recently, Eichengreen, Perkins, and Shin (2012) dived more deeply into Korea's development after the Asian Financial Crisis. In their book, the authors credited Korea's continued growth to the accompanying rise in the labor force, capital stock, and productivity. In another study, Mason (1997) introduced several other variables by studying the six East Asian economies including Korea. This study focused on the relationship between population and economic growth and found that the rapid decline in fertility had a significant impact on growth and living standards in the region.

5.1.2 Criticism of the Existing Studies

Each of these studies contributed to the understanding of Korea's economic growth, but their respective explanations diverged due to differing perspectives: macro versus micro, economic versus non-economic factors, and pre- versus post-1997 Asian Financial Crisis. Several of these studies even contradict the arguments of others. In particular, Amsden (1989) rejected the popular belief that Korea's economic success was due to its export-oriented trade policies and argued that Korea's success through the export-oriented policy was actually combined with other effective government intervention and support policies. In particular, the government disciplined firms by setting strict performance standards to avoid their misuse of government subsidies. Also, in direct contrast to Song (1997), Amsden stated that domestic savings were insufficient to finance necessary investments and instead cited the important role of foreign borrowing at low interest rates.

In order to provide a more comprehensive analysis that builds on these existing studies, Porter's (1990) diamond model can be applied to combine each study's logic behind Korea's rapid growth. One of the strengths of the diamond model is that it incorporates the production factors and other important factors for national competitiveness (Moon and Kim 2006a). Therefore, the diamond model can clearly capture the relevant factors addressed by existing studies. As figure 5.1 shows, previous studies on Korea's economic development have provided useful findings and insights. However, each factor only stands as a partially contributive element to the overall explanation of Korea's success.

Moreover, existing studies mainly address "what" factors led to Korea's economic growth and overlook "how" to achieve the competiveness of these "what" factors. Therefore, they examine the factors behind Korea's development but do not provide practical guidelines for countries that want to replicate Korea's success. Also, while the "what" factors can explain a country's success when it has superior factor conditions (e.g., the

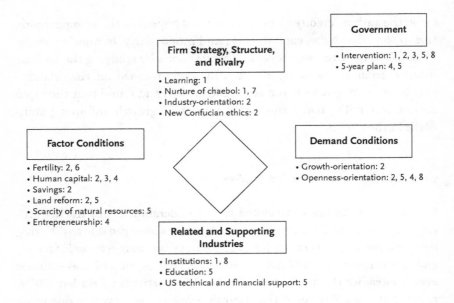

Figure 5.1
Existing Studies on the Success Factors of Korea's Growth
Note: 1: Amsden (1989); 2: Song (1997); 3: World Bank (1993); 4: S. Cho (1994); 5: Toussaint (2006); 6: Mason (1997); 7: Chang (2003a); 8: Eichengreen, Perkins, and Shin (2012).

United States has more capital and higher technology than Korea), they cannot explain the success of one country over another that possesses a similar level of factor conditions such as labor, capital, and technology (e.g., Korea and African countries had similar levels of factor conditions of cheap labor in the 1960s, but how was Korea able to grow faster?).

The aforementioned studies noted such problems, but none of them proposed new approaches to solve them. For example, S. Cho (1994) pointed out that Korea's development should be aligned with the effective use of surplus labor rather than labor itself because not all countries with a surplus labor force in the world enjoy successful economic development. In a similar vein, not all export-led growth strategies and government interventions resulted in economic progress (World Bank 1993; S. Cho 1994). Therefore, in addition to exploring what factors (e.g., technology, labor) led to Korea's economic success, understanding how these factors were implemented is also important for explaining the exceptional success of the Korean economy.

It is worth noting that the "how" approach becomes more significant as the gap in factor conditions among countries narrows. For example, the "what" approach claims that the country with the lowest labor costs will attract the most foreign investment. However, Apple established its production factory in China, although other countries such as Vietnam and Bangladesh had lower labor costs. This is because there are other process variables (e.g., work culture, motivation) influencing the labor productivity in addition to labor cost. For instance, Chinese laborers may be relatively more diligent than other developing country workers and are more willing to work overtime if necessary.

The strategic approach to competitiveness analysis requires research on both structure and process—structure refers to the "what" factors while process is the "how." To cover this, a new model that addresses process advantages is necessary as the success variables of earlier studies cannot fully explain the "how" factors. Before taking an in-depth look at the theoretical underpinnings of the ABCD model, the next section will first review the existing dominant theories on competitive advantages of firms and discuss their limitations.

5.2 BUSINESS PERSPECTIVES ON FIRMS' COMPETITIVE ADVANTAGES

Along with the studies on economic success at the national level, several theories in the field of strategic management have been developed to explain the sources of competitive advantages from either an industry or a firm perspective.[3] Toward the 1980s, one of the hottest fields of research related to economics and industry growth was corporate strategy. As the capitalist system became deeply embedded in Western society following World War II, business schools and consulting firms began to flourish. Also, as competition among firms and industries heightened, demand for superior management strategies increased, and this new wave of change gave birth to many prominent theoretical approaches and frameworks. Some of the most widely accepted theories within the field of strategic management of firms in the modern era are the industry-structure view, resource-based view, dynamic-capabilities view, and institution-based view.

5.2.1 The Industry-Structure View

The industry-structure view (ISV) is rooted in the traditional Bain or Mason industrial organization (IO) model which argues that the industry structure determines the behavior of firms and thus their performance (Hill and Deeds 1996). The traditional IO theorists emphasized the determinant role of environmental factors on corporate performance under the assumption that the firm is influenced the most by the structure of the industry, which is difficult to change. This approach was well-accepted for its pragmatic usefulness and gave birth to the widespread use of modeling techniques for business strategy. A good example is Porter's (1980) five forces model,[4] which was invented to analyze industry structure. According to this model, the five forces are interdependent, and they collectively determine the overall attractiveness or profitability of an industry. Therefore, an increase in threats from the five forces makes the industry less attractive.

However, the ISV soon encountered academic criticism that it fails to address more specific agendas when firms implement strategy. The main criticism is that the ISV is based on the assumption that firms within an industry are identical in terms of resources for implementing strategies. In other words, the ISV does not explain why firms decide to position themselves differently from other players in the same industry. This question is critical in understanding business behavior because there must be sound logic for firms to position themselves differently. In fact, this question led to a theoretical investigation into resources that are firm-specific, which would explain differences in levels of firm performance.

5.2.2 The Resource-Based View

Complementing the ISV, which emerged as an analysis focusing on industries, the resource-based view (RBV) of the firm shifted its focus to the firm's internal factors. The RBV became a popular theory of competitive advantage in the 1990s. Although its theoretical heritage goes further back to the ideas of Coase (1937) and Selznick (1957), it was Penrose (1959) who first developed the preliminary idea of the RBV. Barney (1986) advanced this idea by giving it the name of resource-based theory, which gained further prominence with Prahalad and Hamel (1990). In contrast to the ISV, the RBV emphasizes the determinant role of firms' internal resources on overall performance. Specifically, it argues that firms with key resources will be more likely to have sustainable competitive advantages, which would allow firms to earn above-average returns.

According to this view, firms' resources are the most crucial elements that determine sustainability, and they are defined as capabilities, organizational processes, information, knowledge, and other attributes that enable firms to implement strategies for building or creating new competitive advantages (Daft 1983). However, not all resources are equally important and able to be translated into firms' competitive advantages. Barney (1991) suggested that the resources which satisfy four conditions— valuable, rare, inimitable, and not substitutable (the VRIN), will contribute to achieving and sustaining the competitive advantage of firms.

Later, scholars (e.g., Peteraf 1993; Henderson and Cockburn 1994; Priem and Butler 2001) argued against Barney's interpretation, claiming that resources alone are not sufficient to achieve a competitive advantage but should be combined with firms' capabilities to exploit, leverage, or manage. Also, even though acquiring resources is still a critical factor for firms, the IT revolution transformed the nature of business by allowing easier and more frequent transfer of resources. Thus, coupled with the wave of knowledge-resources, a growing number of firms now engage in alliances for resource sharing. Today, the RBV is considered too static to explain the volatile nature of businesses.

5.2.3 The Dynamic-Capabilities View

The RBV is useful for explaining inter-firm heterogeneity at a specific point in time, but it lacks a clear conceptual model to describe the mechanism of how this heterogeneity arises (Helfat and Peteraf 2003). Also, because it only statically looks at firm resources, it is not sufficient to explain how firms can achieve and sustain competitive advantages in a rapidly changing environment (Teece, Pisano, and Shuen 1997; Eisenhardt and Martin 2000; Teece 2007). To tackle this problem, Teece, Pisano, and Shuen (1997) introduced a new approach called the dynamic-capabilities view (DCV) as an extension of the RBV.

Unlike resources, dynamic capabilities are organizational processes embedded within the firm. Thus, they can only be built internally by the firm and cannot be bought or sold in the market (Makadok 2001). Yet, dynamic capabilities are different from operational capabilities, which allow the firm to make a living in the present and maintain the status quo; dynamic capabilities build, integrate, or reconfigure operational capabilities in order to address the changing environment (Helfat and Peteraf 2003; Winter 2003; Helfat and Winter 2011). Zollo and Winter (2002) addressed the question of how to build dynamic capabilities and suggested that dynamic capabilities are generated and evolved through three learning mechanisms (i.e., experience accumulation, knowledge articulation, and knowledge codification). This implies that dynamic capabilities are path-dependent processes, relying on existing experiences and resource stock.

For the last decade, there have been numerous articles published about the DCV, yet studies show differing and contradictory views. These differences even extend to fundamental issues, such as whether dynamic capabilities are helpful in achieving sustainable advantages (Winter 2003; Peteraf, Stefano, and Verona 2013). While scholars such as Teece argued that dynamic capabilities are a source of sustained competitive advantage, other scholars presented different opinions. For instance, Eisenhardt and Martin (2000) argued that dynamic capabilities might be helpful in achieving a competitive advantage but they are not sustainable. This is because in a high-velocity market, dynamic capabilities are unstable, and thus the duration of any competitive advantage they provide may be unpredictable.[5] Therefore, the debate calls for further efforts to extend the DCV and clarify the conditions under which a firm can sustain its competitive advantage through dynamic capabilities.

5.2.4 The Institution-Based View

Although the aforementioned theories remain highly influential to this day, they were also criticized for ignoring the role of institutions on firms' strategy formulation. This problem arose because the dominant theories are based on studies of advanced countries such as the United States that have relatively stable and market-based institutions (Peng, Wang, and Jiang 2008). However, in emerging economies, government and societal institutions are much stronger and more influential on shaping firm competitiveness (Hoskisson et al. 2000).

The institution refers to both formal and informal constraints. Formal constraints include political rules, judicial decisions, and economic contracts, while informal ones include social culture and ideology (Peng 2002). The most fundamental role of institutions is to reduce uncertainty and provide a stable structure that facilitates interactions (Peng 2006; Scott 2008). Therefore, in developing countries, good relationships with the government could help firms obtain strategic resources, thereby ensuring superior performance (e.g., chaebol development in Korea in the 1960s and 1970s).

In advanced countries, the five forces comprising the competitive structure shape the "rules of the game." However, in emerging countries, institutions significantly affect the shape of a firm's strategy and vision. Therefore, existing theories are more appropriate to explain the competitive advantages of firms in advanced countries, not developing ones. For this reason, the institution-based view (IBV) incorporated the influences of institutions on a firm's process and decision-making. This perspective has attracted attention from scholars since the 1990s and was popularized by Peng (2006). It is viewed as another important theory in the field of strategic management (Peng et al. 2009).

5.2.5 Limitations of Existing Theories and a Need for a New Framework

The ISV and RBV are independent, not contradictory. Rather, they are complementary to explain the sources of firm performance from different perspectives. The ISV does so by emphasizing the external factors (industry environment), while the RBV looks into the internal factors (firm-specific resources). The main contribution of the IBV, on the other hand, is in distinguishing different institutional features between emerging and advanced economies. Hoskisson et al. (2000) predicted that as the market develops in emerging economies, the importance of institutional theory might also decline. Therefore, the IBV may be particularly useful for explaining the drivers which shape business strategy in earlier stages. On the other hand, when explaining the sources of firms' competitive advantages, the DCV emphasizes the way firms create competitive advantages from their existing resources and capabilities in rapidly changing or high-velocity conditions. This shows that unlike the IBV, the DCV approach is applicable throughout all stages of economic development. However, it is still not satisfactory to provide more concrete connections to competitive advantage due to its dynamic and interlocking nature.

Each of the earlier studies filled gaps in the literature and provided meaningful contributions to the field of strategic management. Despite all these efforts, however, none of them could satisfactorily explain the diverse sources of competitive advantages of firms, particularly those of the latecomers such as the Korean firms in their early stages of growth. First, latecomers do not concentrate their resources on R&D expenditures or technological catch-up from the initial stage of firm development. They rather focus on finding the right strategic position among the incumbent industry players. Second, their competitiveness arises by concentrating available resources into increasing sales and market share (i.e., quantity-oriented strategy) rather than focusing on profits (i.e., profit-oriented strategy). Lastly, the DCV scholars explain how firms can generate new knowledge by combining the changing needs with their existing resources. However, the creation of dynamic capabilities still relies on the VRIN advantages, which are less likely to be possessed by latecomers.

Contrary to this perspective, latecomers that succeeded in becoming global leaders, such as Samsung, went through a series of massive restructuring and transformation within a short period of time. This shows that their competitiveness is not only derived from adaptation to contemporary environmental changes but from the ability to radically change and upgrade what they have accumulated in order to achieve a new goal. This reality leads to the need for a new model that can explain the recent success stories of latecomers.

5.3 THEORETICAL BACKGROUND OF THE ABCD MODEL

The ABCD model is the new way to create both corporate and national competitive advantages by maximizing the utility of current resources. It is particularly useful in explaining the performance of a firm (or nation) in comparison with others that have similar resource endowments and capabilities (either inhered or created). People often compare emerging firms (or nations) with advanced ones by pointing out their comparative advantages and/or disadvantages. However, in reality, it is more meaningful to examine the reasons behind the superior performance of firms (or nations) that have similar comparative advantages and/or disadvantages.

This section will review existing studies of business-oriented advantages and link them to the ABCD model. The existing studies are useful to partially explain the theoretical background of the ABCD model. The literature review indicates that the ABCD model, in fact, integrates and complements existing theories rather than replacing them. However, the ABCD model also introduces new features that were previously neglected by existing studies.

5.3.1 Agility: Efficient Management of Time and Accuracy

As the business environment changes more rapidly, firms are pressured by the shortening lifecycles of products and technologies. At the same time, they must produce various products by targeting multiple market segments. Firms can no longer sustain their business by being a one-technology or one-product wonder; a product that is competitive today cannot guarantee its superior market position tomorrow. As a result, agility is becoming more important than ever in today's business environment.[6]

The RBV deals with first-mover advantages, focusing on firms' superior resources or capabilities over rivals. However, the first-mover advantage is neither sustainable nor durable due to the volatile and dynamic nature of today's industries. The first-mover advantage is more effective in stable industries with low levels of competition and long product lifecycles. In high-velocity industries that face hyper-competition (D'Aveni 1998), where the duration of a competitive advantage becomes shorter and thus time should be incorporated as an essential consideration of strategy (Eisenhardt and Martin 2000), firms need to adopt speedy and efficient management processes.

Given the increasing pressure from global competition, firms need to exploit *economies of speed* (along with economies of scale and scope) through faster innovation and delivery (Ito and Rose 2004). Stalk (1988) even argued that time management should be considered as another source of competitive advantage. An early entrance, coupled with a fast-track management process, will accelerate firms' resilience to market disturbances and changes. Therefore, the competitive advantage of "speed" should incorporate both early entry and fast process, in which the latter one is usually neglected in existing studies.

Furthermore, speed should be accompanied with precision. Precision refers to accuracy in all aspects of business to ensure customer satisfaction with products and services. Quality is a growing concern for globally competitive firms (Lakhal 2009), and firms are spending significant efforts to improve the quality of their products and services. In the field of business management, for example, total quality management (TQM) has proven to be an effective method for improving quality. TQM is a source of competitive advantage (Powell 1995) in terms of cost, delivery dependability, and product innovation (Douglas and Judge 2001). Whereas the preceding studies, in which the importance of "speed" and "precision" are often emphasized separately, the "agility" factor in this book incorporates the essence of both.

5.3.2 Benchmarking: Incremental Innovation through Learning Best Practices

The word "benchmarking" is defined as "the search for an industry's best practices that will lead to superior performance" (Camp 1989; Moffett, Anderson-Gillespie, and McAdam 2008). Traditionally, benchmarking was regarded as a practice of imitation, but recent studies contend that benchmarking includes and enhances the firms' abilities to learn and create new knowledge (Massa and Testa 2004). This means benchmarking involves more than learning through imitation but also incorporates elements of innovation. In this respect, "benchmarking" is comprised of two components—learning and best practice.

The RBV maintains the importance of obtaining unique and inimitable resources to sustain competitive advantages. However, creating such unique and sustainable resources is not always possible, as the DCV has hinted. This is particularly true for latecomers who lack the capabilities to engage in such activities. In reality, firms do not have to establish their competitive advantage from the onset if they can acquire it in the open market. This indicates that the safer and more efficient way is to first learn the success factors of leading firms.

Historically, scholars have devalued imitation and respected only innovation. For example, Porter (1996) claimed that firms relying solely on operational effectiveness (OE)[7] cannot achieve sustainable growth. In addition to OE, firms need to engage in unique strategic positioning (SP) to decisively outperform their rivals. However, imitation does not necessarily imply thoughtless duplication or lower quality. It is possible that imitations result in higher quality and lower prices than the original products or brands (Brondoni 2012).

According to Schnaars (1994), imitation can be categorized into two types: *duplicative* (e.g., counterfeits, knockoffs) and *creative* (e.g., design copies, market adaptations, technological leapfrogging) imitation. Nowadays, global competition has demonstrated that imitators can become winners, and imitation has become a definitive way of achieving growth and profit (Brondoni 2012). Imitators can become successful because they can avoid the risks or costs made by the original innovators. In other words, imitation can often be more cost-effective and efficient than independent development. What is more, imitation can even drive innovation, since the savings can be channeled to encourage innovation toward the next generation of technology (Shenkar 2010).

Of course, learning through imitation alone is not sufficient to achieve success. In order to outperform competitors, firms should move beyond the learning stage and create new best practices. However, best practices should not be confused with cutting-edge technology or skills, as sometimes state-of-the-art technology or design is not the best practice that delivers the maximum value to consumers. Taking computer technology as an example, Apple computers were known for their advanced technology in the 1980s, but IBM became the industry standard because of its widespread use and open platform and ultimately took control of the market. The technology used in Apple computers was more advanced but IBM's computers became the industry standard.

Strategically positioning oneself on Porter's (1996) productivity frontier indicates engaging in the current "best practice." Then, how can a firm create new best practice? Strategy and innovation experts often prefer disruptive innovation or radical changes. However, a significant level of commercial value, which better satisfies consumers' demand, can result from incremental changes as well. It should be noted that innovation is never created out of thin air. Innovation occurs most effectively when first imitating and learning the best practice of the time and substantially advancing it to the next generation of best practices. Therefore, the best benchmarking strategy is to learn best practices and improve upon them.

5.3.3 Convergence: Dominant Diversification for Maximizing Synergies

Competitive advantage comes from the entire system of a firm's activities rather than an individual activity. Porter (1996) explained this through his concept of "fit," which is "a position built on systems of activities that are far more sustainable than those built on individual activities: fit comes from the mixture of resources and capabilities." Porter further argued that a proper fit can lock out imitators by creating a chain—an array of interlocked activities. This is an extension of "economies of scope"[8] and can be applied simultaneously to various strategies pursued by a firm (Moon et al. 2014).

"Convergence," as it is defined here, is composed of two subfactors, "mixing" and "synergy creation." The "mixing" strategy can be compared to the firm's business diversification strategy. Scholars such as Teece (1983) claimed that companies tend to expand to other industries if a firm's resources or technology advantages exceed the capacity of the incumbent business. These scholars stated that if there is a surplus in resources or technology capacity, a company will be likely to make use of this excess in other areas. Therefore, according to these scholars, it makes the most sense for a company to diversify its activities into related sectors that can best utilize its current capacities. For example, Coca-Cola should enter the bottling industry since it is an important component of the beverage industry.

On the other hand, Williamson (1975) argued that companies diversify in order to efficiently allocate resources and reduce transaction costs with other companies. Similarly, Lewellen (1971) and Perry (1998) saw diversification as an additional income source to existing industries. Large conglomerates from developing countries, such as the Korean chaebol in their early stage of growth, diversified not because of their excess resources as argued by Teece (1983), but more in accordance with the views of Williamson (1975), Lewellen (1971), and Perry (1998)—they aimed to reduce transaction costs and searched for additional sources of income.

The "mixing" strategy can further be classified into related and unrelated diversification. In general, scholars from advanced countries with well-developed industries assume that unrelated activities imply a risky and ineffective business strategy. This view insists on related-industry diversification where firms launch similar products in related markets to gain brand loyalty and market share (Markham 1973; Baumol, Panzer, and Willig 1982; Montgomery 1994). Through related-industry diversification, a company can extend its existing competitive advantage into new products by utilizing brand loyalty to increase its market share (Markham 1973; Baumol, Panzer, and Willig 1982; Montgomery 1994). Thus, a company can prevent other rivals from entering the market by raising the barrier to entry. This is the context behind Coca-Cola's continuous launch of energy drinks, water, juices, and other beverages.

However, there are different perspectives on the relationship between diversification and firm performance. Some argued that unrelated diversification can be profitable in the face of market failure, which is common in emerging markets (Khanna and Palepu 1997; Ramaswamy, Li, and Petitt 2004). Furthermore, other studies (Jones and Hill 1988; Hill, Hitt, and Hoskisson 1992; Nayyar 1992; Zhou 2011) offered evidence that related diversification might be more costly to coordinate than unrelated diversification in certain situations. For example, Zhou (2011) argued that in order to exploit the synergies from diversification, a firm should deal with the issues of interdependencies between existing and new businesses, however, this causes additional coordination costs. This is because if a firm enters more related industries, it has the potential to share more inputs with existing businesses, which requires more adjustments and coordination efforts with existing relationships.

The mixing strategy itself will not be sustainable, therefore, if firms cannot continuously utilize synergies. Diversification will stop when the synergies shrink to zero (Zhou 2011). Creating synergies involves the combination of inter- or intra-firm activities that allow superior performance. In effect, a synergistic combination provides firms with better access to strategic assets, which enhances the firms' cost or differentiation advantages (Markides and Williamson 1996). It should be noted that a firm does not need to confine itself to either related or unrelated diversification.

A carefully designed "combinative diversification" of both related and seemingly unrelated businesses can reap excellent results. The successful chaebol of Korea, for example, are all characterized by well-designed combinative diversification.

Based on the above discussion, the conditions for synergy creation are as follows (Moon and Yim 2014). First, the strengths of the mixed businesses should be compatible with each other. Second, their strengths and weaknesses should be complementary to maximize the benefits of exploiting strengths and minimize the disadvantages from weaknesses. Third, there should be an efficient and expanded network system to support the operation of mixed activities. Lastly, the partnership should deliver higher commercial value to the market than the separate standalone products.

5.3.4 Dedication: Strengthened Commitment toward an Optimal Goal

Opinions on the sources of competitive advantages have shifted over time. Traditional sources, such as technology, financial resources, and strategic position are still relevant, but they are becoming less important due to the possibility of factor mobility across national borders in today's globalized economy. The new dynamic business environment has given rise to some other sources of competitiveness.

Modern business scholars value organizational culture and effective management of people (e.g., Pfeffer 1994). The corporate culture significantly influences the degree of employees' engagement, which further affects firm performance. If employees are more engaged, they will be more loyal and show extra commitment to the firm (Ncube and Jerie 2012). All else being equal (e.g., wages, skills), dedicated employees will provide a competitive advantage compared to less dedicated workers. The dedication can be broken down into two subfactors: diligence and goal orientation.

Kahn (1990) defined employee engagement as "the harnessing of organization members to their work roles." One important way to increase employee engagement is to improve work motivation. The Hawthorne study has significantly contributed to this, which mainly focused on the effects of external factors such as supervision, incentives, and working conditions (Porter and Lawler 1968). Other studies (Keaveney 1995; Ganzach et al. 2002; Rashid, Asad, and Ashraf 2011) examined internal factors for improving employees' engagement. For example, training and career development help the employees acquire the necessary knowledge and know-how to conduct their tasks. Such enhancement of employees' capabilities could promote new developments and in turn, increase their career commitment (Aryee and Chay 1994). Studies on this subject explored the effects of supervision, incentives, and working conditions, which are external factors of inducing action (e.g., Porter and Lawler 1968). A more comprehensive analysis should thus consider internal factors, which can lead us to the new concept of "economies of diligence."

Diligence is mediated by psychological processes involving goals and self-efficacy (Bandura 1986, 1997; Gist 1987). In essence, diligence and goal orientation reinforce each other, maximizing task performance and efficiency. A number of studies show how challenging goals lead to better performances (e.g., Lee, Tan, and Javalgi 2010). There have also been extensive studies (e.g., Farr, Hofmann, and Ringenbach 1993; Button, Mathieu, and Zajac 1996; VandeWalle et al. 1999; Lin and Chang 2005) on the implications of goal orientation for industrial organization and psychology. Furthermore, Dweck (1986) identified two types of goals: learning orientation and performance orientation. The former is to develop one's competence, while the latter is to demonstrate it. Goal orientation and diligence, the two subfactors of dedication, are particularly important in the business field as they reinforce each other and strengthen the other factors—agility, benchmarking, and convergence by providing motivation for success.

5.4 DISTINCTIVE FEATURES OF THE ABCD MODEL COMPARED TO EXISTING THEORIES

Table 5.1 summarizes the ABCD model and relates the factors and subfactors with the studies that have been reviewed earlier. As seen here, existing theories only partially touched on the ABCD model and do not provide a holistic view of competitiveness. With regard to agility, for example, the first subfactor can either refer to being "early" or "fast." According to existing theories, the first-mover advantage can explain the advantage of early entry, but not fast process or fast catch-up. Therefore, a more refined theory to explain the latecomer advantage, such as the economies of speed is necessary. For the second subfactor, precision, there are some related management techniques such as TQM. However, it is crucial to present a rigorous theoretical framework that explains how to enhance efficiency and precision management.

Table 5.1 DISTINCTION AND COMPREHENSIVENESS OF THE ABCD MODEL

	Established Theories	Emerging Theories
Agility		
• Speed	Early entry advantage	Fast process or catch-up advantage (economies of speed)
• Precision	Automation (from labor-intensive to capital-intensive)	Process techniques with human touch (e.g., JIT, TQM, 6 sigma)
Benchmarking		
• Learning	Resource-based view of the firm	Absorptive capacity (economies of learning)
• Best practice	Innovation, breakthrough technology	Global/local standard, incremental innovation (e.g., Kaizan, creative imitation)
Convergence		
• Mixing	Specialization capability (economies of scale)	Combinative capability (economies of diversity)
• Synergy creation	Related diversification (economies of scope)	Related and unrelated diversification (e.g., Chaebol, smartphone)
Dedication		
• Diligence	Inspiration	Perspiration (economies of diligence)
• Goal orientation	Unique positioning	Continued growth after catch-up (e.g., constructed crisis, extra commitment)

Benchmarking is often understated by scholars who overemphasize the importance of innovation such as the blue ocean strategy (Kim and Mauborgne 2005). However, benchmarking should include both blue and red ocean strategies because firms can also be successful by using the red ocean strategy. The RBV of a firm is somewhat related to the blue ocean strategy because it emphasizes unique resources that are not available to other competitors in the red ocean. However, unique resources such as the state-of-the-art technology are not always in demand nor are they the most commercial—sometimes absorptive capacity or "economies of learning" is a better option for creating higher consumer values. This may be more important in enhancing competitiveness because there is less risk in learning the current proven "best practice" than creating new revolutionary technology.

More recently, convergence has been emphasized as a source of competitive advantage, but few rigorous theories regarding this have been developed. Most of the existing theories of competitive advantage are more about the benefits of specialization or related diversification when firms enter other industries. This leads to the need to incorporate a more specific and rigorous theory such as "economies of diversity" that can effectively deal with unrelated as well as related diversification. This new perspective should be able to explain combinative capabilities and the creation of shared value that can maximize synergy creation.

Dedication has been recently discussed as a source of competitive advantage. However, most of the existing studies, particularly those by Western scholars, have focused on inspiration and creativity rather than perspiration and hard work (e.g., Krugman 1994). This thus raises the necessity to further discuss the usefulness of "economies of diligence." In addition, "goal orientation" is particularly important and it should be understood together with diligence because the effectiveness of diligence can vary depending on the degree of goal orientation.

As introduced in the literature discussed above, there have been a number of studies on competitive advantages. These studies are related to the factors and subfactors of the ABCD model. However, earlier theories were developed independently and do not provide a holistic view of competitiveness or interactions among these sources of competitive advantages. In this chapter, the ABCD model also included important variables that have been understated or neglected in the past. As illustrated in table 5.1, the ABCD model incorporates earlier business concepts and adds new features. It thus offers a more comprehensive and integrative guideline for enhancing competitive advantage.

CHAPTER 6

The ABCD Model

Application to Korea's Three Successful Firms

Chapter 4 introduced the ABCD model by bringing in diverse experiences from Korea's economy, industries, culture, and sports. Chapter 5 deepened the understanding of the ABCD model by connecting it to existing theories on competitive advantage and expounding the differing approaches for creating new competitive advantages. This chapter closes Part II by applying the ABCD model to case studies of notable Korean firms. Although there are other important conglomerates that have contributed to Korea's economic growth, the global firms POSCO, Samsung Electronics Company, and Hyundai Motor Company have been the most successful in creating competitive advantages.

The three firms share some common points. First, they were all established in the late 1960s, and within several decades, became industry leaders in their respective fields. Second, all three firms are highly globalized—each firm was included in the top 100 non-financial global firms from developing and transition economies (UNCTAD 2014).[1] Third, all are major Korean conglomerates. Although previous chapters selectively mentioned examples from each company's history for illustrative purposes, this chapter systematically analyzes these three companies by applying the ABCD model to their success.

6.1 DETERMINANTS OF POSCO'S SUCCESS

POSCO was established in 1968 with minimal capital, technology, and operational experience. However, within 30 years, POSCO became a global leader in crude steel production. After its privatization in 2000, POSCO expanded into foreign countries including Indonesia and India to build production bases overseas. Technology-wise, POSCO enhanced its global competitiveness with newly developed technologies such as FINEX, in addition to its secure supply of raw materials from diverse foreign locations.[2]

POSCO has been ranked among the top 500 companies by *Fortune* for three consecutive years since 2010 (*Fortune* 2014). Through strong technology initiatives, POSCO has also been selected as the world's most competitive steel company for seven consecutive biannual assessments since 2010 (Lee 2015).[3] POSCO has never lost its top ranking while other leading steelmakers such as Nucor (the United States), NSSMC (Japan), Gerdau (Brazil), Severstal (Russia), and JSW (India) have shown fluctuations in their rankings.

The company boasts that POSCO has made great achievements only with a challenging spirit to take action to overcome limits, and led Korea's steel industry up to this day" (POSCO 2015). It is noteworthy that POSCO became a top steel company despite the immense skepticism that it faced when it was founded in the late 1960s. The following section will apply the ABCD model to examine the fundamental reasons for POSCO's success and how it was able to quickly become a global leader in steel production despite its lack of capital, technology, expertise, and other resources for development.

6.1.1 Speedy and Precise Construction Process

The first element of agility is "speed," which is further categorized into two types: early entry and fast process. Compared to obtaining the early mover advantage, it is easier for latecomers at the initial stage of development to improve agility by speeding up every process. Since its humble beginnings as a steelworks company, POSCO has paid great attention to the speed of its construction process. If any part of the process was delayed, workers initiated an emergency plan, working up to 24 hours a day to make up for lost time. This commitment to speed allowed POSCO to construct 23 out of its 26 facilities more than a year ahead of schedule.

More recently, POSCO adopted substantial IT systems to boost its competitive advantage of speed through process innovation (PI). This practice improved the work process and digitized information by utilizing information and communication technology through the enterprise resource planning (ERP) software. The digitized information was then shared across different divisions within the company, as well as with suppliers and other related entities outside the company. This made production and sales planning more efficient and decreased order filling lead times, among other benefits. The increased *e*-procurement rate due to PI has noticeably enhanced productivity. Moreover, the speed management of POSCO allowed the company to reduce its inventory volume from one million to 400,000 tons, while substantially cutting items under maintenance. Table 6.1 illustrates the time reductions of various tasks via the implementation of PI.

The time saved was then rededicated to improving precision. POSCO's commitment to quality is well known throughout the world. As mentioned in chapter 3, CEO Park Tae-jun's unrelenting focus on quality led to the immediate demolition of faulty plants when critical problems were spotted. There are many such anecdotes that show Park's dedication toward precision that appear in business case studies. Park once climbed to the top of a 300-foot tall steel mill frame in order to check for loose bolts, which he found and ordered to fix. He also once led a team of managers to personally inspect all 240,000 bolts for a project and mark those that needed fixing. His thoroughness in the production process earned him the nickname "Dynamite Park" (Kee 2013).

6.1.2 Innovation through Learning Industrial Leaders

In the early 1950s, a new type of steel technology, the basic oxygen furnace (BOF), became commercially available. The introduction of this new technology was remarkable as it reduced the milling time compared to the traditional open-hearth (OH) technology. However, despite the apparent superiority of the BOF technology, few American steelmakers adopted it. On the other hand, new steelmakers in Asia took advantage of the shift

Table 6.1 IMPROVED SPEED MANAGEMENT THROUGH POSCO ICT'S ENTERPRISE RESOURCE PLANNING

Items	Time Reduced
Establishing sales/production plans	60 days reduced to 15 days
Order filling lead time	30 days reduced to 14 days
Budgeting	110 days reduced to 30 days
Monthly closing	6 days reduced to 1 day
Standard costing accounting period	15 days reduced to 3 days

Source: POSCO ICT.

to BOF technology and quickly surpassed American companies (Besanko et al. 2009).

The above example illustrates that US steelmakers failed to keep up with industry best practices. Although there are other underlying reasons for their late adoption, it was essential for them to adopt the global best practice of the time to sustain their competitive advantage. Throughout the history of the steel industry, the location of the top steelmakers shifted from Europe, to the United States, to Japan, and eventually to Korea. While this may be also impacted by structural changes with improving economies and higher living standards in the West, Japan and Korea's success shows how companies successfully learned existing best practices and added their own "alpha" to experience newfound success.

During POSCO's early years, the company needed assistance from the Japanese in all aspects of the installation process for a blast furnace (design, procurement, and construction). In addition, Japanese technicians taught POSCO employees about the best practices in inventory management, production scheduling, and routine maintenance. While POSCO benefited more from the cooperation with the Japanese in the beginning, POSCO employees gradually improved their knowledge and skills and began to take on more senior roles over Japanese engineers (Lee and Lee 2009).

POSCO workers did not simply follow the instructions of their Japanese advisors; they always tried to find other methods to increase productivity and quality. Through these proactive efforts, POSCO engineers quickly became experts and were later approached by Taiwanese and American firms for technical assistance. Over the past several years, POSCO has developed many cutting-edge technologies, such as the FINEX process, strip casting, and endless hot rolling technology. FINEX technology, in particular, was a next-generation, eco-friendly steelmaking process, which substantially reduced construction costs and CO_2 emissions. In September 2013, POSCO exported FINEX technology to China for the first time and went on to construct FINEX plants in other foreign countries. Although POSCO began as an imitator of Japanese steelmakers (who possessed the best practice at that time), POSCO emerged as an innovator in its own right and created a new global standard in steel production.

6.1.3 Global Competition through Effective Diversification

In addition to POSCO's upgrade of productivity through continuous technology benchmarking, the company gained competitive advantages by converging various resources in a synergistic way. For instance, POSCO strategically located processing and assembly lines near ports to substantially lower logistics costs. POSCO also based its entire production process in one location, which allowed for full connectivity among different functions and enhanced the efficiency of the entire manufacturing process. Furthermore, in order to increase worker productivity, POSCO invested in external training, and approximately one-third of its employees were trained overseas. When these foreign-trained workers returned to Korea, POSCO held seminars for them to share the knowledge they acquired from working abroad. By doing this, POSCO was able to maximize benefits with minimum inputs by integrating the foreign-trained workers with other employees.

Prior to 2000, POSCO's primary reason for diversifying into other industries and business areas was to minimize risk. However, as the company matured, it encountered new problems with the rise of Indian and Chinese competitors, a cyclical industry downturn, and ultimately diminishing profit margins. In anticipating these challenges, the company announced its "POSCO Vision 2005" in 1995 to restructure and diversify into new business areas. Since then, POSCO branched out into other less-related (but not completely unrelated) fields such as construction, biology, and power generation, in order to produce synergies for long-term competitiveness.

The qualitative growth of POSCO began to bear fruit in the early 2000s when the company was expanded into other areas such as information technology. Moreover, the synergistic mix of POSCO's preemptive diversification activities proved to be advantageous during the construction of Southeast Asia's first integrated steelworks in Indonesia[4] (POSCO 2013). POSCO's synergy-management achievements also extended to proactive overseas market entry, technology investment, and cost reduction efforts (*Al Bawaba* 2013). Recently, POSCO has received criticism for its overly aggressive expansion into new businesses which has resulted in weak short-term financial performance (e.g., energy and materials development through mergers and acquisitions). However, despite POSCO's disappointing performance in adjacent industries, the company remains the global leader in steelmaking.

6.1.4 From Working Hard to Working Smart

When President Park Chung-hee wanted to create an integrated steel mill in order to make Korea self-sufficient in steel, the country had no capital.

This pushed POSCO to turn to the United States, Germany, and the World Bank for loans which POSCO ultimately failed to secure. Despite these ominous conditions, POSCO did not give up and the founder maintained his strong faith in the company's future in addition to an overwhelming sense of duty to complete the project for his country. During POSCO's early stages of constructing steel mills (which was located on the southeastern edge of the Korean peninsula), Park once famously told his workers to "turn right and jump into the East Sea if we fail in the construction of the steel mill." The strong goal orientation of CEO Park Tae-jun and his employees allowed POSCO to successfully complete the construction of Korea's steel plant.

With Park's extreme commitment, POSCO employees spent the vast majority of their time in the construction site without holidays or vacations. Upon halting construction activities in the evening, workers stayed up late into the night to review and share information and knowledge. To this day, employees at POSCO continue to show diligence by engaging in various extracurricular studies. The top management teams and executives engage in weekly study groups on Saturdays. These sessions cover topics that range from classic Eastern philosophy (e.g., Confucius) to military strategy (e.g., *The Art of War* by Sun Tzu) in addition to Western philosophy and history.

The extra attention to the humanities and other disciplines such as military strategy aims to raise the understanding of human beings and eventually the world at large. Mid- and low-level employees are also encouraged to participate in extracurricular seminars, which occur twice a year on a rotational basis. By doing so, POSCO provides lifelong learning opportunities for everyone throughout the company. If "working hard" merely implies late hours at work, today's goal orientation has changed the paradigm from "working hard" to "working smart," in order to increase productivity in the workplace.

6.2 DETERMINANTS OF SAMSUNG'S SUCCESS

Samsung Electronics Company (hereinafter referred to as Samsung) was established in 1969 and is currently the flagship of Samsung Group. Samsung's early products mainly consisted of electrical appliances such as televisions, calculators, refrigerators, air conditioners, and washing machines. In 1970, Samsung Group established a subsidiary, Samsung-NEC, with Japan's NEC to manufacture home appliances and audiovisual devices. In 1974, the company expanded into the semiconductor business by acquiring Korea Semiconductor, and later the semiconductor business was merged with Samsung and became one of its key business areas. By 1981, Samsung's increased manufacturing capacity allowed it to produce over 10 million black-and-white televisions. In February 1983, Lee Byung-chul declared Samsung's intention to develop its own DRAM. Impressively, it became the third company in the world to develop a 64 KB DRAM within a year. In 1988, the company merged with Samsung Semiconductor & Communications to form the current-day Samsung Electronics.[5]

Samsung grew into a major manufacturer of electronic components such as lithium-ion batteries, semiconductors, flash memory, and hard drives for clients such as Apple, Sony, HTC, and Nokia. In recent years, the company has diversified into consumer electronics and is currently one of the world's largest manufacturers of mobile phones. The company is also a major vendor of tablet computers, particularly its Android-based Galaxy Tab collection, and it is generally regarded as a pioneer of the *phablet* (phone + tablet) market with its Galaxy Note family of devices (BBC 2013b). Samsung has also been the world's largest manufacturer of LCD panels since 2002 and the world's largest television manufacturer since 2006 (Samsung Electronics 2010). Ranking 13th on the Fortune Global 500 list in 2014, Samsung is undoubtedly Korea's number one company.

Despite Samsung's substantial achievements and strengthened innovation capabilities, international media reports tend to undervalue the company for its lack of originality. Most critics attribute Samsung's fast catch-up and success to speed and imitation. Although these factors cannot be neglected, it is obvious that with just these attributes, Samsung could not have achieved its current level of success or outperformed the global industry leaders. In order to better understand the secrets of Samsung's success, the following section will apply the ABCD model to its business strategy.

6.2.1 Top-Down Management and Quality Control

With the sharply shortening lifecycle of memory products, speed and timing were essential to management and production. To meet these challenges, Samsung adopted various measures to significantly shorten the time required for product development and production. For example, to prepare for the production of its first 64 MB DRAM, Samsung completed its development lab in six months. In contrast, it took American and Japanese companies 18 months to do the same. Samsung also planned technology and product development two to three generations ahead of schedule. For example, when the 16 MB DRAM was introduced to the market, the company was already planning for the 64 MB and 256 MB modules (Lee 2011).

Samsung's speed can be attributed to its top-down management style (Barkham 2012). However, unlike the Japanese, who gave detailed instructions for projects, Samsung only provided general guidance and asked individual teams to determine the proper specifications according to their unique situations. Thus, Samsung's top-down management was both speedy and flexible in responding to the rapidly changing external conditions. In 2014, Samsung's speed management was updated to a more aggressive strategy called "Mach Management."[6] This new wording clearly reflects Samsung's continued pursuit of speed. The new strategy aims to maintain competitiveness through further increase of speed in every aspect of business activities whether it be production, design, research and development, or other day-to-day business operations (Kim 2013).

Along with speed management, Samsung was always committed to quality management. Until the early 1990s, Samsung's products were regarded as cheap, low-quality substitutes for Japanese brands. In 1993, the company introduced its concept of "New Management," which aimed to shift its quantity-oriented expansion toward quality-oriented growth. To meet global quality standards, Samsung's various teams adopted a broad range of management quality certifications including the ISO 9000, TL 9000, and QS 9000. In late 1999 and early 2000, Samsung also adopted the Six Sigma process across its entire business operations to improve precision and reduce product defect rates. All department employees were required to participate in these types of training programs. In addition, Samsung built an intranet site called Sigma Park to share reference materials, new benchmarking opportunities, and senior management reports. Moreover, Samsung established an intra-company undergraduate program called Quality College in 1990 and a graduate school for semiconductor technology and operations in 1992.

After the successful achievement of quality control in its products, the company then turned its focus to product design in order to attract high-class consumers. To understand consumption patterns of more sophisticated consumers, Samsung established design centers in advanced countries across the world. Today, Samsung's design capabilities no longer lag behind the global standard and sometimes even set the new global standard, as can be seen by some of the recently launched Samsung products.

6.2.2 Improvement after Technology Catch-up
   ## through Benchmarking

Samsung's product innovations are the results of aggressive investments and an active pursuit of outside knowledge. According to Song and Lee (2014), these capabilities were demonstrated primarily through the improvement of existing technologies and product domains. The business jargon for this concept is "incremental innovation." At first, Samsung accumulated technologies through external acquisitions through a variety of methods including joint venture, M&A, technology license, overseas R&D, reverse engineering, strategic partnership, and recruiting.

After having its initial cooperative venture proposals rejected by Japanese firms when trying to acquire the DRAM technology, Samsung acquired the technology from an American firm called Micron Technologies, which was experiencing financial difficulties at the time. In addition, Samsung acquired a Dutch R&D company, Liquavista, in 2010 for its advanced display technology, and in 2011, acquired a US-based firm called Grandis to gain next-generation MRAM technology. Samsung also established an R&D center in Silicon Valley to stay up-to-date on the latest technology trends, test pilot products, and train Korean engineers. With dedication to learning and continued R&D, Samsung was ultimately able to develop its own signature products and technologies that are world class.

In order to go beyond "catch-up" and become a top company in these product markets, Samsung expanded the technology frontier to create new product categories. This was hinted by CEO Lee Kun-hee, when he stressed that "Samsung must concentrate on setting global standards by growing its intangible assets over the next ten years" (Song and Lee 2014). For instance, Samsung pioneered the first 3D memory chip design and curved-edge technology for LED TVs. Moreover, the company is credited with creating the *phablet* industry and developing the world's first fusion memory and active-matrix OLED displays.

Another example of Samsung's desire to create its own global standard can be seen in their smart-home products—Samsung is aiming to reshape the home lifestyle. To borrow the words of Yoon Boo-keun, the President of Samsung's Consumer Electronics division, "In the future, homes should be customized to their owners, as this technology will be able to display information about owners' households and recommend suggestions to further improve their living quarters." The company claimed that connected appliances could be the next big thing in technology, while also becoming its next major source of revenue (Kim 2014).

Under these efforts, Samsung registered 4,676 patents in 2013 and had the second most patents awarded by the US Patent and Trademark Office for eight consecutive years since 2006. In its early days in the semiconductor business, Samsung used to pay massive royalties to Texas Instruments for various technology licenses. However, the unceasing effort toward learning and innovation has allowed the company to gain strong bargaining power in the industry. Samsung has also turned its attention to design technology by recruiting talented people in the field and empowering design centers in other countries such as Italy. It has registered more design patents compared to its competitors since 2010.

6.2.3 Effective Diversification of Business Structure

Although Samsung's benchmarking strategy contributed much to the strengthening of its technological capabilities, it could not have surpassed the leading firms without its integrated competitiveness through strong combinations of differing resources. Samsung has simultaneously pursued horizontal diversification, vertical integration, convergence of products and services, and regional clustering of major activities. By organically linking these activities across the entire Samsung Group, the company effectively generated synergies from the right mixture of these elements, thereby enhancing its overall competitiveness. Samsung was able to develop new products at a faster pace than global competitors because it had a good mix of related businesses, ranging from intermediate components to final products. Samsung managed to create synergies among businesses that are seemingly unrelated such as manufacturing to finance and services.

The current business structure of Samsung is divided into two subunits: Digital Media Communications (DMC) and Device Solutions (DS). The DMC division deals with end products such as consumer electronics, information technology, and mobile technology, while the DS division covers components such as semiconductors and display technology. The IT and mobile sector has long held the largest share of sales, and this has continued to grow. Much of the sector's success, however, is due to the synergies arising from the integration with other areas that enforce the strengths of the IT and mobile sector.

Samsung's success in the semiconductor business cannot be separated from its close coordination of domestic and overseas research teams, as well as the cooperation among different departments and companies. For example, the company established two product development teams: one in Seoul and the other in Silicon Valley. This not only promoted technology transfer between the two but also pressured the two teams to engage in cooperative competition with each other. The company also encouraged collaboration between cross-functional task forces. It located R&D and production in one area to facilitate interaction and collaboration. The company then had design and production engineers participate in all phases of the development process in order to share information and solve problems quickly (Lee 2011).

In the age of convergence and ubiquitous communications, Korean business groups are uniquely positioned to gain and sustain competitive advantages against foreign rivals that focus on a single business. These business units, under the guidance of their headquarters, share a common corporate culture and philosophy that allows them to handle internal communications smoothly and coordinate interests within their organizations. Samsung has built a business structure that has a strong fit in the era of digital convergence in this sense; it produces everything from core parts such as semiconductors and LCDs to finished products such as digital media and other home and communication devices.

6.2.4 Constructing a Crisis Culture to Prepare for Future Changes

The employees of Samsung are well known for their hard work. For example, when working on the Galaxy S project, employees worked around the clock, only sleeping a few hours a night to achieve their goal (*Verge* 2012). Samsung employees are also famous for their strong desire to learn. They constantly pursue academic programs such as MBAs to enhance their management knowledge and skills. Furthermore, Samsung established an intra-company education system that was customized for the needs of every position, from workers and managers to executives and overseas employees.

Samsung, as a group, has always been highly goal-oriented. By targeting specific industries or rivals, Samsung was able to quickly learn the industry best practices and take proper competitive strategies. For example, Sony was Samsung's first target rival in electronics, but soon after overtaking Sony in terms of market share, Samsung set its target to Nokia and Apple. Samsung employees also display high goal orientation within the company, proudly referring to themselves as "Samsung men." When Samsung made its entry into the semiconductor industry with the "Tokyo Declaration," both internal and external circumstances were highly unfavorable for its business. However, Lee Byung-chul held firm to his belief that the semiconductor industry would be the key for Samsung's long-term success. With the leadership's strong commitment and goal orientation, the company was able to continue its investment despite significant losses during the first several years.

What is unique about Samsung and other Korean conglomerates is that their organizational culture was shaped by a sense of urgency and desperation. Lee Kun-hee, the successor of Lee Byung-chul, is famous for referring to business situations as crises or emergencies, and he urged his executives to adopt the same mindset. Although this kind of "crisis culture" may seem unduly stressful and manipulative, it serves its purpose quite well—employees are always alert and respond to market changes quickly to prevent crises before they turn into disasters. In practice, this allowed Samsung to tightly control the budget and effectively fund its investments into future technology despite initial losses. This is the secret behind Samsung's ability to obtain the most number of patents and produce many of the world's first and finest technologies.

6.3 DETERMINANTS OF HYUNDAI'S SUCCESS

Hyundai Motor Company (hereinafter referred to as Hyundai) was established in 1967 as a subsidiary of Hyundai Group, and it is now the fifth largest automobile producer in the world. Having been labeled as a knock-off company of Ford in the beginning, Hyundai's success was highly unlikely and the company desperately scrambled to borrow technology capabilities from Mitsubishi. However, when J. D. Power and Associates rated Hyundai Motor America vehicles as having lower defect rates than those of Toyota in 2003, the entire industry was shocked. *The Automotive News* reported this incident with the following description: "Man bites dog. The earth is flat. Hyundai builds better quality cars than Toyota" (Rechtin 2004). Although Toyota refrained from publically expressing any strong reaction, the fact that Toyota's engineers and marketing experts secretly travelled to Korea to investigate Hyundai showed Toyota's new sense of urgency (Chang 2005).

In recent years, Hyundai has been acknowledged as a key player for its contributions to the global automobile market. For example, the Genesis model was highly recognized with awards including the "highest ranked midsize premium car in initial quality" by J. D. Power and Associates in 2013, the Automobile Journalists Association of Canada Award (AJAC) for Best New Luxury Car in 2015 (over $50,000), and the Top Safety Pick+ (plus) by the Insurance Institute for Highway Safety (IIHS). Hyundai's brand value also grew by approximately 20% in 2013 and exceeded $10 billion for the first time in 2014 according to Interbrand's "Best Global Brands." The next section will take an in-depth look into Hyundai's growth through the four factors of the ABCD model, and analyze the distinctive strengths of Hyundai.

6.3.1 Speed and Quality Management

Hyundai is well known for the speed at which its senior management acts, dubbed as "Hyundai Speed." Particularly in overseas markets, Hyundai has been adept at recognizing local needs and rapidly creating products that adhere to local consumer demands. Such capabilities have enabled Hyundai to release 21 new models in North America within five years, including the acclaimed luxury model Equus that competes with the Mercedes S Class and BMW 7 series. Hyundai has grown faster than its peers over the past decade.

Hyundai also benefits from the rapid response of executives and mid-level managers. Whenever top executives make a decision, managers mobilize quickly and execute with speed. For example, when Hyundai's CEO visited a parts distribution center in Ontario, he discovered a large pile of faulty transmissions that had failed in quality standards. Upon seeing this, the CEO called for the entire transmission design team to convene in California as soon as possible, and approximately 20 high-level executives arrived from Korea within 24 hours.

Alongside this speed in action, Hyundai also paid much attention to quality control. Until the late 1990s, Hyundai's strategy was focused on quantity over quality—the company increased sales by selling a large volume of cheap cars. However, in 2000, Hyundai took a dramatic turn toward quality when CEO Chung Mong-koo declared "Quality Management" as the new slogan of Hyundai. To keep this promise, Chung established a new quality control division which had the authority to intervene at any stage of the design, engineering, and production process.

In order to further improve "speed management," Hyundai created the Global Command and Control Center in Korea to monitor every operating line of Hyundai's 27 worldwide plants real time. If the quality monitor signals errors or problems, technicians are immediately dispatched to fix them. In addition, after recognizing what consumers wanted, Hyundai introduced the concept of "qualitativity," which combined "quality" and "productivity" to increase customer satisfaction. Such efforts to improve Hyundai's vehicle quality considerably improved the company's brand image; in 2013, Interbrand ranked Hyundai as the 47th best global brand (7th among car companies).

6.3.2 Reverse Engineering of the World's Best Cars

Hyundai entered the automobile business by importing foreign technology. Its first car was Ford's British model known as the Cortina, which was assembled under license in 1967. However, Hyundai soon decided to build its own car, and the company invited a former British Leyland executive to Korea in the early 1970s to assist in reverse engineering the Morris Marina. Hyundai specifically chose the Marina because the model was small, technologically less sophisticated, and cheap—an appropriate design for Hyundai to dismantle and study. Hyundai went even further by purchasing a superior engine from Mitsubishi and consulting Italdesign for the car's exterior (Italdesign was an Italian firm that designed the Volkswagen Rabbit and Passat). With all of these efforts in place, Hyundai produced the Pony model, which was exported to foreign countries.

In order to produce quality cars that were comparable to those of industry leaders, Hyundai carefully studied several "good" models by disassembling, studying, and comparing them part by part. Through this painstaking analysis, Hyundai specifically determined the best practices to follow. During the period leading up to the 1980s, Hyundai selectively adopted various aspects from multiple sources. For example, Hyundai adopted production processes and frame designs from Ford, and operation systems and engine designs from Mitsubishi. At the national level, Hyundai studied engine block, transmission, and rear axle design from Japan; factory construction, layouts, and combustion technology from the United Kingdom; and exterior design from Italy.

Hyundai's primary objective to produce competitive cars never wavered. The company established R&D centers in both Korea and abroad to enhance its technology development and learning capabilities. The Namyang R&D center, for example, was established in 1997 and was acknowledged as a world-class research center that fueled Hyundai's quest to develop its own engine and other technologies. While continuing to improve quality during the 2000s, Hyundai also focused its efforts on exterior design capabilities. Recognizing that the design process of industry leaders was consensus-driven and that designs were largely undifferentiated, CEO Chung Mong-koo proclaimed a new design philosophy for Hyundai, called "fluidic sculpture" in 2009. In order to develop its own unique designs, Hyundai hired internationally renowned experts and promoted internal design competitions for additional ideas.

Accordingly, Hyundai created new competitive advantages by selectively adopting best practices from multiple sources that had different strengths. Hyundai then incorporated its own "alpha" to create globally competitive products. Hyundai's competitive strategy proves that an effective benchmarking strategy through learning plus incremental "alpha" can be highly successful.

6.3.3 Hybrid Production System and Effective Connection with Business Partners

Much of Hyundai's competitive advantage in production can be attributed to its hybrid production system—a combination of Fordism and Toyotaism. Hyundai could not have exceeded other global firms if it selected only one of the two for benchmarking. Hyundai quickly recognized the relative strengths and weaknesses of the two disparate production strategies, along with the practical limitations of implementing either production method at home. As a solution, Hyundai decided to mix these two systems, essentially picking and choosing aspects from each side that best suited Hyundai's needs.

For example, Hyundai followed Ford's strategy of selecting a few models for mass production, as opposed to Toyota's strategy of producing many models in smaller volume. On the other hand, in order to buffer itself from the effects of frequent labor strikes, Hyundai only partially adopted Toyota's production system which places a greater role on employees. Also, Hyundai implemented Toyota's Just-in-Time (JIT) system to reduce inventory space and cost, which allowed Hyundai to utilize production procedures more flexibly.

Hyundai Motor Company has also greatly benefited from other Hyundai companies within Hyundai Group, which can be regarded as a distinctive advantage to its rivals. Within a conglomerate, affiliate companies can conduct businesses more fluidly with reduced transaction costs and time. Hyundai Engineering and Construction Company (1947), Hyundai Motor Company (1968), and Hyundai Heavy Industries (1974) were founded with this very purpose in mind. For instance, if Hyundai Motor needed an additional construction plant, Hyundai Engineering and Construction could build the facilities. Within the automotive industry, a proper mix of quality improvement, design, marketing, and a cooperation with other Hyundai companies enabled Hyundai to outperform its industry competitors.[7]

Hyundai also benefited from its long-term, close relationship with suppliers, and strong coordination of overseas subsidiaries from home. For example, Hyundai built the 5-star Rolling Hills Hotel near the Namyang R&D Center to house thousands of foreign employees who were invited to Korea for training and education. Their VIP treatment along with their exposure to Hyundai's philosophy, corporate vision, and values built strong loyalty to the company. Upon returning to their countries, these employees successfully created a synergistic mix of their domestic knowledge and newfound corporate values.

6.3.4 Improving Human Resource through Education and Training

In the beginning, Hyundai employees had poor skills and training, and the company could not raise its automation capacity due to budget constraints. This presented a critical problem when compared to the highly motivated and trained Japanese workforce in the automotive industry. In order to gain labor competitiveness, Hyundai employees had to simply work harder and longer than their Japanese counterparts to make up for their lacking expertise and infrastructure.

Hyundai's hard-working culture still characterizes the company today, but the content of hard work now puts a higher emphasis on education and training, as Hyundai has continued to advance. In 2012, Hyundai built the Mabuk Campus of the Hyundai Motor Group University in order to provide a variety of educational programs with a university concept. By establishing other regional campuses in Paju, Osan, Cheonan, and Nabu, the university was built to lead all human resource development (HRD) activities by providing a corporate-wide roadmap. The programs are created to act as a performance center, global HRD hub, and corporate culture channel. Through these programs, key corporate values such as shared values and future leadership are taught. In addition, as the curriculum is designed to improve specific work skills, it shows Hyundai's dedication to improving the competitiveness of its employees.

6.4 IMPLICATIONS FOR FIRMS' COMPETITIVE ADVANTAGE

POSCO, Samsung, and Hyundai are the major Korean conglomerates that best demonstrate the power of the ABCD model in creating competitive advantages. All in all, these companies have succeeded in creating new core competencies by exhibiting the characteristics of the ABCD model.

Needless to say, all three companies have exemplified how companies from developing countries can mobilize, accumulate, and expand both tangible and intangible resources to become top global firms. Many of these experiences show how earlier theories and business strategies may not be suitable for companies in the catch-up phase. There must be a different trajectory for these particular companies from under-supplied and under-sourced domestic markets, and the ABCDs are the most efficient ways for these firms to advance from followers to leaders in their respective fields.

Furthermore, the three Korean companies demonstrated a remarkable ability to maximize their advantages despite their increasing corporate size. Common sense says that larger organizations would be much slower in making and executing decisions versus smaller ones. This is because as the organization grows, information flow and decision-making processes are likely to get clogged and conflicts of interest between affiliates and divisions are likely to increase. What's more, agency costs could go up as a greater number of management-level appointments are made. In short, there are a whole host of issues that can obstruct a large company from functioning well. It is important to understand that conglomerates that fail to address these natural impediments will not become successful. In fact, many of the failed *chaebol* in Korea made mistakes or poor decisions around this issue.

This leads to the conclusion that companies, particularly the large ones, must possess the four factors (and eight subfactors) of the ABCD model to produce long-term, positive results. For a large company to curb some of the problems related to size, clear goal orientation must be shared throughout the entire group and by each individual. Therefore, the ABCD model would be most effective when a company first embodies *dedication*. It is the most fundamental factor that has an overarching influence on the other factors of the model.

Once a clear goal is implemented, shared, and practiced in its entirety, the company will be able to move further by acting quickly and precisely. As long as *dedication* is well in place, *agility* becomes the next critical factor as it boosts the catch-up trajectory. This becomes more evident during waning external environment such as a financial crisis. Fast and accurate decision-making and execution capabilities allow the companies to overcome hardships quickly.

The next step is benchmarking the industry leaders, and this is an efficient way to pursue profitable growth. The efficient use of time is not to reinvent the wheel, but taking advantage of the established best practices of industry leaders. Hyundai did this through reverse engineering the automobiles of the industry leaders by thoroughly studying and learning the necessary technology. After the learning phase in benchmarking, companies should and will be able to add their own unique "alpha" to create a superior final product. This is what a successful company continues to do with its products as it adds incremental innovations to existing successful products.

Conglomerates that have pursued unrelated diversification are common even in advanced countries. However, due to the lack of resource efficiencies in distribution and managerial processes, these conglomerates generally become less competitive compared to the specialized firms in specific businesses (Davis, Diekmann, and Tinsley 1994). The reason why Korean conglomerates were able to defy this theory is that they focused on creating synergies with their diversification; while the activities were diverse, they were also specialized. When there is a core competence that is connected to less competent divisions through the sharing of resources (especially knowledge and experience), the overall cost decreases—this is the essence of *convergence*. Brand sharing is a good example where large companies can save time and resources, and this is especially true when a particular brand already enjoys a strong, positive image.

All four factors of the ABCD model provide meaningful implications for all firms because every company, regardless of its competitiveness level, has its own problems. For instance, the industry's leading company may have a greater probability of becoming complacent and relaxing its goal orientation, diligence, or speed, once a certain level of growth is achieved. This becomes a critical problem in the long run. Also, a leading company that has plateaued can still learn something new from other fields as Toyota's research team did with their study of movements of a school of fish to examine accident-free traffic. Leading companies in all industries can benefit from best practices in other fields and incorporate them into their own business. There is always something to learn and when a company can manage to incorporate all of the ABCDs, newly generated competitive advantages will arise.

Part II introduced the ABCD model by showing its theoretical foundation and applying the model in various case studies. The next part shifts the focus to the role of internationalization and examines how the ABCDs combined with the internationalization strategy open up a window of opportunities to further accelerate growth at both the national and firm levels.

PART III

Internationalization

Broadening the Scope of Strategic Choices

As explained in Part II, the ABCDs play an overarching role in boosting Korean businesses and the overall economy. However, there is another key factor to consider—*internationalization*. For a small country with limited resources, such as Korea, having an open door policy allows for far greater opportunities. While often neglected by both scholars and practitioners, internationalization is an essential criterion for the advancement of countries and needs special recognition from those interested in expanding the scope and scale of economic values.

The fundamental reason why the United States is the world's largest economy is its openness. From the beginning, the United States was a melting pot of different people and cultures. As a country founded by immigrants, the development and stability of the United States would not have been possible without being open to diversity while also having a shared sense of identity. The United States was able to procure resources and partners extensively across the world, which contributed significantly to its prosperity. Both US domestic and foreign policies show a continued inclination to remain open despite ongoing criticism from certain interest groups, which demonstrates that internationalization remains a core principle for the United States.

Unlike the Americans, however, Koreans have long been hesitant to open up to foreign influence. In the early stages of Korea's economic development, the government's internationalization policies were skewed to trade (export promotion combined with import substitution), and foreign direct investment (FDI) in Korea was highly restricted prior to the 1980s. In fact, it was not until the 1980s that the government began to liberalize FDI and this continued after the 1997 Asian Financial Crisis in order to overcome the crisis through deregulation and liberalization. Under this effort between 1997 and 2010, Korea carried out its most extensive level of reforms to attract foreign investors. It removed nearly twice as many statutory barriers compared to other developing countries in Asia (see Nicolas, Thomsen, and Bang 2013).

Korea became more internationalized than ever before with these efforts, but still lacks balance in the scale and scope of its internationalization relative to other similarly developed economies. These limits as well as potential improvements will be discussed in the three chapters of Part III. Chapter 7 will discuss internationalization at the national level by focusing on the importance of the government's open policy for national economic development. By using examples of four countries, the United States, Japan, China, and India, the chapter shows how policy direction for internationalization serves as an important cornerstone for national development. Chapter 8 will then examine how internationalization plays into enhancing firms' competitiveness in global competition. Lastly, chapter 9 discusses the cultural aspect of internationalization. Internationalization is often met with criticism within a country and between countries because there are non-economic factors that are emotionally sensitive to the public. This chapter shows how these perspectives can be changed. In addition, Part III suggests how the ABCDs can be used to maximize the benefits of internationalization for all participants.

CHAPTER 7

Internationalization at the National Level

Both developed and developing countries understand that internation-alization is an important factor for economic prosperity and social development.[1] Although an open-door system does not guarantee success, history shows that open countries have had a higher chance of growth than protectionist countries. Korea implemented internationalization measures primarily through international trade in the 1960s, and then by opening up its financial markets to foreign investment in the 1990s. This is in contrast to Korea's old policies in the nineteenth century, when *Chukhwabi* (steles proscribing Westerners) were erected throughout the country. However, Korea was ultimately forced to open its doors from empires such as Japan and Russia. While Korea was not always for an open door policy and was ultimately forced to open its economy, this transition from a closed to an open economy set the groundwork for Korea's economic and social development.

The significant role of internationalization in the economic and social development can also be found in other countries. This chapter shows case studies of the United States, Japan, China, and India's economic growth through internationalization. The four countries are all large economies with populations that exceed 100 million with abundant resources except for Japan. However, there is a vast difference among the four countries in terms of their levels of economic development. The United States is the most advanced, followed by Japan, China, and India—this order is also the same in each country's openness. This chapter demonstrates how the four countries, traditionally self-sufficient, could achieve rapid and continued growth with internationalization. In addition, the chapter provides the theoretical basis for why countries are better off with internationalization and concludes by providing implications for economic development using the ABCD model.

7.1 ACCELERATING ECONOMIC GROWTH

7.1.1 The United States: An Open Country from the Beginning

The Roman Empire often goes hand in hand with the term *Pax Romana* and is the best historical example of national hegemony. The Romans were able to maintain supremacy because of their ability to control international business. Merchants felt secure in conducting transactions under Rome's advanced system and laws, and commerce prospered under this stable environment. Neighboring countries took notice and wished to partake in the Roman system even at the cost of taxation and loss of sovereignty. Countries that refused to join this system, on the other hand, lagged behind economically.

Today's *Pax Americana* is neither as influential nor extensive as *Pax Romana*. While the Romans practically monopolized the world market, it would be hard to say the same for the United States today. American firms such as McDonald's and Coca-Cola are strong in the world market, but there are numerous non-American firms such as BMW, Toyota, Samsung, and Alibaba that are powerful in their industries. Today, the country of origin carries much less weight in assessing the global competitiveness, meaning that any company, regardless of nationality, can become a winner in the global market.

Those who equate internationalization with Americanization often criticize the United States and its spread of American culture and the English language. However, like many American things, English has its roots in other cultures such as Latin. Most people know the famous proverb, "When in Rome, do as the Romans do." The important implication here is not to avoid persecution but to reap the benefits of following a dominant and successful system. It would be wrong to view the import and use of American culture as merely the expansion of American hegemony. The spirit of internationalization rests on the derived benefits of benchmarking and convergence, and many aspects of American culture display convergence with other cultures. In fact, the United States has consistently derived competitiveness from its open-door policies and its spirit of internationalization. When Japanese business methods proved to be effective in the 1980s, American business schools were quick to include case studies and principles of Japanese businesses into their curriculum. This knowledge was subsequently reflected in American business practices, and many American companies exceeded their Japanese counterparts by the 1990s.

Previously, Eastern countries (e.g., Japan, Korea, and China) learned the best practices of their more advanced counterparts in the West in order to achieve economic and social development. In order to obtain national support for adopting Western best practices, which were primarily their advanced science and technology, the Eastern countries came up with slogans that expressed the benefits of learning the West without sacrificing their national identity. The Koreans said, "Eastern Way and Western Technology," the Chinese referred to it as "Making Western Things Serve China," and the Japanese expressed the concept as "Japanese Spirit and Western Bowl." The Western countries' (e.g., the United States) learning from their Eastern counterparts in the 1980s and 1990s is simply the reverse application of the "Eastern Way, Western Technology."

The above expressions imply that Western countries have competitive advantages in technology and machines. However, when combining the strengths of the West with certain Eastern values, Eastern countries such as Korea and Japan are able to supersede the technologically advanced Western countries. This is the essence of "convergence" in the ABCD model. America's success in the 1990s can be attributed to learning certain best practices of Eastern nations and creating new advantages by combining them with their own unique strengths.

Americans have never hesitated to study and learn from others, especially from their Eastern counterparts. A good example is how the United States continuously updates words in its dictionary, by including foreign words from Eastern countries, such as *Kimchi* (Korean) and *Sushi* (Japanese). Although the US government backpedaled into a period of protectionism and paranoia following the 9/11 terrorist attack in New York, American companies continue to show increasing cultural diversity, and this has proven to be helpful in entering new markets, adapting to new environments, and developing new ideas.

It is worthwhile at this point to mention America's immigration policy. As a country founded by immigrants, the United States harbors a core value of diversity. Although democracy and capitalism were both founded in Europe, the United States has best embodied these systems due to its familiarity with diversity, and its preference for open immigration has contributed to this. Despite the post-9/11 changes in immigration policies, the United States continues to be by far the biggest destination for immigration in the world. Recently in November 2014, President Obama announced his executive actions on immigration policy, which provide new protections for undocumented foreigners. Obama said the following (Flannery 2014):

> For more than 200 years, our tradition of welcoming immigrants from around the world has given us a tremendous advantage over other nations. It's kept us youthful, dynamic, and entrepreneurial. It has shaped our character as a people with limitless possibilities. . . . I know some worry immigration will change the very fabric of who we are, or take our jobs, or stick it to middle-class families at a time they already feel they've gotten a raw deal for over a decade. [But] our history and the facts show that immigrants are a net plus for our economy and our society.

America's competitiveness has its roots in its open and welcoming disposition to foreigners. The famous Statue of Liberty, as a symbol of refuge for the oppressed, carries the iconic inscription, "Give me your tired, your poor. Your huddled masses yearning to breathe free." The idea that anyone can achieve the American dream is what differentiates the United States from other hegemons in history. If Americans insist that the United States is only for its citizens, it will lose its key advantage of diversity and raise anti-American sentiment around the world.

There is also statistical evidence that certifies this argument. The current median age of whites is 42, blacks 32, and Hispanics 28 in the United States. With diversified immigrants from across the globe, the United States maintains a relatively young population and does not have to worry about future shortages in labor. This is in contrast to other rich countries that are facing problems due to a rapidly aging, insufficient labor pool and shrinking populations (*Economist* 2015a). At the same time, America also has a strong duty to prevent terrorism while opening its doors to foreigners. These two goals can and must be achieved together as its continued competitiveness rests on convergence and internationalization.

7.1.2 Japan: Opening of Ports since 1853

In contrast to the United States, which was very open to and relied on immigrants from its founding, Japan, as a homogeneous society, had been a closed country until it was forced to open its doors by the United States in the mid-nineteenth century. On July 8, 1853, a fleet of four ships led by US Commodore Matthew Perry approached the Uraga Port of Edo Bay (currently Tokyo Bay). The Japanese people had never seen such large ships before and were terrified by what appeared to be great dragons fuming smoke from their nostrils. When the ships anchored at shore, the Japanese were further daunted by the volume of weapons carried by the foreigners.

From the black tar that coated the exterior to prevent wood decay, the ships received the name *kurohune* (meaning "black ship" in Japanese). Contemporary accounts reveal the emotions of the Japanese people upon meeting Commodore Perry and his men. Some portraits showed Perry as a kind-looking but dull man, while others portrayed him as a fearsome monster. All in all, these different portrayals show the confusion and uncertainty of the Japanese people's first encounter with the Americans. Back then, the only foreigners Japanese saw were Koreans, Chinese, and Dutch. So you can imagine the shock that those people would have felt with this encounter.

Commodore Perry carried a personal letter from President Millard Fillmore declaring America's wish to establish trade relations with Japan. However, Japan rejected all treaty advances in fear of foreign influence. As a result, Commodore Perry returned with twice as many ships the following year and coerced Japan to sign the Convention of Kanagawa in 1854. The treaty forced Japan to open its ports to the United States and in turn jumpstarted Japan's road to internationalization. The Convention of *Kanagawa* was a grossly unequal treaty that affected the Japanese society. Although Japan already had treaties with Portugal and the Netherlands, they were limited to the rights of passage through the Dejima Island and were strictly controlled by the Shogunate of the Edo era. However, the Convention of Kanagawa ceded this control, and Japan soon experienced social and political clashes due to the mass influx of Western culture.

The United States had the upper hand in negotiations due to its advanced cannons and guns. This brought to light the fact that Japanese weaponry and technology lagged far behind those of the West. As Western dominance was spreading throughout the globe, Japan understood that accepting Western technology and values was vital for its continued survival. This promoted the *Meiji* Restoration, which ended the centuries-long feudal system and began a new era of enlightenment and prosperity.

In order to catch up to the Western countries, Japan promoted various policies of modernization in economic, political, and military areas. The so-called "Western boom" spread quickly through the end of the nineteenth century. Japan established a British-inspired constitutional system and embraced Western capitalism and free competition. Socially, Japan advanced the westernization process by adopting British and German education systems. The government also established the Bureau of Translation to further the accomplishments by adopting Western technology.

Furthermore, to promote the transfer of Western technology, Japan hired foreign engineers and managers to assist with building new factories and infrastructure such as railroads. Also, thousands of foreigners from Europe and the United States were hired to teach modern science, technology, and foreign languages. Japan also sent thousands of selected students to study in Europe and the United States through government-sponsored programs. During this time, the Japanese government went so far as to declare, "We have no history. Our history starts now."

However, Japan did not just import Western technologies; it adjusted the acquired products to better fit Japan. For example, when Western machines were introduced to Japan's traditional cotton industry, the Japanese accepted them but made them smaller for efficient usage. Additional modifications included the use of wooden parts instead of steel because the Japanese had easier access to wood. Importing Western technologies and machines not only facilitated Japan's rapid industrialization but also increased the catch-up process to Western countries. In the end, Japan's capabilities of adaptation and renovation played a significant role in building the Japanese competitive products (e.g., consumer electronics and small and medium-sized cars) in the late twentieth century.

Internationalization not only made Japan's entire national system more efficient in terms of economic, social, and other aspects, but also expanded the country's scope from domestic to international, which became an important source of competitiveness. For example, after opening its ports to the world, Japan became a primary exporter of silk and tea, particularly to the United States. Through internationalization, the formerly impoverished farmers of Japan were able to dramatically increase their income because of the enormous demand overseas. Moreover, the liberalization in trade facilitated the emergence of the new merchant class. At that time, foreigners were not allowed to directly source raw materials (e.g., silk and tea) and had to go through Japanese merchants.

All in all, internationalization allowed Japan to succeed quickly relative to other non-Western countries and eventually helped Japan emerge as a global power. Although Japan's internationalization was involuntary and forced by Perry's expedition, the country chose to embrace it. This, as it turned out, was extremely beneficial for Japan's economic growth through the late 1980s and the speed and magnitude of its growth was unprecedented.

After experiencing decades of economic depression from the 1990s, particularly during the 2008 Global Financial Crisis, Japan introduced

Abenomics, which was composed of "three arrows" that aimed to revitalize the economy. The "third arrow" in particular, announced in 2013, attracted significant global attention due to its strong aspiration for growth. This new growth strategy aimed at increasing the productivity of Japan's industries through structural reformation. One of the three components of the growth strategy was "expanding global outreach," encouraging internationalization through regional cooperation in the form of free trade agreements and Trans-Pacific Partnerships. This implies that Japan once again realized the importance of internationalization for achieving sustainable growth.

7.1.3 China: Open Door Policy since 1978

Although China lagged behind Japan in opening its economy to the world, today, China has achieved significant internationalization and has even surpassed Japan in total GDP. China's rapid economic development can be attributed to Deng's open-door policy in 1978. The following is an excerpt from Deng's vision of internationalization shown in a conversation between Deng Xiaoping, Frank Gibney of Encyclopedia Britannica in America, and Director Paul Lin of the East Asian Research Institute of McGill University in Canada (China.org.cn, 1979):

> The aim of our revolution is to liberate and expand the productive forces. Without expanding the productive forces, making our country prosperous and powerful, and improving the living standards of the people, our revolution is just empty talk. . . . In the early 1960s, China was behind developed countries, but the gap was not as wide as it is now. . . . For a fairly long period of time since the founding of the People's Republic, we have been isolated from the rest of the world. . . . However, in the 1960s when opportunities to increase contact and cooperation with other countries presented themselves to us, we isolated ourselves. At last, we have learned to make use of favorable international conditions. . . . To realize the four modernizations, we must follow the correct foreign policy of opening to the outside world. Although we rely primarily on our own efforts, on our own resources, and on our own foundations to realize the four modernizations, it would be impossible for us to achieve this objective without international cooperation.

This shows Deng's keen insight into China's national development. Deng intuitively sensed the flaws in the national development goals constructed by the Gang of Four,[2] who considered it better to be a poor socialist state than to be a rich capitalist one. Since he understood that a country must improve its productivity in order to become a true welfare state, Deng's economic policy was fundamentally different from other socialist plans that focused on equal distribution and economic equality. Instead, Deng, like the Japanese government, chose to pursue benchmarking and constructive internationalization to increase productivity. Deng considered benchmarking to be an unconditional necessity, not an option; he adamantly claimed that China must follow good examples and not merely consider them. Also, Deng emphasized the importance of international cooperation. In that sense, he deserves a great deal of credit for recognizing that China's natural resource advantage could not sustain economic growth without foreign investment, which in turn requires cooperation with other countries.

People often point to China's cheap and plentiful labor, large land, and abundant natural resources when discussing China's economic development. However, these advantages have existed for thousands of years in China. In other words, there is limited correlation between China's inherited advantages and the current level of economic prosperity. These factors may have indeed helped in boosting the economy, but they alone are not the sole contributing factors. Historically, China was at its peak of prosperity when compared to the rest of the world during the Tang Dynasty, a period in which it actively engaged in foreign trade. Other high-growth periods include the Yuan Dynasty, when China actively exchanged with foreigners by calling them "the colored-eye people," and the reform era of the 1970s, when the country began to utilize foreign investments by opening its economy. Thus, a consistent driving force during these prosperous periods is internationalization.

The famous "Black Cat, White Cat" theory developed by Deng Xiaoping claims that "it does not matter whether a cat is white or black, as long as it catches mice." The lesson here is that ideologies should not matter in the face of wealth and productivity. Specifically to China's case, it should not matter whether the government pursues a planned or market economy as long as it results in higher incomes for the people and positive growth for the country. Under this spirit, China maintained its socialist regime politically while adopting competitive principles of capitalism. As a result, it did not take long before China began experiencing double-digit growth in its economy.

In addition to China's economic growth that resulted from internationalization, there is evidence showing that China's increasing degree of globalization enhanced its national competitiveness. In 1990, China's manufacturing output accounted for 3% of global manufacturing in terms of value—this number increased to approximately 15% in 2015. Also, with the increasing number of competitive domestic suppliers, the value of imported components for assembly decreased from 60% in the mid-1990s (peak) to nearly 35% in 2015 (*Economist* 2015b). More recently, following the global recession, China was less impacted than other countries and recovered quickly. In 2010, China replaced Japan as the world's second largest economy in terms of nominal GDP and is seen as the new economic power with significant growth potential.

A good example is the growth of the Guangdong Province in which the local government made efforts to pursue sustainable growth through internationalization and industry advancement. In 2010, I was invited to consult on this region's industrial upgrade and used Korea's experiences of economic development as an example. The Guangdong area was the pioneer that implemented China's reform and open-economy policy. With the opening of the economy a great number of foreign investors were allowed to build factories and conduct other businesses and were able to utilize low labor costs in the Guangdong Province. This type of FDI was the main source of Guangdong's financial resources and technology learning which were required for the region's economic growth.

After the door was open, almost half of China's overall FDI flew into the Guangdong Province between 1979 and 1991 (Tuan and Yeeng 1995).[3] The gross regional product (GRP) of the Guangdong Province increased by nine times during the 30 years from 1949 to China's opening in 1978. After active internationalization and industrial upgrades, the growth rate increased 193 times from 1978 to 2008. What is also significant is that the GRP of the Guangdong Province surpassed the GDP of Singapore in 1998, Hong Kong in 2003, and Taiwan in 2007. Much of this success is attributed to the open door policy that began in 1978.

However, after 30 years of accelerated growth, Guangdong's growth strategy gradually began to show certain limitations. The increasing price of land and labor has degraded Guangdong's cost advantage in the global market. Furthermore, the Global Financial Crisis in 2008 significantly impacted Guangdong where thousands of firms in low-value sectors such as shoes, toys, and clothing were shut down due to slowing foreign demand and increasing labor prices (*Economist* 2008).

Although the financial crisis beckoned Guangdong's most difficult year (*China Daily* 2009), it also provided a good opportunity for Guangdong to promote industries' structural transformation and shift from quantity to quality growth. Although Guangdong embarked on a plan for industrial upgrades as early as the 1990s, only after the 2008 financial crisis did Guangdong promote industrial upgrade and transfer across the whole province. In addition to industry transfer within the region, Guangdong also planned to enhance cooperation internationally by working with Hong Kong and Macau to build basic infrastructure and modern service sectors such as finance, distribution, and intermediary services. As a result, the share of traditional labor-intensive industries such as textile and clothing, food and beverage gradually decreased while the share of modern service industries increased.

Internationalization has both positive and negative influences, yet it is a net positive to national development. However, the magnitude of benefits from internationalization ultimately depends on the government's planning and implementation capabilities as demonstrated in the case of Guangdong.

7.1.4 India: Globalization Strategy since 2000

India began its globalization strategy the latest out of the four countries. After its independence from Britain, India's major concern was to address mass poverty, illiteracy, and health problems that existed nationwide. To achieve solutions in a short period of time, India aimed to achieve modernization and industrialization quickly. During that period, the Indian government observed that while industrialization in Britain took several generations, the Soviet industrialization took only one. With the intention to follow the Soviet system, the first post-independence Prime Minister of India, Jawaharlal Nehru, carefully studied the Soviet model and planned the country's economic policies accordingly. This decision also reflected India's determination to never again be influenced by the West following its independence from the British Empire. Despite India's efforts, however, development was slow and ineffective. On this earlier decision, former Prime Minister and Minister of Finance Manmohan Singh mentioned the following in an interview.[4]

> When India benchmarked the Soviet model and initiated the socialist economic system, it seemed to be operating well in the first five years of its implementation. India's economy worked better than South America or Africa until the 1980s. The country was running quite well by the world standard. However, many economic problems erupted after fifteen to twenty years. The central-planning Soviet system did not bring rapid success as Prime Minister Nehru had intended and many subsequent leaders tried different economic policies to facilitate growth. Gradually, economic conditions of India slowed and faced economic crisis in 1991, which put India on the verge of bankruptcy.

The ineffectiveness of the Soviet model was compounded by the collapse of the Soviet Union in 1991. In contrast, the rapid development of the East Asian countries influenced India to seek alternative routes to prosperity. Particularly, China's great success after Deng Xiaoping's reform and open economy policy showed that the market system was the right way for prosperity. Eventually, India abandoned the Permit Raj Policy[5] and sought radical reforms toward a market economy.

In 1991, the Indian government introduced several reforms toward liberalization and privatization of the Indian economy in areas such as tariffs, exchange rates, industrial licensing, and FDI. With the adoption of the market system, competition increased between domestic and foreign firms. To adjust to this change and compete with foreign countries, India gradually decreased its tariffs and abolished many other protectionist policies. Also, prior to the reform, no more than 40% of foreign investments were allowed in India, and foreign firms were permitted to do business in India only with a promise for technology transfer. However, after the reform, many of these barriers were removed which significantly benefited the Indian economy.

For instance, as the Indian automotive sector was highly regulated and protected, the Indian government implemented many liberalization measures on FDI in the automotive sector in 1991 and the passenger car sector in 1993. Technology transfer from foreign multinational companies (MNCs) was encouraged and majority-owned or wholly-owned subsidiaries were permitted. In the early 2000s, the government even abolished the requirement of local content and a minimum investment threshold (see Kumaraswamy et al. 2012). Thanks to the above liberalization efforts, many global firms entered India.

The drastic changes and reforms under Prime Minister Rao produced positive results almost immediately. There was a substantial increase in trade, FDI, and eventually growth in India's economy. Another notable change was that India's development path was unique as it defied Petty's Law[6] and developed a tertiary industry over its secondary industry. From 2000 to 2011, the service sector contributed to more than 80% of India's overall GDP growth. This is why, in contrast to other developing countries such as China, India's growth is named "service-led growth" (UNTAD 2012).

In response to this view, former Prime Minister Singh explained that India's manufacturing industry lost its competitiveness because it was limited to the domestic market under government intervention. However, the service industry and the IT sector, in particular, were able to operate globally without government intervention. Once again, this example, which is unique to India, shows the importance of internationalization. The growth of the Indian economy has been clearly linked to the promotion of international trade, FDI, and technology transfer.

India was able to come so far because it finally abandoned the closed market system and implemented an international division of labor and open-door policies. Simply decreasing government intervention would not have been enough to overcome its economic recession of the early 1990s. The secret of internationalization lies in appropriate benchmarking and convergence with India's unique advantages. The pledge by the new government elected in 2014 to accelerate economic reform by promoting broad reform agendas also includes India's strong resolution for economic development through internationalization.

7.1.5 The Logic behind Internationalization for National Growth

There is no doubt that internationalization is a critical source of national competitiveness. In theory, internationalization is regarded as an important source for enhancing national competitiveness because it allows countries to complement domestic disadvantages with international resources (Rugman 1991; Rugman and D'Cruz 1993; Moon, Rugman, and Verbeke 1998; Dunning 2003). Almost all empirical studies have demonstrated that open economies grow faster than closed economies (e.g., Yanikkaya 2003). However, it is important to note that value is created by firms, not countries (Porter 1990). This means government policy is important because it provides the institutional environment to attract multinational firms, which can balance out any disequilibrium in the domestic economy.

Small economies rely more on internationalization to gain competitiveness by leveraging global resources (Rugman and D'Cruz 1993; Moon, Rugman, and Verbeke 1998). However, the case studies of Japan, China, and India, show that internationalization also plays a crucial role in countries with large populations. Whether the country opened its doors as a result of foreign pressure (e.g., Japan), social and internal motivation (e.g., China), or failed policies (e.g., India), these countries significantly altered their course with internationalization. As we have seen, internationalization was a common driving force behind the economic growth of these four countries.

Large countries tend to possess comparative advantages from an abundance of inherited advantages, such as natural resources or large populations. However, Auty (2001) discovered that resource-poor economies witnessed better economic performance than resource-abundant countries since the 1960s. The author attributed this to the following: the efficient use of scarce resources, openness, and industry diversification. With respect to the second reason on internationalization, Auty (2001) argued that resource-abundant countries are more likely to pursue a less active trade policy because they can survive without opening their economies. However, in the current globalized era, countries can no longer survive or develop by themselves unless they liberalize and open their economy to the world, as shown in the cases of China and India.

Despite the general agreement on the positive role of internationalization for economic development, there is still controversy on the effects of FDI. For example, Porter (1990) emphasized the importance of outward FDI because it is an indicator of the home country's superior competitiveness. On the other hand, scholars such as Reich (1990, 1991) argued for inward FDI because it contributes to job creation for the host country. In reality, however, both inward and outward FDI are good for both home and host countries (e.g., Moon 2005a) because in the growing globalized world, countries are more connected to each other and they can make up for their disadvantages from a mutual exchange. Therefore, internationalization is important for enhancing national competitiveness, regardless of the country's development level (developing or developed), country size (small or large), and resource endowment (scarce or rich).

7.2 THE ABCDs, INTERNATIONALIZATION, AND ECONOMIC GROWTH

Internationalization can serve as a great impetus for growth, but it can never be done alone. While there are many countries that have implemented open policies, the results vary as seen in the differing economic performance among East Asian and other developing countries. The gap in economic development among countries depends on how countries have internationalize and how they utilize international resources. The following section applies the ABCDs to discuss how countries can most effectively pursue internationalization.

7.2.1 The Sooner, the Better

The timing of internationalization is correlated to a nation's economic wealth. Countries that cooperated with other economies early on currently have more prosperity. For example, the first-tier Asian NIEs (Singapore,

Hong Kong, Taiwan, and Korea, also named as "Four Asian Tigers") adopted outward-oriented policies in the 1960s, the second-tier Asian NIEs (the four Southeast Asian countries, namely, Malaysia, Indonesia, Thailand, and the Philippines) in the 1970s, and China and India much later on. Today, the living standards of these countries correlate with how early they pursued internationalization.

Through liberalization and an open-door policy, foreign firms are allowed to do business in home countries. This pressures local firms to develop faster in order to survive a more competitive domestic market. With increasing domestic competition, local firms are encouraged to tap the global market for continued growth. This competition directly or indirectly increases the speed and precision of firms' operations as they try to maintain their current competitive position or catch up to leaders. Internationalization can thus explain why some countries can grow faster and even outperform those that were previously more advanced.

7.2.2 Learning from Successful Economies

Internationalization provides a variety of choices. By adopting useful practices for benchmarking, a country can gain new sources of competitiveness. Yanikkaya (2003) argued that developing countries can particularly benefit from trading with more developed and technologically innovative countries because this allows access to larger markets and promotes advancement and investment in R&D. Without an open policy, countries such as Japan, China, and India would not have realized the fact that they were far behind other countries.

Some may have concerns that a large-scale entry by foreign MNCs after market liberalization may hurt domestic firms because foreign MNCs usually possess superior technological and managerial capabilities relative to domestic incumbents. However, at the early stage of entry, foreign firms often lack local institutional knowledge and optimal distribution. Hence, instead of establishing wholly-owned subsidiaries, they prefer to form joint ventures or other types of partnerships with local firms, which provide benefits to host countries (Hennart 2009). Therefore, during this stage, domestic firms have opportunities to learn managerial skills and technologies from foreign MNCs. In addition, as they broaden the scope of business by going abroad, domestic firms can also learn the best practices of global markets, which will enhance their international competitiveness.

7.2.3 Creating New Advantages by Combining International Diversity

Enhancing national competitiveness comes from the efficient utilization of domestic and international resources. This is the key to success for countries' economic development. China, for one, achieved substantial economic growth by synergistically integrating the Western market system to its own political system. Similarly, Japan adopted advanced US technologies and combined them with its unique manufacturing system, and outperformed the US firms in many industries. National competitiveness does not always come from superior technological competence, but the capabilities of how to combine diverse resources and create new advantages.

Furthermore, countries can utilize their partners' strengths to complement their disadvantages, by forming economic blocs such as free trade agreements or regional cooperation. For example, the Guangdong Province in China was able to achieve higher growth and better living standards relative to other provinces due to its locational advantage, which facilitated its economic cooperation with Hong Kong. Cooperation among complementary countries results in greater benefits (Moon and Kim 2006b).[7] Countries that have similar endowments and capabilities (e.g., Korea and Japan) can also find a way to complement each other by looking at the subvariables (i.e., more specific or specialized areas) of competitiveness instead of the overall competitive structure. International cooperation at the country level can be more effectively promoted through international clusters. For example, the cooperation among Singapore, Malaysia, and Indonesia through the SIJOIRI growth triangle demonstrates a higher level of cooperation and more benefits among the member countries.

7.2.4 Changing the Goals and Strategies of Internationalization

The purpose of liberalization varies based on the country's degree of development. For example, at the beginning stage, the main goals are often to attract MNCs' financial and technical assistance (Ivarsson and Alvstam 2005). At this stage, therefore, the host countries are more likely to provide many benefits to entice foreign investment (Dunning and Lundan 2008). However, at the later stage, along with the enhanced economic strengths and accumulated technological capabilities, host countries would be more likely to selectively choose FDI that can satisfy their new strategic goals of national development as seen by China's current policy changes.

Likewise, MNCs will also change their business strategies. After a certain period of doing business in the country, they may prefer to have their own subsidiaries rather than joint ventures with local firms (Kumaraswamy et al. 2012). This will subsequently affect the growth and survival of domestic firms. Therefore, national governments should pay great attention to the changing situations and create policies by which the country can maximize the benefits from global resources and minimize adverse effects.

Promoting internationalization will ultimately benefit the overall country, but there will be both winners and losers. The problem results from the loser group, who would most likely have an anti-open policy attitude and be a serious obstacle in achieving internationalization. Similar to other advanced economies, an anti-globalization sentiment is becoming pervasive within Korea's society. Many Koreans still show misgivings or outright animosity toward dual citizenship, foreign nationals, and foreigners naturalized as Korean citizens. They often overemphasize negative incidents and conflicts involving non-Koreans and have an overly pessimistic view of immigration. Of course, internationalization is not without its drawbacks, however, the benefits of internationalization far outweigh the problems and its potential to accelerate national growth should not be understated.

Some people argue that Korea is too internationalized and susceptible to external environmental changes. However, this argument is not valid because Korea's openness is skewed to international trade. Korea's openness in terms of trade is relatively high—more than 100% of Korea's GDP, but its openness to FDI and other indexes such as immigration is much lower than that of trade. For example, the share of Korea's inward FDI in its GDP was just 1% in 2013, which was much lower than other NIEs (7%), China (1.3%), and India (1.5%) (UNCTAD Statistics 2015). Despite many issues and challenges that come with internationalization, in order to maintain sustainable growth, Korea should continue to have a clear goal with diligent and efficient policy implementation, for more internationalization and more balanced internationalization across trade, investment, and immigration.

CHAPTER 8
Internationalization at the Firm Level

Nowadays, consumers are more informed due to the advancement of technology and the Internet. Consumer tastes have also become more sophisticated and diversified. This is because globalization allows consumers to easily access foreign products and compare them with domestic products when deciding which product to buy. As a result, consumers are no longer bound to only domestic brands and make decisions based on globally competitive price and quality. These changes in consumption patterns require parallel changes from firms—they now need to efficiently procure resources globally and serve consumer demand in the most efficient manner at low cost and high quality.

A common trait of successful global companies such as Apple is their ability to maximize utility by selecting appropriate partners and locations across the world to establish the most efficient value chain. This is the essence of the global value chain (GVC) strategy. Firms procure supplies where they are the cheapest, manufacture goods where production costs are the lowest while maintaining a certain level of quality, and sell goods where demand is high and stable. In effect, globalization allows corporations to increase their scope of choices, thereby enabling firms to maximize efficiency and the chance for success. The fact that China is the number one manufacturing site for nearly 80% of the world's air conditioners, 70% of mobile phones, and 60% of shoes (*Economist* 2015b), mainly by the multinational corporations (MNCs) in China, shows how companies are maximizing efficiency by spreading value chain activities globally. Therefore, it is becoming increasingly difficult for firms and industries to operate within a purely domestic context.

However, governments and societies do not always believe that internationalization is a positive shift for the country. For example, the home country might be concerned with the problem of industrial "hollow-out" when domestic firms invest in foreign countries. Host countries, on the other hand, worry about the negative impact of MNCs' operations, and some even consider foreign investment to be a new form of colonization.

The ambivalent perspectives on internationalization show how governments need to have a proper understanding of international business. Governments will directly or indirectly affect the scope and scale of firms' international business, which in turn will influence the overall competitiveness of firms and countries. With this in mind, this chapter begins by comparing the different perspectives of politicians and businessmen on international business and points to the source of conflicts. The chapter will then continue by highlighting the importance of GVC in enhancing firm competitiveness. In order to facilitate the fundamental understanding of firms' global expansion, a concise review of prominent studies on international business will be provided. As firms' global expansion is not separate from national interest, this chapter also examines the impact of foreign direct investment (FDI) on both home and host countries. Finally, this chapter will conclude by demonstrating how the ABCD model can help enhance the efficacy of firms' international activities.

8.1 ENHANCING FIRMS' COMPETITIVENESS

8.1.1 Different Perspectives on International Business

In February 2011, President Obama held a dinner in California with 12 CEOs of major technology companies. With prominent business leaders such as Mark Zuckerberg and Steve Jobs, the discussion centered on facilitating investment and creating more jobs within the United States. In addressing his concerns, President Obama wondered whether the 70 million iPhones, 30 million iPads, and 59 million other Apple products manufactured abroad could be produced inside the United States. Steve Jobs responded by simply shaking his head and said, "No, those jobs aren't coming back" (Duhigg and Bradshier 2012).

Jobs' flat refusal disappointed President Obama. The meeting occurred at a critical time when President Obama had to address the falling employment rate to dissatisfied US citizens in order to be reelected the following year. In fact, Obama was eager to present his plan to increase exports and create new jobs to facilitate private sector growth and employment to the CEOs.

Steve Jobs' response later sparked public criticism for his perceived selfish business behavior. However, the conversation highlights the fundamental differences between politicians and businessmen on firms' international activities. Politicians are primarily concerned with appeasing the public, and therefore aim to satisfy issues such as job security and wage increases. To politicians, voter turnout and public support are the most important issues they must address. Therefore, they tend to focus on popular topics such as domestic industries and job security, even if they may produce short-term benefits at the cost of long-term national competitiveness.

In contrast, a businessman like Steve Jobs is more devoted to corporate objectives of profit maximization by improving the productivity of business operations. To businessmen, having the best cost structure for quality products to satisfy all consumers are more important than creating jobs through domestic production. Businessmen are less concerned about where to manufacture their products and whom to employ as long as the production cost is the lowest and legal and ethical values are maintained. This is the fundamental difference between politics and business, and this discrepancy is well illustrated in the earlier conversation between President Obama and Steve Jobs. Table 8.1 summarizes these differences.

Politicians and corporate executives may clash due to different perspectives on international business. For one, politicians exercise most of their control within the domestic sphere, but executives are engaged in both domestic and global communities. Even on international issues, politicians proceed by representing domestic concerns and interests. Furthermore, politicians are only loyal to their voter constituents, but businessmen must also consider the interests of their global stakeholders, including foreign governments, producers, and consumers.

Table 8.1 COMPARISON BETWEEN POLITICIANS AND BUSINESSMEN

	Politicians	Businessmen
Scope of activities	Domestic	Domestic + Foreign
Interests	Voters	Stakeholders
Objective	Welfare: employment	Profit creation
Method	Protectionism	Efficiency
Production strategy	Made in home country	Made in the world
Global view	Competition	Competition + Cooperation
Result	Income distribution	Survival and growth

Source: Moon (2012d).

Politicians tend to prioritize fair distribution, job security, and the social welfare of voters, while executives pursue profit maximization through business operations on a global scale. In order to satisfy their voter group, politicians may prefer protectionist and export policies, but businessmen need to increase efficiencies by optimizing activities of the GVC. Politicians often view other nations as rivals in competition for exporting home products, while businessmen often view foreign entities as partners for cheaper production and higher sales. As a result, politicians focus on income redistribution and reducing the wage gap, whereas executives focus on creating values to increase the firms' competitiveness.

Apple has well demonstrated these business values in the labeling of its products. Instead of displaying the usual "Made in USA" imprint, Apple products say: "Designed by Apple in California, Assembled in China." The CEO of Li & Fung, the world's oldest textile manufacturer, expressed a similar mindset in an interview with American journalist Thomas Friedman—"We sourced from Asia and sold in America and Europe. Now the rule of survival has changed. Now our motto is to source everywhere, manufacture everywhere, and sell everywhere." This implies that the profit maximization principle is unalterable and internationalization plays an important role in accelerating growth and productivity.

8.1.2 From Trade to the Global Value Chain

Global sourcing by firms such as Apple became a popular trend for MNCs. According to the 2013 World Investment Report, trade in intermediate goods and services accounted for 60% of total global trade (UNTAD 2013). This implies that firms' value chain activities are no longer isolated in a single location. Instead, the value added processes are fragmented across different locations around the world to utilize location-specific advantages. This eventually encourages the emergence of borderless value adding systems, which are referred to as GVC.

In the past, companies invested abroad to exploit or expand their existing competitive advantages. However, recently there have been a growing number of foreign investments aimed at obtaining new competitive advantages by both latecomers and forerunners (e.g., Moon and Roehl 2001). This is because of the substantial changes in the business environment over the past few decades. As the lifecycle of technology shortens, a single or few core technologies can no longer sustain a firm's competitive advantage. Also, the increasingly sophisticated consumer demand requires multipurpose products, and intensive competition pressures firms to continuously create new products in order to maintain their competitive positions. Therefore, rather than conducting all activities internally, firms are more likely to disperse certain activities externally to the most competent firms across the globe. This not only saves time and resources but also enhances firms' product specifications, productivity, and competitiveness, which then benefit consumers in terms of price and quality.

GVC is not a newly developed concept, but the scope of existing studies on GVC has always been narrow, often only emphasizing production processes such as the traded value of intermediary goods versus final goods. For example, UNCTAD's (2013) definition of GVC primarily focuses on the production system and not the entire value chain. The scope of the value chain analysis of these studies is thus limited to upstream activities and needs to be extended to the entire value chain, including downstream and support activities (Moon 2016). Firm competitiveness is no longer determined by a single firm, but the entire network of firms that are engaged in GVC for all business activities.

As MNCs disperse their value chain activities throughout the world, they have to simultaneously determine which activities should be located domestically, and which should be dispersed internationally (UNCTAD 2013). With this added optionality, business decisions become more complex and intertwined with diverse business actors both at home and abroad. As a result, GVC management has become a critical business priority for many MNCs as it relates to the productivity and competitiveness of firms in the global market.

The competition between Samsung and Apple clearly demonstrates the significance of utilizing the GVC effectively to enhance firm competitiveness. International sales account for approximately 90% of Samsung's total revenue. By 2013, Samsung had sales offices in 50 countries. For production, Samsung has been trying to expand foreign facilities and R&D centers across the world. Apple, which has a relatively lower proportion of international sales at 60%, had Apple stores in 16 countries based on 2013 figures, and its entire manufacturing line is located outside the United States; only the high value-added R&D sector is based at home (SERI 2014).[1]

An analysis of both Samsung and Apple's GVC reveals extensive relationships with foreign affiliates. Samsung and Apple work closely with firms in Japan, Europe, and other parts of the world to efficiently source their component parts. The multinationality of the GVC further highlights differences in the configuration between Samsung and Apple's value chains, which provide further insights into the impact of GVCs.

Samsung's procurement was mostly domestic, with 74% of materials and components coming from Korean companies in 2013, whereas Apple's domestic procurement was lower at 25%. This means that Apple procured 75% of its parts from foreign partners. Also, Samsung internally developed 26% of its products and technologies, whereas Apple outsourced all activities except for R&D and design (SERI 2014). These differences between Samsung and Apple could be due to their disparate origins and strategic positioning: Samsung started as a basic manufacturing company, whereas Apple engaged in developing and distributing state-of-the-art technologies.

The growing size and scope of GVC shows that competition no longer involves a small number of companies that sell finished products. As MNCs begin to aggressively utilize GVC to improve the competitiveness of their businesses, competition heightens as a consequence and MNCs must excel in every part of their GVC activities to reap sustainable profits. Therefore, leading MNCs such as Samsung and Apple compete against each other with their entire GVCs, but they also engage in cooperative relationships with their affiliates or other related firms within their GVC. Therefore, in global business competition, the unit of analysis changes from a single company to the GVC of a leading company and its cooperative partners. The leading firms and related firms in the GVC make up the whole business ecosystem. The relationships among related firms within Samsung and Apple's ecosystem are captured in figure 8.1.

Without understanding this new paradigm of firm competitiveness shifting from the single firm to the entire ecosystem, governments may

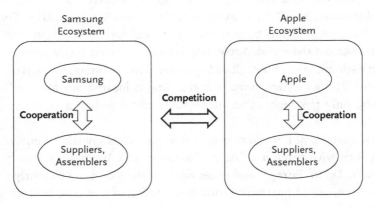

Figure 8.1
Samsung and Apple's Business Ecosystems

make inefficient policy decisions. For example, governments may think that large companies make profits by lowering the prices of component parts procured from their partners that are usually small companies. There are two mistakes about this viewpoint. First, the price of component parts is not unilaterally determined by the leading firms, but through a comparison with competitors' partners (affiliates or subcontractors). For example, the component parts of Samsung's subcontractors need to be more competitive than Apple's subcontractors in both price and quality. Otherwise, Samsung would not be able to compete successfully with Apple in the global market. Second, large firms do not simply exploit their suppliers. In fact, there is ample evidence that suppliers connected to global leading firms earn higher revenues and profits than other suppliers (Choi 2013; SERI 2014). In order to produce high-quality products, leading firms will transfer technology and provide training programs to their partners. Therefore, the government's act of blindly favoring small companies at the expense of large ones could negatively affect both small and large companies (i.e., the entire ecosystem).

In addition, the GVC approach will alleviate contradictory perspectives between governments and firms and even reduce national trade disputes. Most governments, including the United States, still emphasize the significance of trade balance accounts and try to increase barriers to the import from other countries. However, the problem with this traditional approach is that it simply calculates trade figures and does not identify transaction points where value is created.

Let's take the example of the global trade of Apple's iPhone. In 2009, the amount of Apple products exported from China to the United States was $2 billion. Using the traditional approach of trade accounts, the United States recorded a trade deficit against China of approximately $1.9 billion after deducting $121.5 million in the export of certain iPhone parts from the United States to China. However, the GVC approach shows that the United States, in fact, made a value-added surplus because not all of the $1.9 billion in value was created inside China. The value added in China accounted for 3.6% and the value of the US parts comprised 6%, resulting in a trade surplus of 2.4% (i.e., $48 million) for the United States. China was the final assembly place for the iPhone, and most of its components were imported from other countries such as the United States, Japan, Germany, and Korea (Xing and Detert 2010). Therefore, in order to plan and implement realistic trade policies, policy makers should first change the statistical calculation from trade to GVC, which is more accurate in reflecting firms' economic contribution to the country.

8.1.3 Re-examining the Benefits of the Global Value Chain

Firms can enhance competitiveness through GVC as long as they minimize coordination costs among different regions and partners. Otherwise it would be wiser to concentrate all activities domestically or place the entire value chain in a single host country, as most multi-domestic firms do.[2] A similar argument was put forth by Porter and Rivkin (2012). They argued that the recent fall of America's competitiveness as an investment location was due to inadequate government policies in business and indiscreet overseas investment of American firms. According to these authors, American firms failed in overseas markets because they ignored the basic principles of low cost and efficient operations; specifically, many American firms that sought cheap labor abroad overlooked the hidden costs of offshoring and thus failed to create adequate profits.

Porter and Rivkin argued that to choose a better location, an accurate assessment of costs and benefits is needed, by incorporating both direct/indirect and short/long-term views. Many benefits of overseas investment (e.g., low labor cost, tax reduction) are immediate and visible in the short term, but many hidden costs (e.g., wage inflation, regional coordination costs) are overlooked and appear after a certain period of time. Therefore, with comprehensive considerations of the pros and cons of offshoring, a firm or government may determine whether doing business internationally is more profitable. In fact, many US firms have recently experienced such hidden costs, and began to shift their businesses back to the United States. For instance, the high productivity of American laborers was claimed to offset higher wages, making overseas labor markets less attractive. Also, investment funds and transfer costs were said to outweigh the benefits of building new plants in other countries.

Porter and Rivkin did not claim that US firms should always remain in the United States, but opposed frequent shifts from one place to another. This is because firm productivity is often influenced by the investments in individual employees, development teams, and related infrastructure, as well as the entire network. As these investments require long-time commitment, frequent movement will not benefit a firms productivity. Therefore, they suggested that instead of dispersing activities in many locations, it would be more beneficial for firms to select several locations and upgrade the local business environment. Firms will then ultimately achieve large potential benefits from building local clusters and enriching the ecosystem.

Porter and Rivkin's study used Corning Inc., an American manufacturer of glass, ceramics, optical fibers, and LCDs, as an example of a competitive company that focuses primarily on domestic production with selective foreign production. Based in New York, Corning invests heavily in regional research institutes and schools that provide the company with a highly productive labor pool. Citing companies like Corning, Porter and Rivkin advocated for firms to stay at home to generate benefits for both the nation and the company.

At first glance, this argument might sound convincing. However, there are many cases that show opposite results. For instance, the most successful GVC strategy implies that labor-intensive activities are located in developing countries and technology-intensive activities are located in advanced countries. To reorient corporate value chains effectively, however, there should be a different strategy depending on the industry or activity type. In particular, the following four types of activities are better suited for domestic locations for the United States: (1) activities that require high technology and quality (e.g., space technology and aircrafts); (2) activities that are sensitive to consumer health (e.g., pharmaceutical and specialty foods); (3) activities that are insensitive to wages due to automation (e.g., highly automated manufacturing); and (4) activities that need to respond quickly to consumers (e.g., design and delivery services). Activities that do not belong to these categories are better to be located overseas (Moon 2012d).

A good example is that Apple selected the Taiwanese contractor Foxconn to manage human resources and logistics in China, but managed technology development, procurement, and marketing from its offices in the United States. This shows how advanced technology, sophisticated design processes, and components procurement are handled at home, while activities that can reduce production costs occur at cheaper locations. Moreover, marketing and service activities which are highly sensitive to consumer responses are managed locally per region.

A company like Nike, which has a greater focus on labor-intensive activities, has a more diversified GVC and a greater range of manufacturing locations. Only those activities in the value chain related to advanced technology and design are located in the United States. On the other hand, Nike has manufacturing plants and affiliate companies in China, Thailand, Vietnam, Indonesia, and other countries because these regions enable Nike to save costs on production, logistics, and operations. In addition, marketing, sales, and service activities are performed by local partners in each country.

The United States is a country where economic activities and production structures are highly developed. As a result, there are more technology-intensive industries compared to labor-intensive industries, and this has been a staple feature of the United States. In technology-intensive industries such as fiber optics, pharmaceuticals, IT, and aircraft, companies are differentiated more by quality and safety over price. In this regard, Porter and Rivkin's arguments apply to technology-intensive industries, not labor-intensive industries. On the other hand, labor-intensive industries such as footwear and apparel compete heavily on price. Productivity is thus more important in these fields, and overseas labor markets provide more advantages than the American market.

Many Western scholars make the same misinterpretation as Porter and Rivkin because they overlook the differences in production factors between developed and less developed regions. As is the case with Apple and Nike, companies are less concerned with being domestic as long as value creation can be increased by overseas operations. In the real world, companies prefer this type of GVC for its efficiency and cost-saving attributes. Porter and Rivkin viewed Corning as a domestic company because it did not expand abroad and its entire value chain is located in the United States. However, it should be noted that three-fourths of its corporate revenue is created in the overseas market. If you analyze the business spread of Corning closely, it actually operates across Asia, the Middle East, Europe, and South America, with independent value chains in some of these countries.[3] Therefore, firms should choose the most optimal way of utilizing global resources, while considering the characteristics of activities and the specific industry which they are engaged in.

8.1.4 The Logic behind Internationalization for Corporate Growth

The preceding sections discussed how firms can enhance competitiveness through the GVC. This section now looks into firms' global expansion from a theoretical perspective. There are two main tools of internationalization: trade and FDI. Trade is the transfer of intermediary or final goods across national borders, and FDI is the transfer of value-added sources such as technology, management, and marketing skills. The growing importance of FDI is reflected in the value of international production, which has expanded sharply in the last several decades and played a considerable role in shaping the world economy. This is mainly because traditional theories of international trade assume that factors are immobile between countries. The basic assumption of traditional trade theory is that the market is modeled after perfect competition with zero transaction cost. However, in reality, the market system is imperfect and international factor mobility is possible and occurs prevalently by MNCs. Under this business environment, MNCs can benefit by choosing FDI as the means of internationalization.

The most popular FDI theory is Dunning's (1976, 2001) OLI paradigm (or eclectic paradigm). The OLI paradigm is composed of three elements: ownership advantage (O), location advantage (L), and internalization advantage (I). According to this paradigm, the O advantage refers to the assets that are not possessed or accessible by rivals, and it is therefore described as a monopolistic asset. The O advantage benefits MNCs by off-setting some of the inevitable disadvantages that occur from being a for-eign entity (e.g., cultural and language barriers). The L advantage refers to the location-specific advantages of host countries, and it can either be inherited assets (e.g., natural resources, cheap labor, and a large market) or created assets (e.g., institutional structure, value-creating network, and clusters). Unlike the other two, the I advantage is more related to the entry mode for foreign investment. The entry mode with the lowest degree of control is licensing while joint ventures and wholly owned subsidiaries offer higher control. Overall, the O advantage explains why firms engage in foreign investment, the L advantage explains where firms invest abroad, and the I advantage explains how firms invest abroad (Moon 2016).

Despite the dominant position of the OLI paradigm in the field of FDI theory, it is not without criticism. The key assumption of the OLI paradigm is that firms should have an O advantage such as superior technology in order to successfully carry out FDI. However, the outward investments by firms that come from developing or emerging countries do not always possess critical firm-specific O advantages compared to the firms from advanced countries. Their motivations for FDI are often to gain access to ownership advantages in the advanced host countries and to seek new assets that are necessary to be globally competitive.

To solve this theoretical gap in practice, scholars tried to develop new theories and extend existing ones. For example, the imbalance theory (Moon and Roehl 2001) focused on the bottom-up (i.e., developing to developed market) FDI, which is growing in number and scale. According to this theory, emerging firms pursue FDI not because they have superior O advantages, but because they want to increase their competitiveness by acquiring resources from advanced countries to supplement their O disadvantages.

In addition to these FDI theories, the different locations of FDI and the degree of coordination among investment locations need to be further distinguished in order to have an in-depth understanding of the global operations of firms. Porter's (1986) Configuration-Coordination (C-C) framework and Prahalad and Doz's (1987) Integration-Responsiveness

(I-R) framework are the most popular and empirically supported theories for this purpose. Despite the different terminologies, both frameworks fundamentally consider the two criteria: (1) geographical deployment of value chain activities around the world, and (2) the degree of coordination among value chain activities in different locations.

Using the I-R framework, Bartlett and Ghoshal (1989) classified global firms as multinational, global, international, and transnational firms. Harzing (2000) further revised Bartlett and Ghoshal's typology into multi-domestic, global, and transnational firms and excluded international firms due to its ambiguity. There is no universally appropriate choice for all firms—it depends on the industry in which firms compete, the characteristics of value chain activities, and firm capabilities. For example, for downstream activities like marketing, firms prefer to choose the multi-domestic process in order to respond quickly and accurately to local demands. On the other hand, for upstream activities such as production, firms tend to select the type of global strategy that can best improve efficiency through high global integration (Moon and Kim 2008).

8.2 IMPACTS OF FIRMS' INTERNATIONALIZATION ON HOME AND HOST COUNTRIES

In line with the GVC, FDI is the main strategic tool for MNCs to expand their value chain activities globally.[4] Prior to the mid-1990s, people held a more negative view on FDI, but with the recent trend toward globalization, this perspective has changed substantially. However, even today, studies of FDI's impact on economic growth demonstrate both positive and negative perspectives.

For the home country, the negative impacts of outward FDI can be summarized as follows. First, outward FDI could lead to short-term capital outflow and loss of employment opportunities. Second, it might lead to a decrease in home country exports when firms transfer their manufacturing plants to foreign countries. Third, the leading companies' overseas investment might encourage other related firms (such as parts and components producers) to invest abroad, thereby resulting in the industrial hollowing-out problem. The last negative effect is the thinning domestic base of industries with heavy outward investment, which could also influence other domestic industries and deteriorate the overall competitiveness of the home country.

The negative impacts of inward FDI on host countries can be similarly organized. First, inward FDI might cause inappropriate compensation because foreign firms invest to utilize local resources and maximize profits as much as possible. Second, inward FDI increases disposable income for local residents, which also increases the diversity of products and services for consumption. This will often induce unnecessary consumption that exceeds the income level of local citizens. Third, foreign firms may source more parts and components from their existing foreign suppliers than from domestic firms. Lastly, the heightened competition could crowd out domestic firms from the local markets, particularly the ones in infant or less competitive industries.

However, these negative impacts on home and host countries are short term and the positive influences outweigh the negative in the long run. The net results depend on characteristics such as the level of economic development, the economic and industry structure, government policies, motivations for MNCs' investment (e.g., asset-, market-, and efficiency-seeking), and entry mode (UNCTAD 2006). The following section will discuss in more detail the positive impacts of FDI in four areas: capital transfer, trade promotion, industry growth and cluster effects, and technology development and innovation.

8.2.1 Capital Transfer

One of the prime advantages of FDI is the increase in capital transfer. Outward FDI benefits the home country's balance of payments with foreign demand for home-country equipment, intermediate goods, and complementary products, while at the same time there are increasing financial inflows from investment income, royalties, fees, and service charges associated with the investment (UNCTAD 2005). Although outward FDI induces financial outflows in the beginning, this gradually changes as investments begin to yield returns.

For host countries, acquiring capital by attracting inward FDI can directly fund national economic development (Lipsey 2004; Li and Liu 2005). Large MNCs have access to financial resources that are not readily available to the firms of host countries. With the help of these foreign MNCs, local firms can access diverse channels for capital which support their growth. As local governments expect that foreign affiliates will transfer earnings from the host countries to the home countries, they may set regulations to avoid or minimize such transfer. This policy may appear to be a good strategy for local governments to promote MNCs' reinvestment in host countries, but host country governments should be aware that excessive regulations will cause reverse effects.

8.2.2 Trade Promotion

With the increasing number of MNCs engaging in operations abroad, an issue that has emerged is the relationship between FDI and trade. Is FDI a substitute or complement for trade? This question has been crucial for firms to determine whether to trade or invest outside their home borders. Mainstream theories provide arguments for both complementary and substitute links between FDI and international trade.[5] In reality, FDI increases the volume of trade between the home and host countries, particularly through intra-firm trade. Intra-firm trade, which naturally increases with FDI, comprises a significant portion of all global trade. According to the World Investment Report 2013, MNCs were involved in 80% of global trade in goods and services in 2010, and the intra-firm trade between MNC parent companies and foreign affiliates accounted for 42% of total global trade by MNCs (UNCTAD 2013). FDI thus promotes the home country trade.

If MNCs invest abroad to attain natural resources from the host country, outward FDI can increase the imports of those resources, with corresponding exports in the inputs (e.g., equipments and facilities) required for their exploration and extraction. In cases where MNCs engage in FDI for market-seeking purposes, investments will boost the exports of intermediate and capital goods from the home country. On the other hand, inward FDI promotes the host country's export to the third country. For example, in China, much of the dramatic export growth was due to the presence of foreign MNCs that invested heavily in China during the 1990s. Particularly in mobile phones, the subsidiaries of foreign MNCs in China accounted for 95% of China's exports in electronics items (Hill, Wee, and Udayasanker 2012). Overall, FDI increases both exports and imports of the host country.

8.2.3 Industry Growth and Cluster Effects

In addition to the stated impacts on capital transfer and trade promotion, FDI offers many other significant but less visible benefits such as spillover effects for industry growth and increased efficiency through competition. For the home country, the interactions of outgoing MNCs with other home firms have impacts on all sectors of the economy. The more suppliers and affiliates the parent company has in the domestic value chain, the more likely the home country will experience a greater impact. In Hong Kong, for instance, the growth of outward FDI in more advanced-technology industries—mainly "soft" technology—has produced important forward and backward linkages with home-based firms and activities (Chen and Lin 2005).

To the host country, significant contributions of inward FDI include the emergence of new industries or drastic changes in the composition of production. Lipsey (2000) described the large role of US affiliates in the electronics industry in East Asia, especially in the early development of the industry. In the case of Korea, when foreign firms entered the service industry, there was a positive correlation with the growth of other industries, particularly manufacturing. According to Park (2009), 16 manufacturing companies between 1985 and 2003 grew in production with the inflow of foreign investment in service sectors such as transportation, communication, and finance. This shows the importance of inter-industry spillover effects by FDI.

8.2.4 Technology Development and Innovation

Home country benefits arise when MNCs learn valuable skills from their foreign operations in developed countries and bring them back to their home country. This is the so-called "reverse resource transfer effect." Reverse transfer of technology (Hobday 1995b), where knowledge acquired by foreign affiliates is channeled back to the home country, is one of the prominent ways of enhancing the home country's technological edge. Furthermore, with the globalization of knowledge, technology flows are more of a two-way phenomenon, and inflows and outflows mutually reinforce each other, bringing technological spillover effects home.

For the host country, one of the greatest long-term advantages of FDI is the spillover effect on technology and innovation. This is vital to national competitiveness and growth of the economy (Grossman and Helpman 1994; Salomon and Shaver 2005). For instance, local managers trained with the latest techniques of foreign MNCs can improve the efficiency of operations in the host country. Similarly, local personnel, with management and technical training from foreign MNCs can also benefit the local economy when leaving the firm to start their own businesses. Also, the superior management of foreign MNCs may stimulate local suppliers, distributors, and competitors to improve their own management skills.

In order to create and sustain competitive businesses, it is important for MNCs to co-create values with both home and host countries. Rather than emphasizing only the exploitation of local advantages or strategic assets from host countries, firms should maximize the positive effects and minimize the negative ones when investing abroad. Without creating benefits to both home and host countries, it will become more difficult for MNCs to validate their profits though global expansion. Having a concern for social benefits does not mean that firms should deal with social problems at the expense of business, which brings up the concept of corporate social responsibility. Instead, by addressing social issues, firms should create benefits for both firms and the involved countries. This will in turn not only reduce the tension between the firms and countries but also increase benefits for both firms and countries simultaneously.

8.3 THE ABCDs, INTERNATIONALIZATION, AND CORPORATE GROWTH

It is important to note that there are conflicting implications for the two strategies of international trade and FDI. International trade often prompts countries to adopt a competitive stance, leading to trade wars and zero-sum situations among nations. In contrast, FDI induces a more cooperative relationship between home and host countries as the investing firms generate numerous spillover effects, such as capital transfer, trade promotion, industry growth and cluster effects, and technology development and innovation, on both home and host countries.

With an increased scale of globalization, the most important change in international business is that the unit of firm competitiveness is shifting from the single firm to the entire GVC, which refers to the business ecosystem of a leading company that cooperates with its partner companies. Therefore, leading firms do not compete with their suppliers and other related firms but cooperate with them to maximize the efficiency in the whole value chain.

8.3.1 Increasing Agility for Efficiency in the Global Value Chain

The ABCD model can be applied to maximize the benefits of utilizing GVC. First, satisfying the first condition of speed and precision is important for firms participating in the value chain. Firms should deliver the outputs of each activity to the next activity in the value chain on time and with precision. Tardiness or poor quality in any part of the process will ultimately affect the competitiveness of the final product. A case in point is Toyota's substantial loss of revenue due to disruptions in the supply chain caused by the Japanese earthquake in 2011.

8.3.2 Pursuing both Global and Local Standards
for Sustainable Business

Second, it is necessary to learn best practices—local or global—while doing business in various regions. The proper practice to adopt varies depending on circumstances, as some cases will favor local practices while others will favor global ones. For example, McDonald's offers some localized menus (e.g., *Bulgogi* Burger in Korea) while it standardizes its flagship menus (e.g., Big Mac, Cheeseburger) across the world (Moon 2010a). Pursuing only the global standard will not work for all types of businesses. Therefore, it is important for firms to identify and address local issues in a timely manner to ultimately build a sustainable business.

8.3.3 Maximizing Efficiency within the Business Ecosystem

Third, firms should select partners that can contribute the most synergies within the entire value chain. The competitiveness of MNCs depends less on the firms' advantages in superior technology but more on their capabilities of combining different resources to maximize the efficiency of the whole ecosystem. Samsung Electronics' "mother factory," for example, combines and coordinates all of Samsung factories around the world in developing and transferring new technologies and management techniques. Proper convergence of different resources, partners, and locations of investment will become an increasingly important source of value generation.

8.3.4 Building Cohesion with the Local Community

Lastly, as the GVC always involves both home and host countries, firms should consider these countries' social problems in order to achieve sustainable success. By building more cohesion with the local community and governments, it is possible for firms to change the negative stereotypes of foreign companies. This is why MNCs are recently very active in helping home and host societies, which in turn benefits the MNCs. As the spread of globalization trivializes the country origins of MNCs, it will be important for businesses to assimilate accordingly.

Korea possesses limited natural resources and is disadvantaged due to its smaller domestic market and lower technological capabilities. This necessitates an especially active pursuit of internationalization by Korean firms. They must expand abroad to purchase cheaper resources and access broader markets for their products. Also, Korean firms must continue to improve their technology through cooperation with foreign firms. Internationalization ultimately broadens the range of strategic choices available for them.

So far, Korean firms have been successful in internationalization. However, most of the success came from international trade, not FDI. Therefore, for countries like Korea to continue their growth in this era of widespread globalization, firms should more actively and efficiently utilize the GVC. Fundamentally, this is possible when there is a general consensus among different interest groups (e.g., laborers and politicians) that both outward and inward FDI provide more positive than negative effects for the national economy. A healthy and objective view of internationalization must be implanted for the efficient operation of firms, and the next chapter touches upon the cultural perspective of internationalization with this purpose in mind.

CHAPTER 9

Understanding Internationalization from a Cultural Perspective

According to theories, countries with the highest internationalization efforts and open cultures demonstrate the fastest economic growth (e.g., Hofstede 1983; Porter 2000a; Moon 2004a; Moon and Jung 2010). There are many other studies that show similar results. Ironically, however, many nongovernmental organizations (NGOs) across the world continue to advocate against internationalization. Citing issues that range from environmental hazards to human rights abuse and even the corporatism of McDonald's, these groups fight to dismantle internationalization efforts in all aspects of society. Often, these activists resort to violent protests, causing fear and tension in the global community.

While acknowledging certain negative effects of internationalization, it must be noted that the positive influences far outweigh the negative ones. While internationalization may cause certain social issues, most conflicts can be solved through appropriate policies based on a proper perspective. For this, the global mindset is important because it directly influences the decision-making of national policymakers and corporate managers. With a better understanding of globalization, nations and firms can be better responsive to internationalization, avoiding its potential negative impacts and fully utilizing its benefits. Therefore, a global mindset is an important issue of culture.

According to Porter (2000a), countries can build productive economic cultures to shape behavior of people and firms in a productive way as opposed to non-economic cultures, which are more rigid to change. With regard to a productive economic culture, for example, people are likely to work hard under a good reward system. Also, under a sound political system, firms can be guided to act on long-term planning as opposed to opportunistic, short-term benefits (Porter 2000a). Culture is thus an important source of national competitiveness (Moon 2004a).

The overall objective of chapter 9 is to show how the global mindset, or the economic culture, influences the strategies of internationalization. To help achieve this goal, this chapter will first show how a healthy global mindset can solve economic and social problems by using the examples of Korea and other countries. As a global mindset is closely associated with a country's culture, this chapter will review the major existing studies on culture and examine how culture can assist in a country's internationalization and propel growth. The final section of this chapter will provide implications for enhancing a productive economic culture using the four elements of the ABCD model.

9.1 SOLVING ECONOMIC AND SOCIAL PROBLEMS

9.1.1 The Truth behind the Economic Crisis

In the last two decades, Korea has faced two critical crises: the 1997 Asian Financial Crisis and the 2008 Global Financial Crisis.[1] Many people think that the 1997 crisis started in Thailand—the first country to turn to the International Monetary Fund (IMF) for financial support in August 1997. However, the truth is that the crisis first erupted in Hong Kong. On July 4, 1997, Hong Kong was officially turned over to China, and this political event caused investors to withdraw from Hong Kong. As the epicenter of Asian finance, the Hong Kong stock market became volatile and quickly affected neighboring countries. The financial crisis then spread virally, impairing the economies of Thailand, Indonesia, and Korea.[2] However, Hong Kong, Malaysia, and Singapore managed to survive the crisis with relative stability.

Why did the crisis affect some countries more than others? The biggest difference between these two groups was the degree of internationalization in terms of foreign direct investment (FDI) at the time of the crisis. FDI is a long-term investment, unlike short-term lending or financial investments, and it is therefore more difficult to withdraw investment funds immediately once an economy suffers from a crisis. Hence, FDI is a more secure and helpful method for stabilizing the economy and sustaining its growth.

Moon and Bark (2001) studied ten major Asian member countries (Japan, China, the four first-tier NIEs, and the four second-tier NIEs)[3] and examined the relationship between the degree of openness with respect to FDI and the degree of impact from the financial crisis. Surprisingly, the study found that economies that were more open in terms of either inward or outward FDI were less affected by the financial crisis. Korea, at the time, was one of the least open economies and was struck rather severely. With this incident, Korea has since promoted a series of reforms and industrial restructuring to enhance its foreign investment environment, and this ultimately contributed to its quick recovery. In the end, internationalization was not the cause of economic crisis but the source of recovery.

In 1998, the Korean government introduced the new and more effective Foreign Investment Promotion Act by revising the existing Act on Foreign Direct Investment and Foreign Capital Inducement. In the same year, Korea also launched a one-stop service at the Korea Trade-Investment Promotion Agency (KOTRA) in order to speed up administrative procedures for foreign investors. In the following year, the Korean government set up the Office of the Investment Ombudsman in the Korea Investment Service Center to specialize in helping foreigners. Korea continued to expand the scale and scope of internationalization. Thanks to these efforts, Korea recovered faster than anyone had expected, despite being one of the countries hit most severely by the crisis.

The learning experiences from the 1997 crisis and the extensive post-crisis efforts in promoting internationalization played an important role for Korea to safely overcome the Global Financial Crisis of 2008. This crisis, which was triggered by the bursting of the US housing bubble, caused simultaneous economic recessions throughout the world. However, Korea was one of the countries least affected by the crisis, and it made a quick economic recovery without prolonged stagnation (Fackler 2011). In particular, due to the strengthened competitiveness of Korean firms such as Samsung and Hyundai over the years, Korea was able to maintain its high competitiveness in the face of fluctuations and uncertainties in the global market.

As Korea's economy is heavily reliant on trade, its trade volume plays a critical role in the domestic economy. Due to this structural dependence, many Koreans blame the global economy whenever there is a slowdown in the domestic market. Some even argue that Korea's feeble market is due to too much internationalization, furthering the anti-globalization sentiment. However, this is a serious misinterpretation of Korea's economic structure—a small country like Korea can only survive through internationalization.

In most cases, Korea's economic problems are not the result of internationalization but the ineffective policies and governance systems. For instance, the 1997 Asian Financial Crisis occurred due to Korean firms' inefficient corporate governance and lack of astute government policies and institutions for monitoring and regulating the liberalized market (Chang 2003a). However, things had changed significantly by 2008, and Korean companies were able to perform better than their rivals from other countries. Korea managed to effectively promote its FDI strategies on top of improving exports. In addition, Korea gradually diminished its reliance on the United States and Japan by expanding its export targets to Europe and emerging markets. If internationalization is implemented with a proper global mindset, firms can respond flexibly to dynamic market conditions and prosper in spite of global recessions.

Although appropriate policies are important in the face of unexpected events, as demonstrated in the case of Korea, real market leaders do not simply wait for favorable conditions to arrive—they prepare beforehand. Yet, there are many people who simply wait for signs of economic recovery without taking any action. This is analogous to a person standing under a roof and waiting for the rain to stop. There should be less criticism of others' good fortune and more active efforts to realize practical solutions and changes. Similar arguments can be found in the military strategy of Sun Tzu's *The Art of War*.[4] In order to respond well to the complexities of an ever-changing environment, Sun Tzu suggested, "Do not assume the enemy will not come, but always be ready for him. Do not presume that he will not attack, but make yourself strong so that you are invincible." In other words, one should be well prepared to respond appropriately to the enemy's attack, rather than waiting idly with a belief that the attack will not come.

Analogously, one should not take comfort in being safe against the fluctuations of the global market but needs to be fully equipped and prepared to handle unexpected scenarios. When it comes to a firm or economy's internationalization, more is indeed better. Of course, focusing solely on the benefits of internationalization may be dangerous. Disadvantages must be carefully examined along with appropriate measures for successful implementation of internationalization.

9.1.2 The Issue of Foreign Workers

Another sensitive issue surrounding the opening of national doors is the inflow of foreign workers.[5] Recently, the problem of foreign immigrant workers has emerged as a critical issue in the Korean society. Stories abound of foreign workers committing suicide at the threat of deportation and Korean-Chinese (*Joseonjok*) going on hunger strikes due to poor treatment. This is partly because the Korean government has pursued policies that go against both economic and legal principles.

Let's first examine this issue from an economic perspective. In short, foreign workers provide many benefits to the Korean economy. They help resolve problems of labor shortages and reduce the pressure of wage increases. Popular discussions on foreign workers often concentrate on whether they are substitutes or complements for domestic workers. Generally, economists perceive them to be complementary. Most foreign workers take jobs that domestic workers avoid, so in truth they do not seriously threaten the job availability for Korean laborers. In fact, there are many Korean business owners who note that it would be difficult to fill the jobs previously performed by immigrant workers if they were forced to leave.

If foreign workers are prevented from entering the Korean job market, then their replacement by domestic workers will inevitably lead to the rise of labor costs in various industries. The restrictive immigration polices enforced by the Korean government are thus hurting the economy by decreasing the complementary effect of foreign workers and increasing the substitution effect. Countries that openly accept foreign workers generally perform better than ones that do not (Shin and Choi 2015). Some good examples are the United States, Canada, New Zealand, and Singapore. On the other hand, Japan and some European countries, which are less open to foreign workers, face aging populations and stagnant or declining economic performance.

The Korean government's immigration policy also conflicts with legal principles. While it purports to aggressively deport illegal foreign workers, the government exempts workers of small and medium-sized enterprises (SMEs) in the manufacturing sector to avoid potential labor shortages. This is a blatantly contradictory stance that is neither rational nor justified. As a case in point, there are many business owners who are forced to hide their foreign employees to protect their best workers from compulsory deportation. This shows that the government is creating two criminals through this policy—hard-working foreigners who are additive to Korea's economy and their Korean employers who conceal them.

How should this problem be tackled? The answer must be derived from sound economic principles; that is, the government should abolish its targeting of selective businesses on its deportation policy. It is wrong to assume that immigrant workers are needed more at SMEs and not needed at larger companies. According to surveys, there are massive labor short-ages in large construction companies during high demand seasons, and the same is true for other industries. The availability of foreign workers should be left to natural market dynamics and needs. If this simple eco-nomic principle is adhered to, the legal dispute over equality will be natu-rally resolved.

In the twentieth century, countries that actively promoted free trade enjoyed economic success. With the turn of the twenty-first century, the same will hold true for countries that promote open immigration. As trade barriers are dismantled, immigration barriers should be lowered accord-ingly. This is necessary to promote a larger scale of internationalization and achieve national competitiveness. Of course, as some people worry, social problems will inevitably erupt with a sudden influx of foreigners. However, these short-term side effects can be resolved by implementing appropriate polices. Although the social tension caused by mass immigra-tion cannot be prevented in the short run, the inflow of foreigners will help Korea become more diverse and will enhance the economic and social development.

Evidence for this can be found when understanding the prosperity of the technology industry in Silicon Valley. After the dot-com bubble burst in the early 2000s, the employment and average wages of the technology industry declined drastically. The average hourly wage of a technology professional was approximately $200 before the bubble burst, which was ten times greater than the wages of Indian workers. Naturally, American technology companies started to recruit workers from India. With this shift in the technology labor market, the wages of American professionals in Silicon Valley dropped significantly. While many feared the collapse of Silicon Valley firms, the result was just the opposite.

The main industry in the future would integrate all spheres of tech-nologies including information technology, nanotechnology, and biotech-nology. In this regard, companies in Silicon Valley continued to outsource jobs from other countries that require relatively lower skills, while devel-oping other business areas with higher value-add. For example, personal computers were a major source of business during the early 1990s, but as that technology became ubiquitous, the computer industry gradually shifted from hardware to software because of its high profit margins. From the mid-1990s to 2001, the Internet sector emerged and grew rap-idly. Even after the burst of the dot-com bubble, Silicon Valley continued its transformation into higher value-added sectors.

Although overall employment in the high-tech industries declined by 17% from 2001 to 2008, average wages increased by almost 36% during the same period (Mann and Nunes 2009). This implies an increase in productivity per worker. Specifically, the employment of eight industries[6] declined, but there was an increase in three industries (pharmaceuticals, aerospace, and scientific research) in which there was a significant increase in value-add (Mann and Nunes 2009). The changing employment structure thus explains how the inflow of foreign workers actually helped the upgrade of the technology industry in Silicon Valley into higher value-added sectors.

9.1.3 Structural Problems in the Home Country

Domestic structural problems are usually difficult to deal with because they require fundamental changes and reforms.[7] Of course, change itself is not easy. Once a certain level of success is achieved, it becomes more difficult to enact change later on. As countries progress from early to later stages, the goal shifts from creating wealth to maintaining it. Therefore, if a country attempts to protect the competitiveness of existing industries in the later stages, it can easily fall into the trap of isolating itself from the global market and focusing too heavily on remaining unique. The inefficient economic policies of Japan and Europe, as well as their unpopular foreign policies, can be explained with this logic to some extent.

Then, what about Korea? Japan's lost decades came after a time when it was the second largest economy in the world. Korea today cannot claim the same success that Japan once had, so the country would be in a much worse situation if it followed Japan's unsuccessful practices. Some Korean companies must attain the approval of workers before they install a machine in a manufacturing plant. As is the case in some advanced countries, Korean companies are often paralyzed by the threat of confrontation with labor unions, which remains one of the major domestic structural problems. Although the percentage of union members declined to 9.8% by 2011 (half the level of 1989), Korea's labor unions are still very formidable. Some of the labor unions in large Korean companies are so powerful that Korean labor strikes often result in huge economic losses for both the companies and the entire economy. Labor relations have thus been regarded as a key obstacle to foreign investment in Korea.

It is extremely difficult to settle labor agreements when unions and management come into conflict. If management tries to compromise, then strikes will become a regular occurrence. If management does not give concessions, then the strike may turn more violent. Fortunately, extreme conflict can be avoided through internationalization. It allows Korean firms to go abroad, and foreign firms to come to Korea. Korean companies can choose between Korean and foreign workers based on productivity. Likewise, a Korean worker can choose to work for a domestic or foreign company by comparing wages and other benefits. This mutual optimization process will result in a positive-sum game. Both sides can benefit from increased choices. More importantly, the conflict between management and labor can be alleviated through internationalization. However, if a country avoids internationalization and protects the domestic market and labor, it will eventually lead to an inefficient economy.

The following is an example of how Hyundai Motor reduced its labor union problem through overseas investment. In 2002, Hyundai established a local manufacturing plant in the state of Alabama. Among many reasons for its investment in the United States,[8] Hyundai hoped to avoid the influence of a strong domestic labor union (Jo and You 2011), and among the southern states in the United States, Alabama had particularly limited experience with union activities. By investing in the United States, together with other benefits, Hyundai could improve its disadvantaged labor problem, which helped enhance its competitiveness.

9.1.4 Government Regulations against Competition

Some time ago, when Korea announced that it was curtailing its screen quota policy for domestic films, the government, film industry, and citizens all had different reactions.[9] Today, Korean films enjoy significant success due to the spread of the Korean wave, or *Hallyu*. However, back then, many were concerned for the future of the Korean film industry if the government did not protect domestic films. This protectionist view was misguided for several reasons.

First, domestic screen quota does not help improve Korea's competitiveness in film. The policy mandates a certain amount of Korean films be shown in movie theaters to prevent foreign movies from dominating the domestic market. However, this system underestimates the sophistication of local movie watchers and is intended to encourage people to watch Korean movies regardless of their quality. In reality, if there are no good movies worth watching, people will not go to the movie theaters at all. Under this scenario, the entire film industry in Korea would decline and become less competitive.

Second, the film industry does not merit special protection. When the United States and Japan had a trade dispute, the United States pressed to protect its steel industry, while Japan did the same for agriculture under the label of "strategic industries." What is the criterion of a strategic industry? Agriculture, steel, semiconductors, and cultures are all important areas. That is why the government's effort of seeking protection for target industries is not efficient, and distinguishing bad or good industries is wrong (e.g., Porter 2000a). The only thing that matters is productivity because productivity is the sole determinant of a country's prosperity.

In fact, culture includes not only films but also music and art. Since the scope is too broad, it is impractical to design a system that can protect every cultural sector simultaneously. Also, when a nation becomes more developed, government policy should focus more on building an efficient business environment rather than supporting any single industry (e.g., Rodrick 2004; Bianchi and Labory 2006). In this respect, there should be no reason to discriminate between foreign and domestic businesses, and countries should focus on attracting foreign businesses to boost the domestic economy.

Movies that were major hits in the Korean box office successfully appealed to Korea's cultural sentiments while incorporating global standards and features. For example, films such as *The Host, Silmido, Taegukgi*, and more recently *The Admiral: Roaring Currents* and *Ode to My Father*, all had good plots and enhanced graphics derived from Hollywood films, and there was an added "Koreanness" that grasped people's emotions. This is what differentiates Korean films from Hollywood. Both the best technical practices and uniquely Korean elements need to be intricately combined for Korean films to create box office hits (i.e., benchmarking and convergence). The reason Hallyu spread so quickly was that foreigners could easily assimilate to the content while experiencing unique elements of "Koreanness."

The internationalization strategy of Korean films should be applied not only at the production level but also to marketing and sales. The revenues from exporting Korean films have drastically increased, currently reaching tens of millions of dollars per year. In hindsight, it is easy to see that it would have been foolish to continue the screen quota. Korean films are spreading throughout global markets. In a twist of irony, Korea is now a major advocate of free trade in the film industry. Hence, internationalization, which promoted competition in the Korean film industry, enhanced the industry's competitiveness.

High government regulation is one of the major hindering factors of internationalization. Today, another problem in Korea's economy is weak investment. This problem cannot be solved through single monetary solutions such as increased government spending or reduced taxation. Instead, it requires more structural solutions such as lowering popular anti-market sentiment, addressing labor strikes, and scaling back unnecessary government regulation. Among these agendas, abolishing unnecessary government regulation is the most urgent.

Generally, when a country is less developed, there tends to be higher regulation along with less efficient institutions. For example, there are 14 steps required to start a business in Argentina, whereas only one is needed in New Zealand (World Bank 2015). Iran has the highest trade-weighted average tariff rates, while Angola's non-tariff barriers set the highest limits for imported goods to compete in the domestic market, and Venezuela is the most heavily regulated in hiring and firing practices (WEF 2014). Despite the positive connection between high regulation and low development, there are many in Korea who still advocate for higher regulations. They believe that economies face a constant threat of market failure if there is no government policy to correct it, and this is claimed to be still true for Korea. However, their arguments are not convincing for the following reasons.

First, advocates of higher regulation exaggerate the dangers of market failure and understate the role of competition. Naturally, market failure often corrects itself as long as competition is guaranteed. Nevertheless, they insist on maintaining a ceiling for the total amount of equity investment, citing weak corporate governance and transparency of the Korean firms. This argument is not valid, particularly in recent years. When Koreans worried about the malicious acts of chaebol in the past, the chaebol primarily competed with domestic SMEs. However, the competition today is mostly concerned with domestic and foreign conglomerates in the global market. In this context, firms should be allowed to decide on the most appropriate and effective corporate governance strategy for themselves. If a company makes an ineffective decision, it will immediately face criticism from observant consumers and other stakeholders.

Second, corporate misconduct should be left to the legal system and not government policies. If a transgression such as accounting fraud takes place, the legal process should be allowed to run its course without government intervention. Of course, this brings to question the efficiency of a particular country's legal system, as many developing countries demonstrate slow and ineffective legal systems. For example, it took approximately four years to settle a business dispute in Guatemala, while it took five years to liquidate a company in Myanmar (World Bank, 2015). Needless to say, legal procedures must be sped up in these cases.

Lastly, advocates of government regulation assume that governments are, in fact, efficient and benevolent. Even when the government has good intentions, there are times when the results are unsatisfactory. When government regulations are more complicated, there is a greater chance that people resort to informal processes to avoid time delays, complicated procedures, and inconsistent rulings. In addition, with an increase in public officers' discretionary power, companies find it more productive to resort to bribes and under-the-table dealings, which in turn increases business transaction costs and hinders the country's development of healthy and effective institutions.

In fact, corruption in developing countries mostly arises from fundamental structural problems, not from inherent moral shortcomings of the people. For example, some public officials might think that the more complicated the bureaucratic process is, the more opportunities there will be to create and secure jobs. However, the actual result would be different. Unnecessary procedure will not guarantee jobs for civil officers but will incentivize bribery and waste tax money. This will eventually ruin both individual officers and the nation. Thus, reducing unnecessary regulations and building efficient business environments for firms is an important way to enhance national competitiveness and create more jobs. If governments reduce the tax rates or increase other incentives in order to encourage corporate investment, their budget will be under greater pressure. However, removing unnecessary regulations will help the government save both time and money, which can be assigned to more productive areas and create more wealth for the entire economy.

The benefits of internationalization can be magnified when the negative influences of internationalization are avoided. This in turn requires a good global mindset for guiding the collection and interpretation of information in a dynamic global environment. Hence, a proper global mindset can act as the cognitive filter, and the value of a global mindset is to assist a company in making speedy and accurate responses to the global environment (Gupta and Govindarajan 2002). The above examples provide crucial implications of how policymakers' perceptions of internationalization (or global mindset) influence strategies and potential results. A global mindset can be linked to the concept of culture from a wider perspective. In order to give a more general implication, the following section will briefly go over the existing literature on the influences of culture (or more specifically, economic culture) on internationalization and economic growth.

9.1.5 The Logic behind the Open Economic Culture for Economic Growth

Chapters 7 and 8 discussed the role of internationalization in enhancing national and corporate competitiveness from an economic perspective. On the other hand, both government and corporate behaviors are often influenced by the attitudes and values of the people. These elements can be coined together as "culture," which can be divided at the national and organizational (e.g., firm) levels. However, national and organizational cultures are not separate but interact with each other (Naor, Linderman, and Schroeder 2010). For convenience, the following discussion focuses on national cultures.

There are many ways to define culture, and Hofstede's model is one of the most popular models. He defined culture as "the collective programming of the human mind that distinguishes the members of one human group from those of the other; in this sense, it is a system of collectively held values" (Hofstede 1980, 1983). Hofstede then distinguished the patterns of cultural differences under four dimensions: individualism versus collectivism, large versus small power distance, strong versus weak uncertainty avoidance, and masculinity versus femininity.

Although there is no question about the influence of culture on economic prosperity, it is challenging to separate the role of culture from other factors (Porter 2000a). On this matter, Porter said that the appropriate question is not to ask whether culture plays a role, but how culture has an impact. Porter categorized culture into two types: economic and non-economic. Economic culture is defined as "the beliefs, attitudes, and values that bear on the economic activities of individuals, organizations, and other institutions." A country's economic progress is closely tied to its productive economic culture. Porter, however, held different opinions from many other scholars including Hofstede who assumed that culture is stable, inflexible, and less likely to change over time. Porter argued that although economic culture (e.g., work ethic) is "sticky" and not easy to change, it is less so than non-economic culture. Therefore, economic culture can be influenced and changed through external regulations, policies (e.g., social safety net), and economic systems (e.g., reward and incentive system).

On the other hand, national culture has significant influence on a firm's business strategy and international operations (Nakata and Sivakumar 1996; Brouthers and Brouthers 2001; Flynn and Saladin 2006). For example, Brouthers and Brouthers (2001) examined the relationship between nations' cultural distance and international firms' foreign entry mode. They found that firms investing in host countries with larger cultural distances (in terms of the four cultural dimensions of Hofstede's model) would be more likely to select wholly owned ventures as the mode of entry. On the other hand, Moon and Bark (2001) argued that national cultures actually influence the government's international policies. During the 1997 Asian Financial Crisis, the different FDI policies among Asian countries reflected varying degrees of their global mindset. The OUI model

(Moon and Choi 2001; Moon 2004a)—openness, uncertainty avoidance, and individualism—is a revision and extension of Hofstede's (1980) model and it more directly analyzes a nation's degree of "openness" as a cultural variable.

Perlmutter's (1969) study on culture puts a greater emphasis on the cultural factor of openness. He categorized international attitudes into the following three types: ethnocentric (home-country oriented), polycentric (host-country oriented), and geocentric (world-oriented). Ethnocentric attitudes view themselves as more superior and trustworthy than foreigners in overseas subsidiaries. Therefore, the ethnocentric view prefers the "home-country standard" as the universal standard. Polycentric attitudes, on the other hand, acknowledge differences in culture between home and host countries and thus prefer to employ local people to manage local businesses. The world-oriented attitude does not view nationality as an important factor for consideration. Globally oriented firms seek the most appropriate people and products that can best contribute to the company regardless of nationality.

A productive economic culture will be helpful for a country and firm to improve the management of complex situations through proper internationalization. However, such favorable economic cultures do not develop automatically. The following section will describe the role of the ABCDs in cultivating a productive and open economic culture.

9.2 THE ABCDs AND PRODUCTIVE ECONOMIC CULTURE

Although there are many studies that discuss the cultural factors that influence firm or government behavior, few studies have suggested how to build a productive culture. In contrast to other theories on competitive advantage, the ABCD model employs the "how" approach rather than the "what" approach, so it can show insights into how to build productive and open economic cultures. In this respect, the four factors can be viewed as important influential factors for enhancing cultural competitiveness, which will be explained in the following sections.

9.2.1 Acquiring Speedy Culture

Speed is an important factor for creating a productive economic culture. Speed allows for rapid economic and corporate growth, which further encourages firms to go abroad to seize larger international markets and maximize profits. Korea was not originally characterized as a country with a "speedy" culture. Koreans were notorious for arriving late and starting activities past schedule under their own standards of time often called "Korean time." However, after experiencing the Korean War and Vietnam War, Korean people learned the importance of speed in order to survive in hostile environments. Also, during Korea's construction activities in the Middle East, Korean businessmen learned to value speed as a unique resource with which they could out-compete other rival firms. Korea's competitive advantage in speedy management was not inherited, but acquired and improved through efforts.

9.2.2 Continuous Learning and Upgrading

Japan learned how to thoroughly westernize its system, and this practice allowed it to supersede the West and stand as one of the successful economies in the world. However, after its initial success, the hype for Western ideas disappeared, and Japan returned to re-establishing its unique traditions. By becoming content with its past glory and ceasing to learn from other developed countries, Japan's economic growth slowed down considerably. In order to continuously develop beyond the present, a country should never stop benchmarking better models, as there is always something to learn from others. Fortunately, Korea is not yet complacent with its success and is still eager to learn from the West. For example, Korea is famous for its education fervor for studying abroad, particularly in the United States. Despite the small size of the Korean population, there are a large number of Korean students studying in the United States, ranking third behind China and India in absolute numbers (Institute of International Education website), but first when the number is controlled for population size. Studying abroad does not tell everything, but as long as Korea continues to learn from advanced countries, it will not experience the lost decades of Japan.

9.2.3 Accepting and Integrating National Differences

Small countries surrounded by large ones can fill the role of a regional hub for business and other international activities (e.g., Singapore in Southeast Asia, Dubai in the Middle East, and Switzerland in Western Europe). Their role as regional hubs does not arise due to their size but because of their capabilities to smoothly connect different partners and manage conflicts. Dubai, for example, excludes many regulations and cultural requirements for foreigners, unlike many other Islamic states. This allowed Dubai to grow from a small village to one of the most attractive investment locations for foreign capital. International business often involves cross-border activities, which inevitably lead to encounters with different national cultures. In this respect, convergence can be explained as the global mindset of understanding and accepting differences in cultures and synergistically incorporating all the relevant resources for building win-win situations.

9.2.4 Mobilizing Culture toward an Optimal Economic Goal

With strong determination for economic growth, China opened its market in spite of internal political opposition. In the Museum of Reform and Opening-up, in Shenzhen of China, there is a famous passage by Deng Xiaoping, saying "A planned economy is not the same as socialism, because capitalism also has planning. A market economy is not the same as capitalism, because socialism also has a market." This implies that the goal of socialism does not conflict with the goal of capitalism. From this perspective, Deng further argued that socialism cannot survive without reform and opening-up, and without developing the economy and without improving people's lives, there is a way only to death. A country that is not content with its current status and pursues further growth is likely to succeed. Such spirits of strong goal orientation naturally promote continuous growth.

The above illustrations show that by utilizing the four elements of the ABCDs, countries and firms can be more efficiently internationalized not only in physical openness but also in a global mindset. In particular, they show how continued efforts to implement the four factors improved a country that was not originally competitive. Thus far, the three chapters of Part III show the "horizontal extension" of the ABCDs from domestic to international. The following chapters in Part IV will show how to deepen the competitiveness of each of the ABCDs (or "vertical deepening" of the ABCDs), from a less developed to a more developed stage.

PART IV

Korea in the Future

The previous chapters captured the core strategies that led to Korea's unprecedented economic development. By raising national competitiveness through aptly demonstrating the ABCDs and embracing internationalization, the small economy of Korea produced many globally recognized brands and continues to enjoy phenomenal success in other areas such as culture, sports, and entertainment. These achievements of Korea have been applauded and recognized by many countries and experts around the world. In the Graduate School of International Studies at Seoul National University where I teach, the number of foreign students who come to learn about Korea's economic success and *Hallyu* has more than doubled since the school's founding in 1997. Certainly, there is much to learn from Korea's past experiences, especially for many developing countries, where liberal Western ideologies are too advanced and idealistic to immediately replace their extant operating systems.

However, this does not mean that the Korean model is perfect. There are underlying problems that have begun to surface as the country experienced rapid economic and social transformations. Some of the problems arose as natural consequences of industrialization and development, while others occurred as a result of Korea's tremendously fast pace of transformation. One of the biggest downsides to Korea's rapid growth is that certain policy measures that require proper planning and coordination lag far behind its economic development. In other words, the level of economic and business growth greatly outpaced the growth in politics, society, and institutions.

This last part of the book will discuss several key problems that Korea must resolve in order to continue its success. For one, the productivity of the service sector is still nowhere near that of the competitive manufacturing sector, while a greater number of workers shift to small-size services (see Noland 2012; Jones and Urasawa 2013). This inefficiency is further compounded by Korea's exceptionally fast-aging population driven by the declining fertility rate, which is one of the lowest in the world. Other problems are also apparent in the social and political system. Recently in 2014, the *Sewol* ferry disaster revealed many facets of Korea's deeply rooted problems and weaknesses, alerting the entire nation to the reality of Korea's actual level of advancement.

Chapter 10 discusses these major challenges to Korea's next phase of development and provides suggestions for resolving the problems by utilizing the ABCD model. Chapter 11 focuses on the current efforts of Korea in raising productivity and competitiveness. This chapter sheds light on strategic guidelines through deepening and broadening the ABCDs for sustainable growth of Korea. Finally, chapter 12 concludes the book by generalizing the utility of the ABCD model for other countries and firms. In this chapter, strategic implications will be given for both followers and leaders in different stages of development to achieve and sustain competitive advantage.

CHAPTER 10
New Challenges in Korea

Korea maintains one of the highest growth rates among the OECD countries. However, the economic growth rate started to slow in 2010, and structural problems such as a struggling service sector and inefficient small and medium-sized enterprises (SMEs) emerged as critical obstacles to Korea's continued growth. Since Korea's economic problems were both directly and indirectly caused by its fast pace of growth, the traditional catch-up strategy of Korea is now at stake.

Also, due to rising concerns over income inequality, past policies no longer seem to satisfy Korea's general public. The media started highlighting the increasing dissatisfaction of the population and pressured the government and businesses to shift away from growth-oriented strategies toward better balance and equality. Terms like "economic democracy" resonated throughout the presidential election campaigns in 2013. Although economists and academics considered the concept to be nothing more than a political catchphrase for wooing the public, the fact that this agenda remained in the forefront of every political debate showed how people are dissatisfied with the current economic situation.

The problems faced by the Korean government may be natural consequences of development that are common in developed countries. However, Korea's extraordinary rate of growth in a short period, the so-called condensed growth, magnified the problems by depriving the government of much-needed time to accumulate resources and prepare for challenges in advance. The problems to be discussed in this chapter are the unproductive service sector, underdeveloped sociopolitical system, and aging population.

10.1 UNPRODUCTIVE SERVICE SECTOR

Korea's rapid economic growth since the mid-twentieth century is reputable and the earlier chapters focused on the main attributes of its success. As is widely known, Korea's export-oriented industrialization endowed the country with a highly competitive manufacturing sector, and Korea's manufacturing industries continue to be globally competitive. However, this also means that there is limited room for further productivity improvements in manufacturing that can drastically raise the competitiveness of the country.

As the country matures into an advanced state, the dominant manufacturing sector will gradually give way to the service sector. This trend has in fact been confirmed in the Korean economy. Despite these industry transitions in Korea, however, the productivity of Korea's service sector remained low relative to other advanced economies. In 2013, Korea ranked 32nd out of the 34 OECD countries (OECD 2013a). Moreover, the average productivity of the service industries was only 45% of the OECD average between 1990 and 2012 (OECD 2014a). This is again in stark contrast with the productivity level of Korea's manufacturing sector that ranked second only after Norway (OECD 2013b). The problem in the service sector becomes more critical as employment in this sector steadily rises while productivity decreases. This upward trend in the share of the service sector in GDP and total employment is expected to continue in the context of Korea's rapidly aging population.

Growth in labor productivity decelerated by half between 1997 and 2007 in the service sector, while there was 9% growth in the manufacturing sector during the same period. This is why services accounted for only 25% of GDP growth per worker between 2000 and 2006, a low figure relative to the OECD average of 39% (Lee 2013). This shows how the relatively poor performance of services increases the labor productivity gap between services and manufacturing. In fact, labor productivity in services fell from 76% of manufacturing in 1997 to 60% in 2005 (Jones 2009), the largest gap among OECD countries where productivity of manufacturing and services is roughly equal.

Korea's per capita income has reached the point where growth tends to slow down. The slowdown may partly be due to the structural challenges of moving from a manufacturing economy to a more balanced economy in which services play a larger role. In the case of an advanced economy, it is especially important to focus on the development of high-end services such as research and business consulting over low-end services such as housecleaning and small retail. This is a transition that Korea is struggling to make.

Before suggesting possible solutions for Korea, it is worthwhile to mention the three main categories of the service industry (Eichengreen and Gupta 2009). Generally, a nation's service industries progress to the next category as income rises. The first category is traditional services: retail and wholesale trade, transport and storage, public administration, and defense. The GDP share of these activities usually falls noticeably over time as a nation advances. The second category is a combination of traditional and modern services: education, healthcare, hotels and restaurants, and other social services. Their share tends to rise slowly with time. The third category is modern services: financial intermediation, computer services, business services, communication, and legal and technical services. The services of this category significantly increase as a nation advances to the developed stage. According to this classification, the development level of Korea's service sector has not yet reached the third modern group of services, which is a critical cornerstone for Korea's further growth. The following section will illustrate the fundamental problems of the service sector along with possible solutions using the ABCDs as a guideline.

10.1.1 Fundamental Problems of Korea's Unproductive Service Sector

Korea's unproductive service sector is mainly the result of two fundamental problems. The first is a natural consequence of fast, manufacturing-oriented development. Active export promotion of the manufacturing industry resulted in less attention to the high value-added service sectors. For example, the service sector's share of R&D averaged 25% for OECD countries, which shows a clear contrast to Korea's 7%, and over 90% of R&D services in Korea are heavily concentrated in telecommunications and computer-related business services (Jones 2009). Although increased investment in information-communication technology (ICT) can boost growth in Korea (Nicoletti and Scarpetta 2005), the contribution of ICT-related services to labor productivity has diminished since the early 1990s (OECD Productivity Database and Pilate 2007).

At the national level, there is a large inflow of older workers from manufacturing into services. Lacking other alternatives, two-fifths of workers over the age of 55 are self-employed in the service sector. For all ages, one-third of workers in services are either self-employed or family workers, compared with an average of one-fifth for OECD countries (OECD 2014a). This leads to more serious problems for the national economy as a whole, as the growing number of retired workers turning to self-employment (mainly in services) makes labor productivity worse in Korea's service sector.

The second problem is with government regulations. International comparisons suggest that Korea's services are heavily regulated; the OECD's market regulation indicator for the service sector ranked Korea in the top three among OECD member countries in 2009 (Koske et al. 2014). For the economy as a whole, however, Korea was close to the OECD average, suggesting that the stringency of regulation in manufacturing was comparatively low. Unfriendly market regulations damage the spirit of entrepreneurship in services (Nicoletti 2001). Moreover, stringent market regulations are positively correlated with high mark-ups in the service sector, which further weakens competition and efficiency (Hoj et al. 2007).

Due to high regulatory policies in the service sector, insufficient competition in services widened from 1997 to 2005 (Lee, Cho, and Kim 2007). In manufacturing, efficiency gains have been driven by intensified competition as Korea became more integrated into the world economy. By limiting inbound foreign direct investment (FDI), services are more sheltered from allowing global players to enter the competition. These foreign firms are subject to numerous domestic regulations. This further harms Korea's global competitiveness in services.

10.1.2 Strategic Guidelines for Improving Productivity of the Service Sector

Low productivity and low income in service industries go hand in hand with inefficient SMEs in Korea. Compared to the average labor income in larger companies (those that employ over 1,000 people), the average labor income in smaller companies, with 30 to 99 employees, is 72%. This number falls to 60% for firms with 10 to 29 employees and 51% for firms with less than 10 employees (KOSTAT 2013). Also, the average working hours increase with decreasing firm size. This implies that working conditions, in addition to low efficiency, are downgrading the quality of life of SME workers (Kim 2010). Nonetheless, since self-employed workers and small firms are increasing in service industries, the effort to increase the productivity of the service sector should continue. Then how can low productivity in the service sector be improved?

(1) Agility: Reducing Regulations and Increasing Transparency

Korea is now pushing toward becoming the business hub of Northeast Asia. In order to achieve this goal, Korea must provide the most favorable business environment for both domestic and foreign firms. When investing abroad, multinational corporations (MNCs) do not only consider traditional location advantages such as cheap labor and abundant resources but look more at the business system. To this end, the Doing Business Index of the World Bank provides some investment guidelines for MNCs by ranking countries in terms of regulations and procedural complexities. Korea is still behind other competing countries in some areas. Regulations directly affect the speed of business, so they should be eliminated or substantially reduced to create a favorable business environment. Precision, the other subfactor of agility, is affected by the ambiguity of regulations and procedure, and it can be improved by making them more transparent. Reducing regulations and increasing transparency are the most effective ways in enhancing the competitiveness of service sectors.

(2) Benchmarking: Targeting Industrial Efficiency and Fair Domestic Competition

As competition becomes more global, it is no longer appropriate to protect SMEs in the domestic service industry. In the retail service sector, for example, the Korean government restricts the operation of large firms on certain days and in some areas of business. However, in a mature market such as the United States, large retailers such as Costco and Walmart coexist with convenience stores such as 7-Eleven. The Korean government should encourage fair domestic competition, and it needs to consider consumer benefits and industry competitiveness. However, most of the current government support goes to small firms, so growing small firms are hesitant to ascend to the level of successful medium- to large-sized firms (called *Jungkyunkieup*[1] or high potential enterprises). To continue to receive benefits, growing SMEs often curb their employment to retain their SME classification. Therefore, the government policy of supporting SMEs has not been always effective because it has the unintended consequence of removing incentives for SMEs to grow. In order to be more globally competitive, Korea should further enhance competition between large and small firms.[2]

(3) Convergence: Gearing International Resources for Greater Spillover Effects

In service industries, in addition to the lack of competition between large and small firms, there is also a lack of competition between domestic and foreign firms. Since the service industry has been shielded from FDI and there is a relatively low level of trade in service goods, there is a corresponding lack of spillover effects that could allow the Korean firms, particularly SMEs, to learn and grow. The service sectors that are particularly protected from international competition include law and finance, which are very important foundations for expediting the growth of other industries. It should be noted that the reason the Industrial Revolution fledged from England was that law and finance were better developed than in other European countries in the eighteenth century. On a similar note, the competitiveness of Silicon Valley is not solely due to its high-tech firms and institutions, but the well-developed infrastructure of the service sectors. The development of service industries is important not just for their own sake but also for the synergies with other industries.

(4) Dedication: Directing Strategies for Value Creation

Governments are highly sensitive to economic indicators, and the Korean government is no exception. One of the most important economic indicators for the government is the employment rate. In Korea's economy, large firms such as Samsung have higher productivity but a lower employment rate relative to SMEs, and this is mainly why the government wants to support the SMEs. In more democratic societies, like Korea in recent years, governments tend to favor this policy in order to gain popularity from the general public. SMEs, which are relatively more involved in service sectors than large firms, are expected to hire more employees and contribute to the important economic indicator.[3] However, the government should realize that true economic achievement comes more from productivity growth than simple quantitative, employment growth. Instead of focusing on short-term performance and political popularity, the government should implement strategies for maximizing value creation.

10.2 UNDERDEVELOPED SOCIOPOLITICAL SYSTEM

In May 2014, the International Institute for Management Development (IMD) announced the 2014 World Competitiveness Rankings. Unfortunately, Korea's ranking dropped by four places to 26th out of 60 economies. The details of the report, however, revealed that in business, Korea has increased its competitiveness. A similar result was published in Fortune's 2014 Global 500 rankings—a total of 17 Korean companies appeared on the list, compared to 13 or 14 companies since 2011. The reason Korea declined in the IMD rankings is that in addition to firm activities IMD utilizes a more holistic view of competitiveness by including other areas such as politics, society, and culture. The 2014 rankings revealed that Korea had high marks in areas related to business and economy, such as domestic economy (rank 13th) and employment (rank 7th). On the other hand, areas such as government policy and regulation were far below Korea's overall ranking—Korea's business legislation ranked 42nd, while social framework came in at 36th. Other reports on national competitiveness by international organizations such as the World Economic Forum (WEF)[4] and Institute for Industrial Policy Studies (IPS)[5] showed similar results.

These reports identified Korea's low government efficiency and ineffective regulations as major weaknesses. This glaring fact was thrown into the public spotlight with the 2014 Sewol ferry disaster. The tragedy exposed many of Korea's underlying problems that had been neglected in the past. One significant difference between developed and developing countries is their capacity to manage emergencies, which require long-term planning and investment. Since these events require the government to financially support a complex web of issues, developing countries with less competent governments have difficulty coordinating and managing crisis-prevention measures. This is why advanced countries are able to avoid or mitigate crises, while developing countries undergo similar crises over and over again. Although Korea has achieved rapid economic development, it still lags behind advanced countries in social and political areas.

10.2.1 Fundamental System Failure in the Sewol Ferry Disaster

In April 16, 2014, the MV Sewol sank en route from Incheon to Jeju Island, resulting in hundreds of deaths as well as tremendous outcry in the nation. An investigation revealed that this was no ordinary sea accident, and the uncovering of deep bureaucratic problems shocked the entire public. The affair also exposed the government's incompetent response to emergencies, and many questions arose regarding the government's ability to manage emergency situations.

Following the crisis, I was asked by the media to give my opinion on the matter. The key point I wished to get across to the public was that the problems in this case extended far beyond the faults of the captain and crew-members who failed to conduct proper rescue protocols. At the time, the media and public expressed outrage against the authorities in charge, and the sinking was characterized as a result of individual failures. However, as the investigation revealed, the responsibility did not lie with individuals but the entire administrative system; the problem was much more fundamental and amounted to a system-wide failure. In my analysis of the Sewol disaster, I was able to draw up a useful comparison with the sinking of the *Titanic*.

On April 15, 1912, approximately a hundred years before the Sewol case, the British passenger liner *RMS* Titanic sank in the North Atlantic Ocean. The Titanic was the world's largest vessel at the time, and its sinking was the worst sea accident to date. Similarly, the Sewol sinking was Korea's worst sea accident, and both the Sewol and Titanic disasters were viewed as manmade tragedies that could have been prevented. The aftermath of these two unprecedented accidents were catastrophic—in both cases, more than 60% of passengers lost their lives. However, the Titanic sank in spite of good recovery efforts, while the Sewol sinking was caused by numerous lapses in judgment. As a result, the media quickly turned its attention in the coming months to structural problems such as the government and institutional inefficiencies.

There were numerous ways in which the casualties of the Sewol accident could have been minimized or prevented altogether. If Chonghaejin Marine, the company operating the voyage, adhered to national safety laws, the result could have been quite different. Also, if the crew had received proper safety training and emergency preparation, the subsequent rescue missions could have been significantly more impactful. The number of victims could have been reduced if any of the procedures were kept properly.

The Titanic was heralded as a ship that even "God himself could not sink," and this overconfidence may have had a part in its demise. On the contrary, the Sewol began its last journey with numerous pitfalls and deficiencies. While the average life of ships is 15 years, the Sewol at the time of its voyage was already 20 years old. Moreover, the Sewol carried improper design modifications that increased the load capacity to a dangerous level—the addition of 240 passenger cabins and 239 tons of weight which disturbed the ship's balance. For the Sewol, it was complacency that allowed those in charge to neglect potential dangers.

The Sewol sunk because of a sharp turn that caused it to lose balance and take in water. At this point, it was crucial to inform the passengers of the situation and immediately begin the emergency evacuation procedures. However, the captain and crew of the Sewol lacked any determination to save the passengers, and 300 students were allowed to continue eating breakfast in the cafeteria. This is the most striking difference between the sinking of the Titanic and Sewol. The captain and crew of the Titanic possessed the utmost sense of duty to their passengers and displayed strong goal orientation in carrying out their emergency obligations. Sewol's captain Lee, however, spent most of his time on board sleeping, and he and other senior crewmembers were the first to escape the capsized ship. They showed none of the responsibilities required for them.

The Korean public was enraged at this fact and pressured the court to charge the leaders with homicide, punishable by death. On this issue, however, I raised a different viewpoint—Were the captain and crewmembers simply immoral and irresponsible people? The truth is neither the captain nor the crew of the Sewol received proper safety training. It was soon reported that the company had only spent two dollars every year on the captain and crew's emergency training (Choe et al. 2014). Since there are established safety protocols that must be satisfied for a company to gain a license to do business, the training of the captain and crew was the responsibility of the company and, by extension, the government. When these facts are put together, it seems unreasonable to solely blame the captain and crew that fled the scene.

The web of problems underlying the Sewol ferry disaster may seem like an overstatement of Korea's structural problems. However, building a system with quality emergency management and social security requires significant long-term preparation and investment. These issues are among the core problems that Korea needs to address in order to stand as a truly advanced country. To borrow the words of Sun Tzu, an ancient military strategist, "Winners only go to war after full preparation that will ensure victory, whereas losers go to war blindly without adequate preparation." Here, Sun Tzu highlights the importance of complete preparation and prior training to achieve success.

10.2.2 Strategic Guidelines for Building an Advanced Sociopolitical System

To strategically counter sociopolitical problems and emergencies, effective policies can be divided into three phases—pre-crisis, crisis response, and post-crisis. If Korea can plan and prepare for these three scenarios, many future problems can be prevented or minimized. In my analysis published in an article on the Sewol ferry disaster, I further elaborated by including a strategic guideline to improve Korea's current system for crisis management.[6] Although the analysis in this case is situation-specific, it also holds important implications for other social and institutional problems that require systematic change.

(1) Agility: Immediate On-Site Decision-Making

The most effective and critical decisions that minimize the scale of a crisis occur during the immediate response in the early phase. The "golden hour" must be accurately pinned down and utilized. To do this, there must be an efficient system already in place that can handle the given circumstances. Therefore, once a crisis arises, the responsible parties on site should not waste precious time. The "Miracle on the Hudson" serves as a good example of this kind of action. Captain Chesley Sullenberger of US Airways Flight 1549 immediately and accurately assessed the situation when his aircraft lost both engines. Accordingly, he ditched the flight and proceeded with an emergency landing onto the Hudson River without power within six minutes. What could have turned into a disaster instead became a showcase of textbook emergency response and rescue efforts, and all 155 passengers on board were saved. As this example demonstrates, the fast and accurate action of the first responders plays a critical role. When there is an emergency, well-defined manuals and protocol determine how decisions are made.

(2) Benchmarking: Regular Training prior to Crises

Although a good manual is necessary for response agencies to react to a crisis in a timely manner, it is important to educate and train members while evaluating standardized protocols under different scenarios. Reports reveal that prior to the Boston Marathon bombing in 2013, police officers, firefighters, emergency medical personnel, and public safety agencies planned for mass casualty disasters by conducting inter-agency and cross-jurisdictional exercises. Experts said that the "Boston Strong" response was not due to chance. Instead, it was the product of years of hard work by people across multiple jurisdictions. The reason that Boston was so prepared was that the United States had become more alert since the 9/11 terrorist attack and multiple hurricanes. The United States had learned from past traumas to plan for any future threat. Boston also learned much from Israeli emergency personnel, who had become proficient in "terror medicine" over the years. Korea and other countries can learn much from the regional and national crisis prevention measures taken by some well-prepared advanced countries.

(3) Convergence: Combination of Command and Coordination

The next vital necessity for crisis control is effective communication and cooperation. This is facilitated by the leadership of top authorities who can effectively command and coordinate the situation. Crisis experts advise senior leaders to command at the unified strategic level in order to directly oversee basic operations. Also, a nationwide disaster control center should be in place to carry out the coordination processes more effectively. Since time is so crucial during these moments, field decisions may be made on the ground, but well-designed coordination is important for efficient operation. In the United States, the Federal Emergency Management Agency (FEMA) takes on this role and coordinates organizations across multiple disciplines. The coordination process of FEMA is carried out in the form of the Integrated Emergency Management System (IEMS). The effectiveness of this system was demonstrated following the collapse of the I-35W Mississippi River Bridge in 2007. The ensuing rescue mission lasted only 81 minutes. The administrator of FEMA at the time stated, "Perhaps the most important initiative we must undertake is to recognize our efforts are part of an interconnected plan of action" (DHS 2011).

(4) Dedication: Fostering a Professional Mindset and Strong Responsibility

Having dedicated people is a crucial factor in all social events. For instance, the Hippocratic Oath outlines the responsibilities and ethical obligations of physicians: "Whatsoever house I may enter, my visit shall be for the convenience and advantage of the patient; and I will willingly refrain from doing any injury or wrong from falsehood" (Lloyd 1983). Another good example is expressed in the mantra of American firefighters, "first in, last out." During the most horrifying moments of 9/11, many firefighters did not hesitate to rush into the collapsing buildings to rescue people, knowing that they may not come out alive. In total, 343 emergency medical service workers and firefighters of the New York City Fire Department, including the department chief and first deputy commissioner, sacrificed their lives while carrying out their duties. The reason these people were so committed to their duty is that a good system and matching attitude were firmly in place. The system provides the necessary training and education for competent workers. Meanwhile, a healthy society that understands the commitments of a job fosters respect for vocational integrity. What appears to be a cultural or personal phenomenon on the outside may in fact be the outcome of a strong system and social infrastructure.

10.3 AGING POPULATION

The final and perhaps the biggest fundamental challenge that Korea faces is its rapidly aging population. Until the 1960s, demographers forecasted the total global population in 2050 to surpass 16 billion. Recent demographics, however, have gone back on earlier predictions and adjusted the number to 9 billion—slightly more than half of the prior forecast. What is alarming is that most of the 7 billion in reductions are attributed to declines in birth rates in Asian countries (McDonald 2000). One of the reasons for the decline could be the active promotion of fertility control and family planning programs by Asian governments. Also, the side effects of industrialization, improved education, and a higher quality of life all lean toward smaller families, and Korea is no exception.

Despite some of the positive effects of a decreasing population, the overall prospect for Korea's future looks grim. The decrease in population from lower birth rate and higher life expectancy generally results in aging population. This phenomenon is happening faster in Korea that caught up very quickly to the qualities of industrialized countries. The aging population also results in a decline of active human capital, which further hinders economic growth. Therefore, countries around the world are becoming increasingly concerned with this trend, as fewer productive workers will be left to shoulder the growing burden of supporting the elderly.

By 2026, Korea will become a "super-aged society," where the proportion of people over 65 exceeds 20% (OECD 2013c). Although Korea currently has one of the youngest work forces in the OECD, it is likely to have one of the oldest by 2050, just behind Japan (Keese 2003; Hong and Kim 2009). Furthermore, the elderly dependency ratio (i.e., the population aged 65 years and over as a proportion of the population aged 20–64 years) is projected to increase from 11% in 2000 to 68% in 2050 (Heller 2006). Although this trend exists broadly across countries, Korea's case deserves special attention because Korea has the fastest aging population and lowest fertility rate among OECD countries.

10.3.1 The Double-Edged Sword of Rapid Economic Development

Historically, the rapid change in demographics in Korea was facilitated by the interaction of fast socioeconomic development and full-scale adoption of family planning programs since the 1960s (Kim 1992). Under the first Five-Year Economic Plan (1962–1967), the GNP grew at an annual rate of 7%. The GNP growth for the next five years was even higher, reaching up to 11%. Accompanying this rapid economic growth was the adoption of a national family planning program in 1962, which was implemented to prevent unwanted childbirth (Kim et al. 1996).

In addition to the family planning program, the rapid socioeconomic and demographic changes have made Korea a prime case for examining the relationship between education improvement and population aging. Population aging and education expansion are worldwide phenomena, but the pace of these changes in Korea has been exceptionally fast. For instance, the degree of women's education is negatively correlated with the level of fertility. According to a study on the relationship between women's education and fertility rates, women without formal schooling have 4.1 children on average, and women with a high school diploma have 2.9 children (Kye et al. 2014). Husbands' education, on the other hand, does not influence the level of fertility much—men with some secondary schooling have the same indistinguishable level of fertility as those with no schooling. All in all, improvements in women's education slightly worsen the overall generational support ratios as their education affects fertility.

Among others, economic factors have become increasingly important in explaining the low fertility in Korea, to the extent that many scholars argue that economic determinism has become the sole explanation for fertility decline (Eun 2007). The high cost of childrearing is particularly an important factor. Due to poorly equipped facilities of public childcare, the vast majority of Korean families must handle childcare privately. Provision of childcare by grandparents or other close family members has traditionally been the best solution. However, rapid urbanization, a high rate of migration, and a shift toward nuclear families have weakened the capacity of close relatives to provide childcare. As public and private sources of affordable childcare services have become less accessible, the cost of childrearing has soared in Korea.

10.3.2 Strategic Guidelines for Dealing with the Aging Problem

Compared to other developed countries, Korea's aging problem started much earlier in the development process, creating a situation where the government and social structure were hopelessly unprepared. In advanced countries, the super-aged population (i.e., over age 65 composing more than 20% of the nation's population) happened slowly and gradually, but Korea is undergoing the change faster than these countries. The labor force between ages 15 and 64 was estimated to peak in 2016 and decrease from then on; however, this peak arrived in 2007, much earlier than expected (Song and Park 2012). The following will suggest some strategic guidelines for relieving the social issue of an aging population according to the ABCDs.

(1) Agility: Focusing on Labor Productivity with Selective Programs

Tackling the multiple issues surrounding an aging population is not an easy task. The issue requires appropriate strategies to evaluate which policies and programs are the most effective. The first step, however, is to shift away from approaches that only seek to directly control population numbers. Rather, solutions should first aim to improve the productivity of the given labor pool because this is a much more significant figure than absolute population. This is not to say that policies to promote increased childbirth are unimportant or unnecessary. However, the benefits of these types of policies take years to bring about noticeable changes. While pursuing the policies of increasing childbirth, we should look for a more immediate and precise solution that would be to raise the productivity of current workers by improving their quality and skills. Since productivity improvement is directly connected to corporate competitiveness, the government should engage the private sector for faster and more accurate implementation. By closely working with firms and industries, the government can solve much of the employment and aging problems. Specifically, firms can improve labor productivity by actively training and educating new talent. In addition, if the society is concerned with the increasing burden of supporting an aging population, extending the retirement age can be another solution.

(2) Benchmarking: Utilizing the Older Labor Force by Learning from Business Sectors

As a new member of the fast-aging country group, Korea can learn from advanced countries that had more years of experience to prepare for this problem. Particularly, there are many lessons that can be adopted from successful MNCs that are trying to solve the problem at the firm level. The German company, Siemens is a notable example that succeeded in preparing for the aging workforce by creating a career development program called the Compass Process. This system is operated through workshops and one-on-one counseling, and it is a highly personalized procedure for the participants. Open to workers older than 40, the program has four steps, beginning with an overall assessment of the worker that incorporates feedback from relevant people including managers, colleagues, and clients. The second step is to construct a detailed career development plan based on the given feedback. Then, with top managers and human resource personnel, workers discuss their potential roles within the company by going through the plan. The final step involves progress evaluation as well as follow-up planning. The program benefited Siemens by allowing the firm to increase the utility of older employees that possessed firm-specific knowledge.

(3) Convergence: Synergistically Engaging Different Policy Agendas

At its core, the problem of an aging society can only be resolved through mutual support among different disciplines and policy areas. Increased birthrate and female employment, in the short term, are conflicting issues that are difficult to address simultaneously. Immigration policy, which is also an important factor for human resource, brings about serious conflicts of interests as well as delicate sociopolitical agendas. Nonetheless, the aging population problem requires all of these issues to be brought to the negotiation table for effective solution. Due to the inherent complexities of the problem, many governments have been criticized for ineffective policies. This area requires extensive country-specific research and a comprehensive judgment call from the public and government. Policies such as family planning, labor, immigration, finance, business and industry, education, and social security must be sorted by priority. When the government is able to set its own optimal outlook on short-, mid-, and long-term goals, policy design becomes much more efficient.

(4) Dedication: Turning Diverse Interests into the Creation of New Values

Tackling the massive aging population through a productivity approach is the most immediate and easiest way to produce results. The competitiveness of workers has been the core success factor for Korean companies. However, many of them now find it difficult to motivate the new workforce as the spirits and attitudes of young people have changed. They no longer wish to work incessantly to earn for their family. The rise in living standards has raised the awareness of personal values and happiness, and young people are motivated by factors that are entirely different from those of the old generation. The role of the government and businesses is to cater to these diverse interests and turn them into the creation of new values. Many of the new employees now have high and diverse qualifications that they have accumulated in pursuit of employment. This means the fresh graduates are competent interest holders who have much to contribute when properly guided. The companies should engage more directly with the workforce to utilize this valuable human resource. All in all, the goal should be to improve productivity of the labor force before tackling welfare policies to support growth in the nation's birthrate.

This chapter discussed Korea's current three main economic and socio-political challenges, which should be resolved in order for Korea to achieve sustainable development and transform it into a truly advanced country. As explained in chapter 2, Korea's economic development history is a continuous process of solving current problems and creating new advantages. It is firmly believed that after overcoming the current problems, there will be new competitive advantages waiting for Korea. This chapter also employed the analytical tool of the ABCDs as guidelines for overcoming these three challenges, which shows that the practical scope of the ABCD model can be extended from economic to social and other important issues.

CHAPTER 11
Upgrading Korea's Competitive Advantages

I n many areas such as entertainment, sports, science, and technology, Korea has shown great leadership in the world stage. However, if Korea settles on its current success and does not further pursue proper national strategies, the long-term success of Korea will not be guaranteed. The main objective of national strategy is to enhance competitiveness and a wrong strategy can bring about negative outcomes. Ideal strategy for competitiveness at the global stage strives to create a win-win situation for all stakeholders versus a one-sided positive-sum game.

In an increasingly competitive and volatile economic environment, economists and governments have sometimes turned to military strategies for advice. Although there are many useful lessons that can be drawn from military strategies, if this approach is inappropriately used, the result could be extremely dangerous to both nations and firms. This is because military strategies view victory as synonymous with defeating the opposing party. However, this outcome is not always desired in business—a company can succeed along with the growth of its rivals (e.g., Coca Cola and Pepsi, Apple and Samsung Electronics). Moreover, one's success may even depend on its rivals' enhanced competitiveness. This changing paradigm of business competition is often referred to as the "business ecosystem."[1]

Another modern misconception is that Korea's competitiveness would diminish with the rise of China and the recovery of the Japanese economy. Many have argued that Korea's "neo-sandwich crisis" will hurt Korea's economy. However, the truth is that none of these three countries has to fail—Korea, China, and Japan can all continue to grow and reap success. Therefore, instead of contemplating the unpredictable fate of countries through a geopolitical approach, it is more beneficial for actors to focus on enhancing national welfare through appropriate economic and social development strategies.

The previous chapters focused on explaining the success strategy of nations and firms using the ABCD model. This chapter will discuss how to use the ABCDs to upgrade current competitive advantages for long-term growth. For each element of the ABCDs, the section will compare the success strategies of other countries, examine Korea's current status, and provide useful implications for Korea's economy and firms going forward.

11.1 AGILITY: TECHNOLOGY DEVELOPMENT AND INNOVATION

Overcoming disadvantages is crucial to sustaining competitive advantages. This is what Korea has been pursuing since its early stages of development. First, by resolving the weaknesses that hindered its growth, Korea succeeded in creating the foundation to increase productivity, which maximized outputs with limited inputs. A country needs to be aware of its disadvantages and quickly act to fix them.

Although Korea's speed is widely known in the world, its precision still lags behind many advanced countries. Going forward, Korea needs to improve its precision in addition to demonstrating high speed in order to enter the next phase of development. In order to realize this, Korea needs to develop better technologies in a more precise and well-organized manner. There are similar examples in history where many advanced countries have achieved success by creating new advantages while overcoming disadvantages through appropriate innovation.

11.1.1 Examples from Other Countries: Overcoming Disadvantages through Innovation

Today's advanced countries (e.g., Japan, Germany, the United States, and Australia) all underwent this process of overcoming disadvantages at one point.[2] After the end of World War II, Japan and Germany were nearly torn apart from defeat, yet these countries soon rose to the highest level of prosperity. The companies in these two countries revived themselves by overcoming their weaknesses and increasing their competitiveness. Japan's strategy involved producing light, thin, short, and small (the so-called *kei-haku-tan-sho*) products. This was because Japan had scarce natural resources and small land. Thus, Japan worked on manufacturing products that required less resources and space, in addition to increasing their technological capacity.

In fact, the competitiveness of Japanese companies increased after several crises, as demonstrated by their resurgence from the 1970s oil shocks. Japanese firms had long been vulnerable to energy shortages because the country depended heavily on foreign energy supply. Due to the severe lack of natural resources, Japanese firms focused on inventing highly resource-efficient automobiles. This strategy, which was created out of necessity, worked to their advantage when Japanese products received worldwide recognition for the efficiency in their automobiles. Eventually, Japanese automotive firms were able to break into the US market following the oil shocks. With the Japanese firms' early efforts and large R&D investments, they have become the world leaders in the energy-saving technologies. The above examples show how Japan turned its disadvantages of scarce natural resources into its strong competitive attributes by continuing to invest in technology development.

Similarly, Germany lost nearly everything from their defeat during World War II. While Britain and France had colonies to fall back on, Germany lacked such sources of income. Among Germany's many obstacles, the most serious problem was the limited supply of natural fiber for the country's formerly competitive industries. To overcome this problem, German companies began to develop chemical industries (e.g., synthetic fibers and dyes) under the slogan of "chemistry rather than colonies" (Porter 1990).

On the other hand, the primary problem of the United States was a shortage of labor, which pressed the country to develop labor-efficient technologies. This strategy helped the United States establish efficient manufacturing operations. For example, the unprecedented success of Ford's Model T was due to the substantial decrease in labor and massive automation in factories. Today, some products are more efficiently designed and manufactured in the United States relative to other countries because its scarce labor force has to be most effectively utilized.

Countries such as Australia and New Zealand that have abundant natural resources were able to join the list of wealthy countries by overcoming their disadvantages as well. As a strategic measure, they developed advanced technologies in the exploration, processing, and distribution of their rich natural resources. While Australia was successful in implementing advanced technologies to further build upon its inherited advantages, many other resource-abundant countries failed to achieve strong economic growth because they relied on their comparative natural resource advantages and neglected to address their weaknesses. These countries are still developing countries today.

11.1.2 The Case of Korea: Future Technology Development

Although Korea has had significant technology achievements, there is room for improvement in certain areas relative to advanced countries. Korea now faces the challenge of sustaining its past competitive advantages in the future business environment. The world is now witnessing technological breakthroughs in various areas such as information technology, biotechnology, nanotechnology, cognitive technology, and green technology. How should the Korean government and companies respond to this extensive transformation? This is an extremely important matter for Korea as a nation, and both the public and private sectors of Korea have set out to resolve this issue.

The Park Geun-hye administration, in particular, made innovation a central point of government policy through the promotion of the "creative economy." The creative economy is defined as "the convergence of science and technology with industry, the fusion of culture with industry, and the blossoming of creativity in the very borders of different fields" (Park 2013). In June 2013, Park announced a comprehensive plan called the "Creative Economy Action Plan," aiming to generate new industries and employment through creativity and innovation (Connell 2014).

Overall, the strategy of the Korean government in supporting future technology is divided into two main objectives. The first is to become a top global leader in some strategic technologies and the second is to develop more practical and commercial technologies. These objectives are to guide the investment behaviors of public and private sectors, and to further contribute to Korea's strengths in technology development. The viability of Korea's technology development strategy and its implications are assessed in the following section.

11.1.3 Implications for Technology Strategy

This section provides general implications for Korea to establish an effective strategy to develop future technology. In general, technology can be divided into four types: foundational, original, applied, and converging technologies. The first three types focus on the development of a single technology, while converging technology emphasizes the combination of two or more technologies. In the narrow perspective, converging tech-nology involves the integration of different technologies; in the broader perspective, it also includes the convergence of various fields such as eco-nomics and culture (Moon 2012g).

Let's take two contrasting examples of Japan and Singapore to illus-trate different policies on technology development. Japan, in particular, promoted the nationwide strategy of the "50–30 Project" in 1990, which aimed to raise 30 Nobel Prize winners in science in 50 years. Due to these efforts, it is no wonder that Japan was able to produce many Nobel laure-ates in science: while the country produced only five Nobel Prize winners between 1901 and 1999, Japan had 15 Nobel prize winners from 2000 to 2015 (nearly one laureate per year). This shows that Japan focused more on foundational technology than converging technology.

By contrast, Singapore had a different strategy. Since the country did not possess significant foundational or original technologies compared to other advanced countries, it turned to developing an integrative system that connects important technologies such as biotechnology, medicine, and ICT. Based on this model, businesses were naturally linked to form an efficient ecosystem. Foreign universities, research institutes, and com-panies were invited to supplement Singapore's weaknesses in technology and skilled labor. This allowed Singapore to become a hub of converging technologies. This is an ambitious national goal of Singapore that seeks to transform itself from an isolated "intelligent island" to a technologically connected location (Moon 2010a).

An interesting article of "Now and Then" published in *The Economist* highlighted the recent changes in the process of invention. In order to give more specific evidence, the scholars at Oxford University conducted research that compared the patents issued by the United States Patent and Trademark Office. They found an interesting point that during the nineteenth century more than 50% of patents were of fundamentally new classes of technology. However, today, approximately 90% of techno-logical inventions are created by recombining existing technologies. This result signifies the rising importance and practicality of converging tech-nology in the real world (*Economist* 2015c).

Recently, major conglomerates in Korea have made substantial invest-ments in new industries such as renewable energy. However, few compa-nies have achieved success. Even if the industry seems promising, there is little chance for success if they do not have a strong infrastructure of efficiently liking related technologies. If Korean companies enter seem-ingly promising industries in the future based on the "me too" strategy of the past, a significant waste of time and resources is inevitable. Therefore,

Korean companies should be careful in selecting new industries and carefully analyze their competitive advantages and disadvantages when deciding to pursue a new technology strategy.

Currently, there are two challenging issues for Korean firms. The first is that they lack foundational (or basic) technologies, and the second is that the future of these technologies is uncertain. The second issue is particularly important because although a certain technology may be the most scientifically advanced, there is no guarantee that it will be widely used in the industry. Under these situations, it is not desirable for firms to invest large amounts of human and financial resources in a speculative future technology that is uncertain. A firm may fail in developing desirable technology. Even if a firm does develop a breakthrough technology, it may not be commercially successful. There are many such cases of advanced technologies that failed to achieve their potential, including Nokia's highly advanced Symbian operating system which was not successful.

Two important strategic guidelines can be derived from this discussion. Korean firms' competitive advantage lies in converging technologies, so they should continue to quickly and efficiently combine commercially viable technologies that exist today. However, Korea also needs to develop certain foundational technologies that can serve as the basis of converging technology. While doing so, Korea needs to be careful not to enter noncore technologies that are not synergistic to what they are doing today. Noncore technologies can be better acquired by establishing alliances with other competitive companies and institutions. The "speedier" and more "precise" way for Korea to gain competitive advantages is to work with others in converging technologies rather than developing new technologies on its own in noncore areas. Trying to become a leader in new, unrelated areas will result in massive costs. In today's era of rapid technological change, it is critical for companies to accurately assess their strengths and weaknesses and selectively apply strategies to new industries while maintaining their global market position.

11.2 BENCHMARKING: DIFFERENTIATION STRATEGY IN THE NEW COMPETITIVE LANDSCAPE

In the previous chapters, the benchmarking strategy was primarily focused on learning technologies and other production techniques. Firms can expand the scope of benchmarking by carefully studying the demand side as well as the production side. However, the most important point in this perspective is not always to find a large or new market but to further satisfy the needs of consumers in the existing market in a more value-added way. Consumers are no longer interested in products that are simple imitations of other products. This is not only true for existing markets in advanced countries but also for consumers in emerging markets who prefer differentiated products at a reasonable price. Supplying differentiated products is the key to attracting consumers, and it also helps establish the new best practice and raise one's bargaining power in the market.

Consumers in major international markets do not hesitate to purchase luxury goods when they see value in the product. People are willing to pay for expensive luxury products such as high-end automobiles, designer clothing, and exquisite wine despite their high prices. This is because these products are differentiated. Korean firms should utilize this characteristic of consumers to develop more advanced and customized products. If Hyundai, Samsung, and LG move beyond the imitation stage and begin to produce truly differentiated products, they will be able to become new leaders that set the global standard.

11.2.1 Examples from Other Countries: Differentiation Strategy

Italy is a country that best utilizes the differentiation strategy for success in apparel and fashion industries. Italian consumers are well-known to have highly sophisticated taste. Italians are the trendiest and the first to purchase new designs and models. This unique and sophisticated feature of the Italian consumers led companies to prioritize commercial luxury goods over high-technology investments. Luxury fashion companies represent the main competitive industry of Italy today. As Italian consumers are selective when considering features such as design, fabric, and color, Italian companies learned to be more intricate and sophisticated in producing competitive products.

Let's look at some other cases. The United States was able to emerge as the global leader in sports, movies, and music because the United States had a broad range of sophisticated consumers in these industries. American consumers show a lot of interest in these areas and are willing to pay premium prices for quality entertainment products. The medical industry in the United States is also more advanced than other countries because of the sophisticated nature of American patients. The consumers are highly knowledgeable about medical services, requiring doctors and related personnel to provide high-quality services to meet the demand of sophisticated consumers.

This same concept applies to the Japanese electronics industry. Japanese consumers have high standards of quality and service and possess detailed knowledge on electronic products with a preference for high-quality products. Thus, the consumer demand for the best and most up-to-date items led to product innovation and continuous efforts for related R&D (Kim 2004). Recently, however, the Japanese electronics industry declined because Japanese firms did not understand the demand of global consumers. While Japanese electronics are still competitive in Japan, they are no longer competitive in the global market. Therefore, in today's global market, firms not only need to understand domestic needs but also global consumers' demands.

The fundamental reason why apparel in Italy, medical services in the United States, and electronics in Japan have grown more successfully relative to other countries is that their respective consumers have sophisticated tastes. These industries have been developed by producing differentiated products in order to meet the market demand.

11.2.2 The Case of Korea: Differentiation Strategy in Market Entry

Sophisticated consumers in a country help industries grow competitively in the global market. Korean companies have utilized this fact as an impetus to develop new markets in some areas. Once products are initially developed to satisfy sophisticated consumers in one's home country, obtaining global market share is a matter of time. A good example is Korea's electronics industry. The reason why Korean electronics companies such as Samsung and LG are doing so well in the global market is that they are able to serve the unique, sophisticated Korean market, while carefully incorporating the best practices of the global market. Today, Korean electronics companies have outgrown existing market leaders and are now setting new best practices for others to follow.

Korea's automobile industry is another example of success. Korean automakers have proven to be successful in emerging markets, particularly in India. Toyota entered these markets first, but underestimated the purchasing power local consumers because of the country's low GDP per capita and only introduced older and cheaper models. Toyota did not understand that although India had low GDP per capita when looking at the country as a whole, the higher-end consumers that would purchase these automobiles would be willing to pay for slightly better cars with more options. On the other hand, Hyundai entered India with a localization strategy. While the company introduced models that were similar to

Toyota's, Hyundai included more options and also catered to local preferences, for instance, by raising the height of the roof for the vast majority
of the Indian male population who wore turbans. While adopting the best
practices, not necessarily most advanced technologies, of the global automobile industry, Hyundai tried to meet some unique needs of the host
markets (e.g., India, the United States) as well as the home market (i.e.,
Korea).

One of the strengths of Korean companies is that they do not impose
their own idiologies when entering new markets. Korean firms have a
strong ability to adapt to new market environments—they catch on to
local preferences quickly. However, firms from advanced countries tend to
be less aware of differences in local customs and preferences, often believ-
ing that what works best at home will work well in other countries. Most
advanced countries have acclimated to the West in terms of culture, systems, and ideologies. This means that they have less experiences adapting to a foreign environment, particularly those of developing countries.
Korea, on the other hand, started off by having to adapt to new cultures
and systems, and this experience allowed Korean firms to enter emerging
markets more effectively. However, Korean firms now face serious challenges as emerging countries have caught up to a level that threatens the
sustainability of many Korean firms. The following aims to provide useful
implications for Korea to establish an efficient differentiation strategy.

11.2.3 Implications for Differentiation Strategy

Although not as popular as it used to be, the Blue Ocean Strategy (BOS)
(Kim and Mauborgne 2005) was once a famous business strategy in Korea.
The BOS details the way a firm can carry out a differentiation strategy—
according to BOS, the first step is to leave the red ocean behind. Breaking
away from the intense competition among existing products (i.e., the red
ocean), the BOS argues that firms should create new or untapped markets
that lead them into the blue ocean. However, disregarding the red ocean
may not be the best solution in all situations as there are industries where
the Red Ocean Strategy (ROS) is more effective. This is because the probability of finding an entirely new, untouched market is extremely low, in
which case, a hasty BOS would not be fruitful. In fact, this is why many
ventures fail despite strong government support and entrepreneurship.
For a business owner, deciding whether to stay in the current business or
enter a new field with limited resources and capabilities is an extremely
difficult task that requires rigorous research and analysis.

For easier understanding, let's take the example of a new owner of a local pizza store. There are two options for making profits: (1) developing an entirely new, revolutionary recipe that could transform the current state of pizza, or (2) finding a top-rated pizza parlor and learning and improving its business practices. The first option sounds bold and attractive. However, the uncertainty and costs behind developing a new recipe lowers the chance for success. The second option is the benchmarking strategy of the ABCD model. As long as the owner properly learns the secrets of successful pizza stores, the potential for success is much greater. The first strategy is the blue ocean, in which returns are uncertain and remote, while the second is the red ocean, in which returns are more certain and immediate.

Then, when does BOS work? It is when the pizza store is already successful and wants to develop the next-generation pizza. If the owner has a passion to bring in more ideas and efforts to improve the existing products, then the BOS will be helpful. For instance, existing pizzas are delicious but high in calories, and consumers have now become more concerned about a healthy diet. In this case, finding ways to reduce the calories by studying Italian flatbread pizzas or changing the sauce or other ingredients could lead to the next best-selling pizza.

In most cases, the BOS is best suited for existing leaders, while it is easier and faster for followers to adopt the ROS. Then, what about firms like Apple that dominated the market instantly? As mentioned earlier, the secrets of Apple and Microsoft's success in introducing revolutionary products were in fact due to their careful observation of the red ocean. To the existing best practices at the time, they added their own "alpha." Therefore, in the new wave of competition where technology life cycles are shorter and the value of convergence is higher, the efficient way of differentiation is to benchmark the leading firms first. If the company is already a leading firm in the market, it can benchmark other related sectors, which can be a safe and tested source of innovation.

11.3 CONVERGENCE: THE CO-EVOLUTION STRATEGY

For convergence, this book has previously focused on combining technologies and skills in different fields. The benefits of convergence can be more efficiently achieved by forming clusters through sharing advantages and encouraging competition. Chapter 8 illustrated that firms' competitiveness tends to be more determined by the soundness of the entire business ecosystem rather than by the competitiveness of a single firm. In a similar vein, the determinants of a country's competitiveness are also shifting from a single country to an international cluster that expands beyond national boundaries.

Using the concepts of economies of scale and reduced transportation costs, Paul Krugman linked trade theory with economic geography. According to Krugman (1992), regions are divided into a high-technology urbanized core and a less developed periphery. However, a more systematic approach to the same topic had been forwarded by the business economist Michael Porter, who pioneered the cluster theory. According to Porter (1990, 1998a, b, 2000b), the cluster helps reinforce the competitiveness of firms through cooperation of sharing resources and knowledge. Furthermore, it can help maintain competitiveness through alliances that act as buffers against the weaknesses of individual players, which can cripple the entire system. The platform architecture and its governance can increase the efficiency of coevolution. This means a competitive business environment of a well-functioning cluster possesses a good combination of competition and cooperation.

11.3.1 Examples from Other Countries: International-Linking Clusters

Although Porter's framework is useful and comprehensive in analyzing the cluster, it is limited to an individual country and neglects international scope (Moon and Jung 2010). Identifying the limitations of Porter's cluster concept, Moon and Jung extended the boundary of clusters from domestic to international.[3] They distinguished the clusters into four stages: regional cluster, regional-linking cluster, international-linking cluster, and global-linking cluster as shown in table 11.1.

The first stage is the regional cluster which is identical to Porter's original concept where each cluster is independent. Prominent examples of this stage include the early form of Silicon Valley. The second stage is the regional-linking cluster where the combination of related clusters within the national boundary generates synergistic effects. The American entertainment cluster consisting of Hollywood, Disneyland, and Las Vegas is a good example. All are located in the Southwest of the United States and create synergies with each other. These attraction points reinforce each other because travelers usually visit more than one place in the same visit, making this regional-linking cluster more competitive than when they are separate from each other.

Table 11.1 THE CLUSTER STAGE MODEL

	Domestic Cluster		International Cluster	
Type	Stage 1: Regional Cluster	Stage 2: Regional-Linking Cluster	Stage 3: International-Linking Cluster	Stage 4: Global-Linking Cluster
Description	Independent and separate clusters	Regionally linked by neighboring clusters	Internationally linked by neighboring countries	Globally linked by neighboring/ non-neighboring countries
Example	The early form of Silicon Valley	Linking Hollywood, Disneyland, and Las Vegas	Linking Singapore, Malaysia, and Indonesia	Linking Silicon Valley and Bengaluru

Source: Revised from Moon and Jung (2010).

The third stage, international-linking cluster, is an effective form of cooperation among neighboring countries. It is beyond the scope of free trade agreements because it incorporates and surpasses the benefits made from other types of economic cooperation. The SIJORI (Singapore, Johor in Malaysia, and Riau in Indonesia) growth triangle in Southeast Asia is a good example of an international-linking cluster. Singapore has advantages in capital, technology, financial infrastructure, and access to the global market; Malaysia has advantages in related infrastructures of airports and harbors, cheap labor, and natural resources; and Indonesia has underdeveloped land, cheap labor, and abundant natural resources. Through the SIJORI growth triangle, the three countries can share their advantages while complementing the others' disadvantages. Thanks to this international cluster, the SIJORI has become the Southeast Asian hub of manufacturing as well as commerce and tourism.

The final stage is the global-linking cluster where the clusters are located in distant areas but are still linked to produce maximum synergies. In the technology industries, for example, the link between the United States (Silicon Valley) and India (Bengaluru, renamed from Bangalore in 2006) on the other side of the globe is a good example of a global-linking cluster. In fact, the evolution of Silicon Valley from a regional to global cluster provides an important implication. Silicon Valley started off as an independent regional cluster but rapidly expanded its scope into neighboring cities. Silicon Valley then connected with other clusters in foreign countries and then India to form a global-linking cluster of high-technology sectors such as computers and software.

11.3.2 The Case of Korea: Broadening the Scope of Internationalization

Korea has built several well-performing regional-linking clusters in its homeland, but it has not been successful in building international and global-linking clusters, including one with North Korea. A notable example of a cluster with North Korea is the *Kaesong* Industrial Complex, located in North Korea slightly north of the demilitarized zone. The project was initiated in 2003, and South Korea provided the main financial support for economic cooperation. South Korean firms, mostly in the clothing and textile industry, utilized North Korea's cheap labor for low value-added activities in this industrial complex.

The geographically closer production site benefited South Korean firms by decreasing transportation costs (versus China or other developing countries). In addition, due to the common language and culture of the two countries, costs for communication were also very low. On the other hand, North Korea also benefited from the earnings made in this industrial complex. This was an important source of North Korea's inflow of hard currency (BBC 2013a). However, due to the vulnerable political relationship between the two countries, North Korea closed the complex unilaterally several times, which imposed significant economic losses to South Korean firms. In order to solve these types of problems that arise from political conflicts, the industrial cluster has to be internationalized by attracting multinational corporations (MNCs) from other foreign countries. North Korean will then be less likely to change policies and impose threats on MNCs in the region.

This brings up a point on fundamental strategy for other countries in similar situations. When there is political tension in an international cluster, two strategic solutions can be provided. One is to carry out more internationalization and the other is to increase commercialization. The Kaesong cluster is not successful because it lacks internationalization, and the Tumen River cluster, which will be explained below, is not successful, because it lacks commercialization.

The Tumen River Area Development Program (TRADP) was first launched by the UNDP as a regional cooperation program in 1991. The promotion of TRADP was divided in two stages: the first stage was during the period of 1991–2004, where China, North Korea, and Russia were involved; the second stage began in 2005 and is ongoing, and the program was renamed as the Greater Tumen Initiative (GTI) under the leadership of China. The business sectors for cooperation include transportation, trade and investment, tourism, energy, and the environment. Mongolia and South Korea joined as members, but North Korea withdrew due to political reasons.

Despite significant elapse of time since its inception, the program has not achieved the expected results of economic development for the participating countries. This is because both TRADP and GTI are intergovernmental programs led by governments and are therefore considered more political than economic or commercial. They are driven by political objectives and are overly dependent on government support, which means they are frequently affected by government policy changes. The critical problems of TRADP and GTI are the shortage of private investments and an unfavorable business environment, which hinder economic interest and confidence of business sectors. While this cluster is internationalized, it is not fully commercialized.

11.3.3 Implications for Cluster Strategy

As for the nation's internationalization strategy, Korea is still focusing on increasing trade rather than encouraging foreign direct investment (FDI) and international clusters. Korea ranks in the top 10 in global trade but lags far behind the world average on FDI. Korea must understand that trade alone does not promote industry advancement. FDI, in the form of international transfer of production factors (i.e., capital, labor, and technology) brings more benefits to the industry. If Korea wants to remain competitive, it should shift its focus on international strategy from trade promotion to building international clusters, which include FDI and other types of international alliances for mutual efficiency and productivity growth. To this end, some strategic guidelines can be suggested for Korea to enhance competitiveness.

First, independent domestic clusters should be connected to other international regions and clusters rather than being focused on increasing individual competitiveness. Global firms serve as the main connecting blocks of different regions. Therefore, the government should create an environment that makes the outgoing and incoming investments easy and convenient. Currently, most outward FDI in Korea is concentrated in low value-added industries, whereas inward FDI is in high value-added industries. Both of the industries should be able to come and go smoothly in order to develop Korea's industries to the next level. Korea already has several domestically independent and regional-linking clusters and the next stage should be to increase internationalization by attracting more MNCs and linking these domestic clusters to other international clusters, including Silicon Valley, Southeast Asia, and potentially Kaesong and Tumen River.

While doing so, the government needs to understand that the service industry is just as important as the manufacturing industry. In the world, there are more foreign investments in services than manufacturing. Also, globally competitive clusters in the United Kingdom, Singapore, and Hong Kong have well-developed service industries such as finance, distribution, and law. In contrast, Korea is highly competitive in certain manufacturing industries but is weak in many service sectors. In order to become a truly competitive cluster in Northeast Asia, Korea has to further encourage service sectors and build balance between manufacturing and services.

For attracting investments to build a competitive cluster, discriminating different types of foreign investments is also dangerous. For example, a perspective that prioritizes new investment through greenfield FDI while undervaluing Merger and Acquisition (M&A) must be changed, because M&A is equally important as greenfield FDI. In addition, a negative perspective on private equity funds and hedge funds needs to be corrected, and legal problems such as copyrights need to be addressed properly. If Korea wants to develop a competitive global cluster, every form of investment should be welcomed as long as it is legal and ethical. When foreign investors choose Korea as a strategic base, the location will serve as a global network that allows growth in business throughout the world. Also, when foreign firms actively invest in Korea, domestic components and related industries will grow further. This will additionally help Korea learn how to efficiently manage resources and develop related technologies.

Finally, from a cultural perspective, clusters increase diversity by giving society the chance to embrace foreign cultures. This will be a meaningful change for many Koreans, who live in a relatively homogeneous society. Learning to accept cultural differences is an important step in transforming Korea to attain new competitive advantages. In this manner, making the country mature in cultural and ideological aspects is a necessary cornerstone for Korea's further development. More fundamentally, government bodies, both national and regional, can enhance bureaucratic efficiencies and improve transparency by dealing with foreign firms and people. A cluster is not simply the physical combination and connection of different partners, but the convergence of many different and invisible things, such as cultures and values.

11.4 DEDICATION: MAXIMIZING SHARED VALUE AND BUSINESS OPPORTUNITY

In the twenty-first century, the most common problem for corporate governance is the pressure for corporate social responsibility (CSR). This has been addressed in many business conferences today where topics such as sustainability, corporate philanthropy, and shared value are key agendas. These were the themes that emerged as global challenges for governments and businesses as people around the world have become widely concerned with the growing discrepancy between different types of labor, education, and environments.

This is not just a social problem related to justice, equality, and good virtue. The imbalance within income groups eventually brings down the potential for further economic growth. It turns into an economic problem if the imbalance causes deterioration in the market and impairs productivity and efficiency. However, many experts and governments only address this problem by looking at how rich or profitable businesses can share some of their benefits with those in need. Although this may seem like a positive and benevolent behavior, the topic needs to be approached more holistically with a sustainable outlook.

11.4.1 Examples from Other Countries: Nobel Brothers in Azerbaijan

In the beginning of 2011, I spent about a month in Azerbaijan as an economic consultant to the government, and I found several important implications for economic development and CSR from my experiences in the country. Azerbaijan has a rich reserve of oil and natural gas, and exports in these two natural resources have soared since the turn of the century. Due to the global fluctuation in energy prices throughout the world, Azerbaijan has received much attention from international organizations that offer consultations and development plans. These reports all addressed the issue of government corruption, fostering more small and medium-sized enterprises (SMEs) over large businesses, and diversifying the industry away from oil for broader economic development. Most of the solutions and recommendations were given with these goals in mind.

However, if a developing country wants to achieve fast growth, there must be a substantial role of MNCs.[4] This was quite true for Azerbaijan in its earlier days. In the beginning of the twentieth century, Azerbaijan emerged as a leading oil nation thanks to the two Swedish brothers

Robert and Ludvig Nobel, the older brothers of the famed Alfred Nobel. After being handed down his father's war supply factory as the eldest son, Robert Nobel often visited Azerbaijan to obtain wooden materials, gunstocks, and other supplies. During his visits, he discovered the potential of Azerbaijan's oil industry and suggested to his younger brother Ludvig that they should start a company and eventually, in 1879, Ludvig and the rest of the brothers jointly founded Branobel (meaning Nobel Brothers).

Back then, oil-refining technology had not yet been developed, so Ludvig brought in talented scientists and engineers to find the most efficient refining methods. This led Ludwig and his teams to build more than 80,000 oil facilities dealing with everything from oil extraction to production. It is thus no exaggeration to say that much of today's oil-refining and production technology began with Ludvig Nobel. Furthermore, he introduced some techniques necessary for shipbuilding, oil pipelines, and metal oil tankers.

From a business strategy perspective, the company expanded through a vertical integration of related and supporting businesses. Ludvig focused on integrating his oil and related businesses in order to increase business opportunity and efficiency. All business activities from oil exploration to extraction and commodification were integrated under a single system. Compared to today, transferring oil back then was extremely costly. Oil firms could not enjoy the benefits of economies of scale due to the slow and inefficient transfer of oil through camels and other pack animals. To rectify this problem, Ludvig devised a new, inexpensive, and safe oil transport system—the world's first tanker. When Ludvig encountered difficulties with the construction and transportation due to the large size of the fleet, he decided to complete ship welding on the Baltic Sea as the parts arrived from Sweden. This was a remarkably innovative idea at that time. Eventually, this led to the creation of other related businesses such as fleet construction that further contributed to the development of oil tankers that could sail cheaply and safely across the Caspian Sea. The fact that Baku became the world's busiest port during those years proved the success of Ludvig's innovations.

Among many successes, perhaps the most significant impact of the Nobel family was their contributions to the well-being of Azerbaijan's society. Although Ludvig and his son Emanuel were known as pioneers of business, their efforts to improve the livelihood of their employees were extraordinary. They made a system that ran on creating value for employees. This was a highly progressive approach during a period when labor was seen as an expendable resource to owners. The Nobels established a cooperative bank for employees and provided social areas such as dining spaces, leisure rooms, libraries, and conference rooms where public speeches and discussions were held. They also built houses for workers near the Villa Petrolea estate and they offered a shuttle boat between the city and the harbor. In addition, the Nobel family spent considerable effort on educating employees (and even provided scholarships for employees to study abroad) and donated funds to local schools and hospitals.

Unfortunately, all the efforts of the Nobel family came to a dramatic end with the Bolshevik Revolution in April 1920. Hoping to survive on Baku's oil money, the Bolsheviks seized the country and nationalized Nobel's assets. The country came under chaos as the revolutionists killed everyone who resisted. In the midst of this turmoil, local employees protected the Nobel family as "good citizens" of Azerbaijan and risked their lives to assist the Nobels' escape from the country.

The above narrative gives a detailed account of the Nobel family's contribution to Azerbaijan. The Nobel case is interesting and there are many similar cases of corporate social activities in modern times, which successfully brought benefits to both society and company. All these cases present the same message: when social problems are seen as opportunities to improve existing practices and reorient the company's value chain activities more productively, the resulting solutions can benefit both the society and company. This shows that social well-being and corporate strategy do not have to be treated as separate, exclusive agendas. The fundamentals of social responsibility contribute to changing a company's objective and way of thinking, which ultimately influence its entire business behavior. All in all, this is the proper way to head toward sustainability for the society. Particularly for Korea and its firms, social value can be connected with dedication regarding strategic guidelines for a sustainable growth strategy.

11.4.2 The Case of Korea: *Chaebol*'s Role in Society

Many people in Korea criticize chaebol by pointing to the social problems they have long caused. However, conglomerates often bring greater efficiencies to a nation. Especially in the early phase of economic development when industries struggle to compete, fledgling industries cannot survive if other activities in the value chain are weak. This is where conglomerates' internalization can help improve efficiency. For example, despite Ludvig Nobel's efficient oil enterprise, the firm could not have sustained itself with weak transportation and logistics. Nobel knew this well and developed all related and supporting sectors.

In Korea today, the biggest socioeconomic conflict lies between top chaebol and SMEs. The stratification has pushed the government to design policies to protect the "weak" (SMEs) against the "strong" (chaebol). The Korean government addresses this social problem through strict policies that often go against natural market dynamics, which hinders productivity. On the other hand, chaebol massively and publicly demonstrate charity activities to improve the company's image. Although the trend is slowly changing among chaebol, there once used to be seasonal events, sponsored by top chaebol during the winter, such as briquette delivery and kimchi making for the elderly and families with low income. These two events were popularly held throughout many companies in Korea to be portrayed as a "good" company (Moon 2012b).

Although these events help those in need with an immediate supply of heating and food, conglomerates can do more than directing their resources to one-time events that only produce transitory benefits. By matching corporate strengths to social problems and vice versa, even overwhelming national challenges can be solved without hindering firms' growth. Samsung's vocation program for students in Africa and Southeast Asia is a good example. When Samsung entered these countries, there was an immediate need to hire employees who were familiar with electronics, particularly Samsung's. Also, since these countries had huge pools of labor, Samsung saw the potential to recruit a competent labor force. These emerging countries, on the other hand, were struggling to raise the level of living through education and proper job training.

With such mutual benefits that result from matching the needs of Samsung and the society, Samsung decided to launch programs to encourage local students to enroll in Samsung's education and training program. By granting them the opportunity to learn Samsung's technology, competent students were granted jobs in customer services or manufacturing, depending on the company's job functions in the region. Through this initiative, both the company and local society could enjoy win-win solutions and shared benefits. Therefore, firms should engage in social problems by viewing them not as a responsibility but as an opportunity for mutual benefits (Moon and Lee 2014).

This type of methodology can be applied to other social tensions that are blamed on chaebol. For instance, the conflict between SMEs and conglomerates can be resolved when chaebol engage in joint technology development with the SMEs that supply parts and components. Often, the competitiveness of chaebol is closely linked to the competitiveness of SMEs. In reality, large and small firms cooperate in producing the finished products (as shown in chapter 8). Simply concluding that large firms always exploit smaller firms does not help because it limits all situations and relationships to zero-sum games. In fact, there is a much more cooperative than competitive relationship between large and small firms, and business and society.

11.4.3 Implications for Strategic Goals

Early academic studies of corporate social activity focused on the social responsibility of businessmen, the individuals who became rich through their business activities. Howard Bowen's 1953 book titled *Social Responsibilities of the Businessman* is widely known to mark the beginning of modern CSR, where he argued that social responsibility is not a panacea but contains important truths for guiding businesses in the future—businesses alone cannot solve social problems, but it can create solutions to alleviate them.

Drucker (1984) provided some important insights into this fact as well. He compared two business leaders and corporate philanthropists, Andrew Carnegie and Julius Rosenwald, to delineate the proper role of business in society. Carnegie is well known for his contributions to the community by building libraries and schools using his wealth. On the other hand, Rosenwald similarly realized the importance of social improvement but defined it in line with his business. Rosenwald believed that the wealth of his customers was directly linked to business profits, and he sought ways to increase business value by tackling the social problems that limited customers' welfare. On this note, Drucker argued that the Rosenwald-type of business philanthropy is more appropriate. Drucker went on to highlight the importance of opportunity by addressing how firms could realign the value of self-interest to solve external social problems. According to this approach, the immediate challenge is to find the right opportunity, and when this is tackled with business value and firm competitiveness, the resulting benefit can be shared with other members of the society (Moon and Lee 2014).

Drucker (1984) argued, "The proper 'social responsibility' of business is to turn a social problem into economic opportunity and economic benefit, into productive capacity, into human competence, into well-paid jobs, and into wealth." The importance of implementing strategy in solving social challenges is logically explained in Porter and Kramer's analysis on the efficiency of charity and philanthropic organizations (Porter and Kramer 2002, 2006). The main purpose of their study arose from a concern with the problem of inefficient funding and operations of nonprofit organizations. Eventually expanding their scope of research to business philanthropy, Porter and Kramer (2011) developed the concept of creating shared value (CSV) where building a coherent value between business and society will allow mutual benefits.

A conflict in Korea and many other countries revolves around the issue of growth against social welfare. If resources were unlimited, granting the best welfare options would be possible and encouraged. However, the conflicts occur because governments have limited funds. This requires governments to settle on second or third best options as long as they are optimal under the given circumstances. Therefore, a sound welfare policy is the one that allocates resources in the most efficient way. What is more important, if the country wants to become the best welfare state, it must first become the most productive state. In this regard, the ABCD model can again play an important role for increasing productivity of the economy.

While the preceding chapters of this book primarily dealt with explaining the past and current success of Korea's economy and firms, this chapter emphasized how to upgrade Korea's competitiveness through the ABCD model. Korea has been highly competitive in speed but still lacks precision. Thus, this chapter suggested solutions through future technology development. Korea has demonstrated great success through its fast catch-up strategy, but in order to further advance, Korean firms need to reposition themselves as more differentiators than just followers. For this, this chapter provided the guidelines to establish efficient and realizable methods in the transitional stage. This is related to the upgrading of the benchmarking strategy, particularly on the demand side through satisfying sophisticated consumers.

For convergence, the chapter suggested developing international-linking clusters to incorporate the advantages of other nations and firms to complement Korea's weaknesses. Lastly, for dedication, this chapter discussed the social responsibility of business, which involves the shared value of both business and society. By reviewing the existing arguments and showing relevant cases, we can see how a firm's competitiveness can be enhanced, together with the sustainable growth of the society.

All of the issues emphasize how to pursue sustainable growth through the ABCDs. As seen, the ABCD model is not only useful in explaining how Korea has been successful as a follower in the past but also provides implications on how the country should pursue further growth in the future. From this perspective, the ABCDs provide useful guidelines for both developing countries on how to catch-up and developed countries on how to sustain growth. This will be discussed in the next chapter.

CHAPTER 12
The Generalization of the ABCD Model

I n 2011, I was invited to speak at the annual meeting of the International Conference for National Competitiveness held in Brazil. Over the course of the discussion, I had an interesting encounter with a representative from Argentina. I asked him why Argentina was currently struggling when it used to be an economic powerhouse on par with the United States. His response was simple—it was too easy to make money in Argentina back then. When he asked me the same question about Korea's success, my answer was the opposite—it was extremely difficult to make money in Korea in the past.

Although overly simplified, these explanations reflect the fundamental forces of economic development. In resource-abundant countries like Argentina, it is relatively easy to earn money by making use of resources. However, these economies often become heavily reliant on their resources and complacent. Furthermore, usually, only few elites benefit from the abundance of natural resources, which consequentially widens the income gap. In many cases, the wide availability of natural resources may appear as a blessing, but it can be a curse in disguise. Few countries in the world have been able to advance their economies just with their abundant natural resources, commonly known as the "resource curse."

On the other hand, in countries with scarce resources like Korea, the initial stage of development is exceedingly arduous and bleak. Every industry requires an input of resources, small or large, and it is difficult to develop competitive industries with costly resource imports. However, if the people are diligent and guided by a proper development strategy, the country can overcome these initial disadvantages to achieve economic success. The lack of natural resources may appear like a curse in the beginning, but if the government and people work together, the curse can turn out to be a blessing in disguise. Evidently, this applies to the economic growth of the Asian newly industrialized economies (NIEs). All of these economies worked tremendously hard to reap the fruits of dedication. In this respect, perhaps Krugman (1994) was correct when he described Asia's driving force as "perspiration." However, this is related to only one factor (i.e., dedication) of the ABCDs and neglects other important variables that have contributed to driving the economic growth of these countries today.

So far, this book has focused on illustrating the success and challenges of the Korean economy and firms using the ABCD model. As the final chapter of the book, chapter 12 will show how the model can be generalized to build and sustain national or firm competitiveness regardless of the level of development. In order to achieve this goal, the following section first begins with an analysis at the national level. It touches upon the earlier development trajectories of Asian NIEs and examines how the ABCDs can explain their substantial economic development. Then, the chapter will look into whether this framework can also be used to provide direction for other countries' future development. Finally, the chapter will illustrate how the ABCD model can be extended to explain the success of other emerging and developed firms.

12.1 THE GENERALIZATION OF THE ABCD MODEL AT THE NATIONAL LEVEL

Going back to my conversation with the economist from Argentina, earlier theories that focus on inherited advantages (e.g., traditional trade theory) could not explain why Argentina's economy declined while Korea's improved. As echoed throughout this book, the ABCD model fills this gap by showing how the combination of different factors results in economic success. The model serves in formulating an optimal development strategy for national development. In this regard, the orchestration of the ABCD model is visible in the development experiences of the four Asian NIEs—Singapore, Hong Kong, Taiwan, and Korea. Since the preceding chapters have clearly demonstrated the usefulness of the ABCDs in explaining Korea's economic success, the following section shifts its focus to illustrating the rapid growth of the other three economies of the NIEs.

12.1.1 Different Types of Governance System: Korea versus Other Countries

In the past, economic theorists did not give much consideration to the differences in state governance. Instead, they generalized the models of advanced countries and applied them to developing countries. However, this generalization is highly ineffective because it neglects the conditions of developing countries and blindly prescribes the elimination of corruption and the promotion of technology or skills as solutions. Contrary to popular belief, corruption is not the cause but the result of poor economic performance and advanced technology is not as critical as primitive factors like basic labor in the early stage of economic development. In fact, it is inappropriate to focus on advanced production factors from the onset of development; such advanced growth should only be pursued once an economy reaches a certain level (Moon, Parc, and Yin 2012).

Modern analyses of the political economy discuss various concepts of different political and economic systems.[1] For example, capitalism is an economic system principally based on the free market, and democracy refers to a governance system where decisions are based on popular consent. *Democratic capitalism*, which is also known as *Liberal democracy*, is the combination of these two systems and can thus be defined as *a free economic system where the rules are made by popular (or majority) vote or representation*. The United States serves as the prime example of this type of economic and political system. The antithesis of capitalism is socialism, where regulations are imposed by the government with the purpose of protecting social ownership. Accordingly, *democratic socialism* can be defined as *a regulated economic system where rules are made by popular decision*, and many European states fit this model.

Although many states have adopted democratic systems (especially after the Cold War in the 1990s), there are still many others that display varying political features. Some states are ruled by authoritarian governments, and under this system, major decisions are made by small interest groups that hold power. The combination of authoritarianism and capitalism (or *authoritarian capitalism*) is *a system where decisions are made by political leaders with the strong support of interest groups based on a market economy*. Under this system, if leaders construct appropriate economic development strategies, the market and society can experience rapid growth. Singapore and Korea serve as modern examples of this type of system. These countries did not follow in the footsteps of the United States or Europe. Instead, an elite group within each country utilized its political insights and economic expertise to implement strategic development programs to expedite growth.

At the other end of the spectrum is *authoritarian socialism, a system where a single dictator or minority leadership regulates the national economy.* This system is especially vulnerable to economic deterioration and includes despotic and communist states in the Third World. In order to enhance growth, they must shift from an authoritarian system to a democratic one (democratic socialism) or from socialism to capitalism (authoritarian capitalism). History has shown that a state's transition out of an authoritarian socialist system is more likely to succeed under authoritarian capitalism and not under democratic socialism. Again, the cases of Korea and Singapore serve as good examples.

Another good example is China, which continues to receive attention for its ongoing development. Maoist China was under clear-cut authoritarian socialism, but with the opening of its doors to market reform, today's China more closely resembles an authoritarian capitalist state. In addition to China, other Southeast Asian countries such as Vietnam are following a similar track. Interestingly, China and Vietnam had both publicly announced that their economic development benchmarked Korea and Singapore. This is because following the Korean or Singaporean track seemed the most plausible and effective. As these two countries show, the governance system of authoritarian capitalism may provide important implications for developing countries today. For this purpose, the following section compares and contrasts Korea with Singapore and other NIEs.

12.1.2 The Newly Industrialized Economies: Korea's Competitors

There are similarities and differences among the four NIEs, as summarized in table 12.1. Singapore and Hong Kong have more in common with each other, and the same is true for Taiwan and Korea.

Table 12.1 COMPARING THE FOUR ASIAN NIEs

	Singapore	Hong Kong	Taiwan	Korea
History	British colony (Western)		Japanese colony (Eastern)	
Economy Size	City state		Middle-sized country	
Trade Policy	Open door		Selective open door	
Growth Strategy	State Capitalism	Free Capitalism	Balanced (SMEs)	Unbalanced (Chaebol)

First of all, a major division can be made in history and governance—Singapore and Hong Kong were deeply influenced by Western (i.e., British) colonialism, whereas Taiwan and Korea were mainly influenced by Japan's governance architecture. At a deeper level, the former two economies gained important tools for facilitating international transactions and business via their familiarity with Western culture and English language. In terms of country size, both Singapore and Hong Kong are relatively small city-states. Moreover, both are regional hubs whose influence extends beyond their borders, serving as *de facto* capitals for industry, finance, commerce, information, education, and culture (Vogel 1991). Most importantly, both carry out active open door policies to invigorate commerce and industries to compensate for their small domestic market.

Taiwan and Korea are the opposite; both countries were colonized by Japan, and had the remnants from the Japanese ways of administration, education, and commerce. Also, both faced communist military threats, although the situation was much more serious in Korea than in Taiwan. Compared to Taiwan, Korea started with a smaller industrial base and lower GDP per capita. Regarding trade policy, the governments of both Taiwan and Korea protected their fledgling firms through trade measures in the form of tariffs and legal restrictions for entry, while promoting exports and only selectively allowing imports in certain areas.

Despite some of the evident similarities, the growth strategies differed significantly among these economies. Singapore's Prime Minister Lee Kuan-yew believed in government-led enterprises, along with other common socialist features such as government provisions of social security, housing, and medical care. One interesting fact is that Singapore's public enterprises provided a close link between business and politics, with leading businessmen also serving as government bureaucrats. Although Singapore is a highly regulated economy, it has achieved great success due to close and effective collaboration between the government and private sectors and active globalization of the economy.

Hong Kong's growth strategy was much different from that of Singapore's. Hong Kong, which reached the per capita income level of its colonial motherland by 1990, is often referred to as the best example of free-market capitalism (Vogel 1991). However, Hong Kong has often gone beyond free-market principles. Indeed, the government's civil servants greatly facilitated industrial planning and the development of local industries. These government officials used public funds to develop industrial estates and then made the land available to manufacturing firms at prices below market value. Also, there was strong leadership by the government in promoting exports and local textile firms. Yet, despite the shadow role of the government, the businessmen of Hong Kong remained in the fore-front in stimulating businesses and industries.

Taiwan pursued a rather different growth strategy that was char-acterized by balanced growth and a heavy focus on small and medium-sized enterprises (SMEs). Unlike other developing countries that tried to break away from primary industries, the government of Taiwan put great emphasis on agriculture. This is mainly because agriculture is more fam-ily-oriented and benefits the nation with a greater sense of community and security. The main political leaders of *Kuomintang* who fled from mainland China had difficulty blending with the locals in the region. Therefore, the Kuomintang government wanted to bring stability and order by encourag-ing kinship or family-centered business and balanced growth. This is the political backdrop of SME growth in Taiwan, which is quite different from Korea's unbalanced, chaebol-led growth.

12.1.3 The Distinctive Features of Strategies: The Newly Industrialized Economies

Despite these different histories and backgrounds, the four Asian NIEs succeeded in achieving rapid economic growth and industry transforma-tion. In the past, many scholars classified economic growth as a natural progression through various stages (e.g., Rostow 1959, 1990). Collectively, these theories influenced the way modern economists thought about the specific steps for economic development. However, they all tended to have a narrow focus on production and market systems and did not provide a comprehensive framework for dealing with all of the important factors for economic development. The following section applies the ABCD model to the other three Asian NIEs (Taiwan, Singapore, and Hong Kong) to show how their prominent economic development has been achieved.

Agility of Asian NIEs—The NIEs had a readily available labor force that was eager to work. With industrialization beginning to take shape, each of these societies had a large dislocated population that was anxious to find a new basis for economic livelihood. In Taiwan, there were over 1.5 million people who had fled from mainland China by the early 1950s. In Hong Kong, refugees from China constituted over half of the popula-tion after the closing of the Chinese border in 1950, and in Singapore, there was a substantial population of immigrants who flew from Malaysia and Indonesia. With these demographic dynamics and the modernization movements in these countries, the laborers were hungry for any and all opportunities to work hard for their own livelihood. Consequently, this propelled the labor force to work fast and productively, which ultimately served as a valuable human resource for the Asian tigers.

On top of a productive labor force, a meritocratic bureaucracy was developed by hiring and allocating highly competitive individuals to leadership positions that require special expertise. Together with merit-based performance acknowledgment in the government, the East Asian bureaucrat systems were effective in generating economic achievements. The level of effect was enhanced when modern bureaucrats monitored the economic progress of the West and granted more independence to private enterprises while maintaining a certain level of control (Vogel 1991). With their increased expertise, the heightened sense of responsibility enabled the bureaucrats to expedite the most adequate policy construction for national growth.

All in all, it became clear that the government's role was to help the private sector prosper and eventually help the nation grow into a stable economy in a "speedy" and "precise" way compared to other developing countries. This belief has continued until today in NIEs where most of the governments and leaders have made huge contributions to economic development. In short, the NIEs benefited from the vast pool of human resources who were willing to work productively, and this is what allowed each of the NIEs to achieve fast growth.

Benchmarking of Asian NIEs—In the early phase of development, the NIEs learned the Japanese model of technology and investment.[2] Sharing many similarities with Japan, such as a dense population and a short supply of natural resources, the NIEs adopted Japan's industrial patterns. Some of these include the transition from labor-intensive industries to capital- and technology-intensive sectors by using income from exports. In order to increase exports, they engaged in original equipment manufacturer production with top MNCs, which helped in learning technologies and skills from Japan, and later the West. As their economies developed, they continued to improve the quality of their products and services. As a result, the NIEs have moved further to provide differentiated services and products.

In Taiwan, companies such as HTC, ASUS, and Acer have emerged as new market leaders with their differentiated computers and electronic products. In Singapore, Singapore Airlines has received a rare five-star rating from Skytrax, and its food service industry has flourished due to its unique multinational culture. Singaporean dining franchises such as Mr. Bean and Jack's Place can be seen in numerous regions throughout Asia. On the other hand, Hong Kong boasts strong competitiveness in hotel services and logistics as it utilized its position as an international hub. For example, Hong Kong companies such as Swire Resources have established joint ventures with global MNCs to optimize and differentiate their logistics for customer service.

As these cases demonstrate, the NIEs have been driven to different industries by enhancing product and service quality. However, the key to the success of these four countries is their learning of Japan and the West. As a result, they succeeded in appropriately upgrading their competitive industries. Compared to other developed countries, the NIEs did not possess superior technologies and high-tech products in the beginning. Their success is attributed to an efficient benchmarking strategy of best practices rather than their own innovation in technology and product.

Convergence of Asian NIEs—Initially, the industrial and commercial infrastructures of the NIEs were extremely weak. Taiwan was essentially forced into an island with no commercial base to begin with. Singapore came into possession of a British naval base since its independence, but by that time, the port was in such poor condition that it needed a complete overhaul before it became operational. Hong Kong, on the other hand, had access to ports but completely lacked related infrastructure to jumpstart its industries. Therefore, as Taiwan, Singapore, and Hong Kong reached the next phase of development, they focused on cementing industrial infrastructure and creating a competitive business environment that could attract investment.

As early as the 1970s, Taiwan devoted itself to building manufacturing complexes. Twenty cities, including Jilong, New Taipei, and Taipei were established by the government for this purpose. Additionally, specialized zones such as the Central Science Industrial Complex, Shinju Science Industrial Complex, and Southern Science Industrial Complex were created to oversee the growth of the semiconductor, computer, communication, and biotechnology industries. Singapore carried out similar initiatives by building the Jurong Petrochemical Complex and Seletar Aerospace Park. From the onset, the Singaporean government had a clear vision to engage in petrochemicals and logistics and invested accordingly. Today, the Jurong complex is one of the world's three largest petrochemical complexes, and the Seletar complex is known for being the most connected station with the rest of the world. Hong Kong was no exception and it invested early and heavily to build a strong industrial base. Recently completed projects such as the Hong Kong Science Technology Complex, Hong Kong Science Park, and the InnoCentre reflect a concerted attempt by the government to develop new competitive industries.

Singapore and Hong Kong now boast strong industrial complexes that serve as gathering sites for MNCs and experts in business and finance. The Economic Development Board of Singapore continues to push hard to transform Singapore into a global business hub that connects global business. The same holds true for Hong Kong. Ranking among the top countries in terms of trade value (tenth in exports and ninth in imports according to 2013 UNCTAD statistics), Hong Kong is a highly converged economy that strives to maintain its position as a global business hub.

Dedication of Asian NIEs—It is no surprise that three of the four Asian Tigers were characterized by strong authoritarian governments in the early stages of development (the only exception, Hong Kong, was under British rule). Leaders Chang Kai-sheik, Lee Kuan-yew, and Park Chung-hee exercised tight control over government policies, and the regimes are often described as tyrannical due to their oppressive political actions. However, the motivations of these governments are entirely different from many authoritarian governments of other developing countries in Africa or South America, which pursue individual gains over national development. In fact, the governments of the NIEs have directly contributed to their nations' progress and can be labeled as benevolent developmental dictatorships.

Under a developmental dictatorship, the political environment is relatively stable, albeit at the cost of democracy. In the case of the four Asian Tigers, a stable political and social system combined with proper guidance from the state propelled economic development by raising the efficiency of economic policies. This particular path to development has proven to be highly effective, and it remains a defining characteristic of NIEs' economic development.

However, it is important to approach the development agenda from a more fundamental perspective—the motivation for success. This is because industrial development can follow a proposed model only if there is a corresponding motivation from the society. More specifically, leaders have to be motivated themselves first before motivating their citizens, which again shows that political and social stability is crucial for inspiring hard work. The growth experiences of Taiwan, Singapore, and Hong Kong clearly demonstrate the people's strong motivation to improve their standard of living.

For instance, Chiang Kai-shek was expelled from mainland China for advocating a liberal and anti-communist nation. He used these two ideologies to fuel economic development and successfully emerged amidst difficulties. Singapore acquired independence from Britain as a federal state of Malaysia. However, following a series of conflicts, Singapore was expelled by Malaysia's federal government, placing it in a precarious economic and political situation. Nonetheless, the state had a profound motivation to protect its newfound independence and did not stumble. In case of Hong Kong, a flood of refugees sought new lives by escaping from the communist government of the People's Republic of China.

In the beginning, the NIEs were among the poorest countries and lagged far behind other regions such as Latin America. The success of the Asian Tigers is often attributed to foreign aid, a favorable global environment, and export-driven government policies. However, this view cannot explain why other countries failed under similar policy directions and conditions. The missing piece is the strong motivation and desire for a better life, which fueled diligence and motivation.

12.1.4 Korea and the Newly Industrialized Economies: From Competition to Cooperation

The NIEs started off as major competitors in labor-intensive manufacturing in their early stages of economic development, but now there is room for more cooperation than competition due to their different competencies. Fortunately, decades of experience allowed the four NIEs to find their own competitive advantages. Hong Kong is now a center for finance, Singapore is a reputable hub for logistics, Taiwan has its prominent world-class electronics companies, and Korea has prominent industries such as steel, electronics, and automobile.

Due to these different industry structures, Korea engages more in cooperation than competition with other NIEs. Many Korean firms currently operate regional headquarters in Singapore to serve the Southeast Asian markets, have buying offices in Hong Kong to have easy access to China, and source electronics parts from Taiwan. Firms from Singapore, Hong Kong, and Taiwan also make substantial investments in Korea. In the past, the NIEs competed against each other in international markets, but they now engage in more collaboration through cross-investments and sharing of differentiated competencies.

While the Asian NIEs are well on the path to further growth and show leadership in the global community, there are also concerns about their future sustainability. With the rise of China and other emerging countries, the world has shown interest in learning and following the four dragons' economic growth experiences. Fortunately, their growth continues and this can also be explained by the ABCD model. In order to better understand the future of national competitiveness, the next step is to discuss the fundamentals of strategy in greater detail and expand the application of the ABCDs.

12.1.5 The ABCD Model: Stage Approach to National Growth

The four elements of the ABCD model—agility, benchmarking, convergence, and dedication—are each broken down into two subfactors. The first four subfactors—speed, learning, mixing, and diligence—constitute the "basic" factors for enhancing competitiveness in the early developing stages, and the other four subfactors—precision, best practice, synergy creation, and goal orientation—are the "advanced" factors for developed stages. This distinction is important because it shows a different prioritization of strategy factors for developing and developed economies.

Agility—In developing countries, the general trend is that markets are less efficient and demand exceeds supply. Additionally, consumers tend to look for goods to fulfill their immediate needs and put relatively little importance on quality. Under these economic conditions, firms can easily earn profits by simply producing products that are in demand without much concern for quality. Therefore, in the developing stage, the speed of entering the market is a crucial element, and profit seekers must move ahead of others to gather resources, produce products, and sell them in the market. However, firms that serve more developed countries can only survive by creating additional values for consumers. Furthermore, consumers in advanced countries are usually more sophisticated and discerning in their tastes and preferences, so companies must thoroughly understand these needs to serve them in order to remain competitive. Accordingly, in the developed stage, the entire business process should be more carefully designed with higher precision.

Benchmarking—Innovation does not appear out of thin air; it requires significant investment. An investment, in turn, involves a certain degree of risk. Considering the limited capabilities of competitiveness in the developing stage, learning and imitation are often much more effective than taking on the inherent risks of innovation. In practice, many firms in developing countries establish competitiveness by learning rather than creating new products and ideas from scratch. However, in the developed stage, firms should continually be up to date on best practices (although not necessarily the highest technologies in their fields) and create new best practices to sustain their positions within an industry.

Convergence—In the developing stage, firms that diversify into unrelated industries can make profits by servicing excess demand in unrelated fields. For example, Samsung, which is largely known for its electronics business, was once involved in a variety of industries including sugar, textiles, and media. In the developing stage, mixing is important for not only creating industry synergies and additional values, but making profits in individual businesses. However, as the economy matures, firms have to be more concerned about creating proper synergies to strengthen and mutually reinforce the competitive advantages of related businesses. Otherwise, they may not be able to survive the highly competitive environment of the developed stage.

Dedication—Economic progress comes from diligence more than anything else. Under this context, nationwide campaigns such as Korea's *Saemaul* movement of the 1970s provide important lessons. It motivated villagers to overcome poverty through their own efforts and put forth the notion that problems can be overcome through diligence. However, once the economy develops to a certain stage, the motivation for further growth may subside. As an example, the so-called "lost decades" of Japan may better be explained by lost motivation rather than unsound macroeconomic policies. In the developed stage, therefore, a clear and sound goal-oriented mindset is needed for continued economic development.

I have discussed the division of the ABCDs into two groups (each with four subfactors) based on a nation's level of development. However, this does not mean that only certain subfactors should be utilized by developing countries and certain ones by developed companies; all subfactors are important for countries to maintain sustainable growth. The division is simply meant to prioritize the more relevant variables for developing and developed countries in order to make more effective policies.

12.2 THE GENERALIZATION OF THE ABCD MODEL AT THE FIRM LEVEL

In 2014, I was asked to speak at an international conference in Europe. The topic of the conference was the competitiveness of future industries, and distinguished speakers from other countries such as France, Germany, and Japan came to participate in the discussion. As important industry leaders and scholars, the representatives from these countries were eager to share their assessments of their home countries' innovative technologies and industries to promote business competitiveness in their countries. The session began with a Japanese scholar highlighting Japan's tremendous investments in R&D for developing new competitive industries. While the presentation focused on Japan's superior technology base for creating new, promising industries, the discussion that ensued with other participants were primarily centered on Japan's "lost decades."

When it was my turn to speak, I assured the audience that Japan does indeed possess top technologies in many industries despite its low economic growth. However, I also pointed out that in our current business environment, state-of-the-art technology does not always equate to success. In other words, technological innovation does not always promise market value. The ABCD model can be used to explain the success cases of firms from developing countries that do not possess superior innovation and technologies, such as Xiaomi, as well as industry leaders from developed countries, such as Apple.

12.2.1 The Competitive Strategy for Followers: A Case Study of Xiaomi

The Chinese company Xiaomi made headlines in 2014 with its rapid rise in the Chinese smartphone market. Xiaomi's devices sell for approximately $100, while Samsung's high-end Galaxy smartphones typically cost more than $500 (Dou 2014). Production and shipment of Xiaomi phones have exceeded those of Samsung in the Chinese market. With this effective cost leadership strategy, Xiaomi became the number one smartphone provider in China and the fifth largest in the world in just four years since its inception (Olson 2014). Their business goal is to target the low-end smartphone market and sell cheap, decent quality phone accessories, while integrating these products with their own Internet service and user interface. Xiaomi's business strategies, which seem to be complicated, can be easily captured by the ABCD model in the following.

Agility of Xiaomi—Xiaomi demonstrated agility by limiting sales to online channels. This was a huge success because its main target, young consumers, was heavy users of the Internet. These consumers did much of their shopping online and shared their experiences through social media. By focusing on online sales, Xiaomi saved themselves the trouble and costs of securing offline retailers and distribution channels. Xiaomi's global strategy in speed was also apparent when the company targeted the Indian smartphone market which is the second largest after China. According to Manu Jain, the head of Xiaomi India: "One of our focuses is to reduce the time lag between China launch and India launch to under two months" (Dutta 2015). With the mobile device rivalry quickly shifting toward wearable products, Xiaomi sold one million Mi Band fitness trackers in just 100 days since its launch, ranking as China's top wearable tech product and possibly the world's bestselling fitness tracker. All these show how Xiaomi quickly and properly addressed the dynamic and fast-changing market.

Benchmarking of Xiaomi—Moreover, Xiaomi demonstrated good benchmarking by learning from the top companies in each of its three business divisions (phones, software, and the Internet service). Xiaomi's smartphone designs are somewhat similar to those of the iPhone but are sold at only half of the iPhone's price (Wohlsen 2015). As for software, Xiaomi launched its Android-based MIUI firmware, which was made to resemble Samsung's TouchWiz and Apple's iOS. Its Internet service was made by carefully learning from other Internet-based companies. Furthermore, Xiaomi's CEO, Lei Jun, closely imitated the dress and presentation style of Steve Jobs; he favored simple black shirts with jeans, stood in front of large visual displays, and even used Jobs's trademark "one more thing" phrase at the conclusion of each presentation.

Convergence of Xiaomi—Xiaomi, however, did not stop at learning or imitating the market leaders. In fact, Lei Jun always stated that Xiaomi's core business strategy does not revolve around smartphones, which clearly sets it apart from Apple. Rather, Xiaomi more closely resembles companies like Amazon with some elements of Google, and the Internet service is where most of its profits are made (Reuters 2013). This shows that Xiaomi's linkage of its three core business areas can be understood as convergence. The Internet serves as the platform that enables profit growth in the surrounding ecosystem for mobile phones.

Dedication of Xiaomi—Xiaomi's dedication is shown in the meaning of the company name—"mi" is commonly understood as an acronym for "mission impossible" (although originally intended to stand for "mobile Internet," Lei Jun wittily uses this concept in public). Lei linked the "Xiao" part to the Buddhist concept that "a single grain of rice of a Buddhist is as great as a mountain," suggesting that Xiaomi focuses on one small thing at a time, instead of striving for immediate perfection. The name tried to capture the earlier obstacles that the company faced when it was first founded. Lei's play on Xiaomi's name is intended to reflect the impossible missions that Xiaomi had to accomplish to stand where it currently is. This shows clear dedication with setting high targets and working hard to achieve one goal after another.

The Xiaomi case provides an important strategic implication. It is very difficult for a company to maintain its position over time as the market leader of best practice, especially when the industry is dynamic and volatile like the smartphone industry. This is why unique positioning of the company on the competitiveness frontier is crucial to maintaining a competitive advantage. When the market already has high barriers to entry due to competitive incumbents, it is difficult for new entrants to break into the industry. However, when a company like Xiaomi succeeds in doing this, other firms must realign their positions on the competitiveness frontier to avoid being left behind and ultimately "stuck in the middle" (as long as the switching cost is not prohibitive). This will then raise the question of how market leaders such as Apple continue to sustain their competitiveness.

12.2.2 The Competitive Strategy for Leaders: A Case Study of Apple

The preceding section illustrated how the ABCDs can explain the success of latecomers. The following section explains how the ABCD model can also be applied to incumbent market leaders that already have superior competitive advantages. A good example of this is the iPhone developed by Steve Jobs of Apple.[3] This section systematically explains the secrets of its success using the ABCD model.

The components of the iPhone are almost entirely borrowed and are not invented by Apple. This is not to say that the iPhone is insignificant or non-innovative, but that the proper combination of existing good technologies can generate competitiveness. Here, I use the word "good" instead of "best" to point out that the individual functions of the iPhone are not the most up to date according to current technology standards. For instance, Nikon makes better cameras than Apple, and the iPhone camera does not produce the same quality photos that the Nikon D3100 does. However, a greater number of people use their smartphones to take pictures instead of using specialized cameras. This trend is putting camera companies like Nikon in a difficult position. As the camera functions of smartphones continue to improve, the market demand for cameras will further decrease.

Another example that demonstrates the need for technology products to be commercial is Nokia. Although Nokia invested four times as much into R&D as Apple from 2001 to 2010 (Troianovski and Grundberg 2012), it was completely ousted from the market within several years of the iPhone launch. Although several case studies point to problems with Nokia's strategy and management, it is evident that Nokia failed because it was not abreast of industry's best practices when developing its own operating system for smart phones. The truth behind Apple's rise and Nokia's fall does not lie in innovative technology but other factors such as the ABCDs, which will be explained in detail in the following.

Agility of Apple—Steve Jobs was more of a business strategist than a technology specialist. The inscription on the back of every iPhone—"Designed by Apple in California, Assembled in China"—illustrates this point. This shows how Steve Jobs not only created an innovative product but also keenly calculated costs and future competition. He was well aware that other competitors would soon enter the smartphone race and produce products of similar caliber. Therefore, in order to maintain price competitiveness and outdo rivals in the global smartphone market, he chose to produce Apple products in China. However, Jobs also knew that basing all production in China might lower the quality and image of Apple, so he had precise designs performed at home. In the process, Jobs was extremely careful in ensuring product quality. For example, he changed the plastic screen of the iPhone to a glass screen only one month before the final launch because he found dozens of tiny scratches in the plastic screens. This shows that the iPhone's first competence comes from agility—speedy manufacturing by a vast pool of Chinese workers with low wages and precise design with minimal defects.

Benchmarking of Apple—Many consider Steve Jobs as the king of innovators. However, he, in fact, cleverly carried out the "learning plus alpha" strategy. One of Jobs's favorite quotes was Pablo Picasso's "Good artists copy, great artists steal." He also proudly said:

> We do not grow most of the food we eat. We wear clothes other people make. We speak a language that other people developed. We use mathematics that other people evolved. . . . I mean, we are constantly taking things. It is a wonderful, ecstatic feeling to create something that puts it back in the pool of human experience and knowledge (Levy 2000).

Of course, success requires more than simply taking the creations of others. Nevertheless, values can be most efficiently created when the best practice is properly utilized and incorporated with new and meaningful contributions. You do not need to be innovative in everything, and you do not have to always create a breakthrough innovation. A major innovation ultimately comes from good benchmarking. While the result may be innovation, the process stems from learning. This is the essence and true value of the benchmarking strategy.

Convergence of Apple—The combination of the iPhone's various components is its best portrayal of Apple's competitiveness. The iPhone contains many features such as a mobile phone, camera, recorder, Internet, and other key functions that consumers enjoy. However, none of these functions were developed by Apple alone. The beauty of this product is in combining many useful functions into a single device that is convenient to use. Of course, there are also new features that Apple developed independently, but from the perspective of scientific innovation, these features were quite modest. By properly converging a phone, a camera, the Internet, and other valuable functions, Apple produced synergies among the functions for greater user-friendliness. In all of Apple's products, including the iPod, iPhone, and iPad, Steve Jobs enhanced synergies among different features through the iTunes platform. With iTunes, Apple users could easily connect and sync their personal accounts and download files and applications. This connectivity aided in producing more value and convenience for the consumer as well as increasing their reliance on Apple's platform.

Dedication of Apple—Among many quotes attributed to Steve Jobs, perhaps the most popular one is "Stay hungry, stay foolish." This quote nicely captures the clear goal-oriented mindset that is required of successful people; it talks about pursuing one's dream while working hard for it. Steve Jobs was diagnosed with pancreatic cancer in 2003. Despite this knowledge, he remained a dedicated and passionate business leader until he eventually passed away due to the disease in 2011. Facing his own mortality, Jobs provided people with an inspiring lesson to embrace when he stated—"If today were the last day of my life, would I want to do what I am about to do today?" The lesson here is to carefully assess your priorities and pursue them accordingly. As anyone can die on any given day, every day should be spent doing something meaningful. It was this dedication to life that allowed Steve Jobs to create a masterpiece like the iPhone.

12.2.3 The ABCD Model: General Guidelines for Both Followers and Leaders

The previous sections utilized the ABCD model to analyze the success strategies of Xiaomi (a follower) and Apple (a leader) in the smartphone business. In order to take this analysis to a more general level, this section shows how the ABCD model can explain the catch-up and success of other companies or business leaders in practice.[4]

Agility—For many years, Ford was the leader of the US automobile industry. However, Ford did not possess leading technologies during its heyday. There were other German companies like Mercedes Benz that had better technologies for both their products and production processes; they had already implemented the conveyor belt production system to increase the speed of production and even automated the process to improve precision. With these existing technologies that were developed by more advanced German auto companies, Ford expanded his business operations to further benefit from scale and speed. Later Toyota improved process techniques and systems (e.g., Just-in-Time); Then, Hyundai increased the speed of production while maintaining a high level of quality control. The first principle of competitive strategy is to be quick and precise while taking advantage of existing technologies.

Benchmarking—US Steel was able to develop its competitiveness by first adopting European practices and then developing its own system of iron processing. This invention ultimately allowed US Steel to enhance its production speed and enjoy economies of scale, dominating the previously European-led steel industry. Japan's Nippon Steel then took over as the new leader by reducing the cost of extracting natural resources and increasing manufacturing efficiencies through learning best practices from the United States and Europe. Korea's POSCO then benchmarked both Japanese and Western steel technologies and developed its own FINEX technology to further reduce costs and environmental damages. Continuous technology improvements with careful learning allow new entrants to supersede earlier leaders. This is the second principle of competitive advantage—benchmarking plus alpha.

Convergence—General Electric (GE) was originally established as an electrical company, but it eventually diversified into finance, airplane engines, and healthcare. On the other hand, Sony was originally an electronics business but diversified into areas such as music and entertainment. While GE's diversification strategy can be classified as "narrow diversification," SONY's is broad and has lower synergies among businesses. Samsung has businesses in electronics, finance, construction, trade, and services. From these categories alone, it seems that Samsung and GE have a similar level of diversified portfolios. However, the portfolio of business reveals that Samsung's electronics division makes up more than half of all revenue. This type of diversification can be called "dominant diversification" and has proven to be more synergistic than other types of diversification. Therefore, regardless of the degree of relatedness, it is important to diversify around a company's dominant business where the company has its core competence. The third principle of competitive advantage is convergence—maximizing synergies through business diversification by focusing on one dominant business.

Dedication—One of the foundational American ideals is the Protestant work ethic. The moral obligation for hard work allowed the new country to surpass the economies of Europe. Similarly, during the golden age of Japan, the Japanese were the most diligent in the world, even superseding the Americans. The Japanese were highly motivated to bring prosperity to their nation and families. Although this type of ideal has subsided somewhat today, Japan's foundational "samurai spirit" still remains. Korean people today also display this kind of hard-working and goal-oriented mindset, dating back to the Saemaul spirit of the 1970s. All firms of the United States, Japan, and Korea in high growth periods resemble each other in this aspect. The fourth principle of competitive advantage is thus dedication—diligence with strong goal orientation.

The cases discussed in this chapter show the usefulness of the ABCDs for both latecomers and leaders. With new challenges for businesses caused by shorter product life cycles, agility becomes more important in gaining and sustaining competitive advantages. The essence of business is not to defeat competitors but to create new values. Therefore, a successful strategy involves firms and industries mutually sharing their core competences, which can be achieved through effective benchmarking. In today's global environment, the unit of competition has changed from individual companies to global value chains or ecosystems, and the convergence of technologies through cooperation among firms has become a key strategic element. Finally, remaining complacent with past successes will only bring backwardness and demise, and it is therefore important for firms to stay motivated and work hard for continuous growth.

This final chapter discussed the generalization of the ABCDs at both the country and firm level. While acknowledging the usefulness of strategic values of the model, some may argue that the four elements of the ABCDs do not seem to reflect tangible, unique resources such as technologies, and can easily be copied by other firms and nations. However, in today's fast-changing and volatile environment, even superior competitive advantages such as technologies may be quickly undermined by other rivals. Therefore, rather than trying to create non-imitable advantages (often advocated by conventional theories such as the resource-based view), the continuous upgrading of current advantages, by using the ABCD strategy, is more important and practical.

Conclusion

A. AN ACCURATE VIEW OF ECONOMIC DEVELOPMENT

People often misunderstand the fundamental factors that have contributed to Korea's economic growth. Factors such as cheap labor, export promotion, perspiration, and Confucian ethics are not entirely correct because not all countries that had such factors achieved economic growth. Then, what are the real fundamental factors behind Korea's success?

First, while the Korean labor force was cheap, it was also productive. Korean workers are speedier and more precise relative to others (i.e., agility). The reason why Korean construction firms were able to win business in the Middle East during the 1970s and 1980s was not just cheap labor (other countries such as Egypt, Ethiopia, and Sri Lanka had cheaper labor and the Western MNCs hired the workers from these countries), but their ability to complete projects the fastest while maintaining precision. Given that the Middle East countries desired to develop their infrastructure and economies quickly, they were attracted to the agile Korean firms.

Second, in addition to promoting exports, Korea focused on learning global best practices and achieving economies of scale. Through learning global best practices (i.e., benchmarking), Korean firms could compete with other international rivals. This is an important and positive result of an export-promotion policy compared to an import-substitution policy. Firms may lose competitiveness under an import-substitution policy that only focuses on domestic demand while neglecting international markets and global standards. In addition, firms will be unable to achieve economies of scale when serving only the domestic market.

Third, Koreans had perspiration, but more importantly, combined with inspiration and other practices (i.e., convergence). While working hard, Korean workers are adept at combining the best practices of the West with their own strengths, which generates synergies. Perspiration is crucial and usually characterizes the people of developing economies. However, as economies begin to advance into more developed stage, they have the ability to add their own inspiration and other practices, which enhances competitiveness. The Korean chaebol are good examples that originally started with a "me too strategy," but gradually developed into global competitors with differentiated products.

Lastly, Koreans supplemented effective leadership and bureaucracy of Confucian ethics. There are two important elements in Confucianism. The first is to maintain the status quo, especially prevailing power relations between rulers and subordinates, and seniors and juniors. This is essentially a developmental setback because economic development entails improvements or changes to the current status, including changes of power relations. The second element of Confucianism is the responsibility of leaders with diligence and strong goal orientation (i.e., dedication), which contributes to economic development. However, in order to support leadership, political stability and competitive bureaucracy are also necessary.

B. OVERCOMING DIFFICULTIES TO CREATE COMPETITIVE ADVANTAGES

Koreans embodied these characteristics while overcoming various difficulties, which allowed them to create sustainable competitiveness. While all of the Asian NIEs experienced hardships after World War II, Korea faced even more challenges due to the subsequent outbreak of the Korean War. Koreans needed to be faster and work harder in order to survive their dire circumstances. The hardships that Korea faced were a blessing in disguise for its long-term economic development.

Under the continued threat from the North, Koreans worked even harder to overcome difficulties, and this helped enhance the competitiveness of Korea's workforce. President Park Chung-hee further improved the Korean economy with well-constructed policies as discussed in chapter 2. Unfortunately, there are two common misunderstandings regarding President Park's economic policy. The first is that the intensive government intervention reduced market efficiencies, when, in reality, President Park created globally competitive firms. The other misunderstanding is that he only favored a few big chaebol, but in fact, President Park supported only the most competitive firms in order to maximize the utility of the country's scarce resources.

It is important that policymakers correctly understand the market and firms. The market is often more efficient than policymakers think, and firms do more good than bad to society. The effectiveness of the market and firms varies at different levels and situations of the economy. Other Korean presidents, who followed President Park, have also contributed to the country's economic achievements, although some policies have been controversial. As Korea continues to develop into a more advanced economy and require solutions to various problems, the ABCD model will serve as a useful tool in determining the appropriate path forward.

C. PROPER DIRECTION FOR KOREA'S FUTURE ECONOMIC POLICIES

Some say that Korea should change its "speedy" culture to a "precise" one as the country seeks to advance in its economic development. However, there is no need to sacrifice speed for precision as the two do not have to be trade-offs—it is possible to have both. The Korean conglomerates—POSCO, Samsung, and Hyundai—created sustainable competitiveness because they were fast (despite being large) and precise (despite operating in many different businesses). Speed, as the core competence of the Korean economy and business, should not be sacrificed, but complemented by enhanced precision.

Likewise, Korea should not give up imitation and learning to focus on innovation. Even one of the most innovative places in the world, Silicon Valley, is not focused on the creation of breakthrough technologies. Silicon Valley was founded upon an entrepreneurial culture that efficiently promotes innovation. The region provides a collaborative environment for all people to share best practices across different fields. This environment allows everyone to learn the global standard and add incremental "alphas" to existing best practices. Competitiveness can be efficiently enhanced from benchmarking, which is an important message to Korean firms. If they continue to seek and learn best practices across relevant industries, the incremental alpha (i.e., innovation) will come naturally.

The third misconception is that Korean firms should concentrate on specialized businesses rather than broaden their business scope. In practice, however, it is difficult to maintain competitiveness if a firm is competent in one or very limited areas because its competitors have similar competences. In this situation, the firm can compete more effectively if it has other strengths that its competitors do not. Otherwise, latecomers will be able to surpass first movers by adding their own alpha to existing best practices. Therefore, rather than focusing on extreme specialization, Korean firms should pursue the continuous "mixing" of best practices of related fields and developing their own unique strengths to enhance "synergies."

Finally, some argue that Koreans work too hard, and should therefore work less and enjoy more leisure time. If this happens, Koreans will face the risk of a similar situation to the lost decades of Japan. Sustainable success requires continuous learning and hard work, and at the most advanced stage of success, people work hard because they enjoy their work. A love for what they do is a common trait in all successful people across various areas of business, sports, and arts. While this is not easy for all individuals to achieve, if Korean firms create an enjoyable work environment and support employees to work in fields that they most enjoy, people will work harder with greater satisfaction.

D. DEEPENING AND BROADENING STRATEGIC OPTIONS

The ABCD model places less emphasis on natural resources and innate talents. With the ABCDs, anyone can create one's own competitiveness. Internationalization is a similar concept in that it relies less on inherent resources, but creates a system that enhances the competitiveness of all participants by increasing the number of strategic options. All successful countries today are internationalized despite differences in history and the endowment of resources. The level of economic development is positively influenced by the degree of internationalization. For instance, while the BRIC countries once received much attention for their economic potential, China and India are experiencing significantly higher growth relative to Russia and Brazil because they have been achieving significant internationalization. The internationalization strategy broadens the scope of strategic choices while the ABCDs deepen the value creation of strategic resources. We must realize that the fundamental sources of competitiveness are not necessarily tangible competencies such as technology, capital, and natural resources, but more importantly, intangible competencies of internationalization and the ABCDs.

In addition to developing countries, developed countries can also derive useful implications from the strategic guidelines of the ABCD model. For example, firms from developed countries tend to place more emphasis on precision than speed. This allows them to maintain a decent competitive position and command premium prices for their products and services. However, this will remain true only if their competences are noticeably higher than their competitors. In recent years, however, the quality gap between developed and developing countries has narrowed with the global availability of first-rate technologies and management skills. While products made in the United States or Japan were more differentiated than those made in Korea or China in the past, there is significantly less differentiation today. In order to make up for this diminishing competitive advantage, developed countries and their firms need to consider other strategic tools such as the ABCDs to maintain competitiveness.

This book outlines a new analytical framework that comprehensively identifies the factors behind Korea's rapid economic growth. However, despite such growth, Korea is not without its problems (as discussed in chapters 10 and 11). The good news is that Korea will be able to achieve continuous growth by re-embracing the model that has brought the country to where it is today—the ABCDs. Korea was one of the world's poorest countries about half a century ago and its rapid development would not have been possible without the help of advanced nations. Now, as a country that has the ability to help those who are less privileged, Korea has a duty to pass on its knowledge to other developing countries. I hope that countries around the world will find the ABCD model as an effective guideline for achieving advancement and prosperity.

NOTES

INTRODUCTION
1. This example is abstracted and modified from Moon (2001).
2. See Cho and Moon (2013a) for details.

CHAPTER 1
1. Human capital contributes to economic growth in two ways. First, human capital embodied in a human being increases that individual's productivity, leading to an increase in total production and economic growth. Second, the human capital embodied in an individual also contributes to the productivity of all other factors of production. These are respectively referred to as internal and external effects of human capital. For more information, see Coleman 1988; Lucas 1988; Woolcock 1998.
2. See Gelb 1989; World Bank 1989; Roubini and Sala-i-Martin 1992; King and Levine 1993; and Fry 1995.
3. For more information on the debate, see Solow 1962; King and Levine 1993; and Arestis and Demetriades 1997.
4. There are two approaches to measuring and analyzing input factors' productivity. The first is the fundamentalist view, which focuses on technological progress as the source of increasing TFP, and the second is the assimilationist view, which deals with the acquisition and mastery of foreign technology. For the fundamentalist view, refer to Young 1992, 1994a, b; Kim and Lau 1994; Krugman 1994; and Collins and Bosworth 1996. For the assimilation view, refer to Dahlman and Westphal 1981; Hobday 1994, 1995a; Pack 1994; and Pack and Page 1994.

CHAPTER 2
1. This chapter is abstracted and extended from Moon (2011b, 2012c), and Moon, Parc, and Yin (2012). This chapter particularly added more implications for other countries' policy development.
2. For more information, see Haggard and Moon 1990.
3. For more information, see Shinohara, Yanagihara, and Kim 1983; Clifford 1994; Kim 1997; Harvie and Lee 2005; and Noland 2012.
4. Low oil prices, interest rates, and currency value (i.e., weak US dollar, strong Japanese yen, and weak Korean won). These three conditions were very helpful for the Korean economy because low oil prices decreased the nation's energy costs, low interest rates reduced the cost of domestic borrowings, and the weak Korean currency made the Korean products more competitive in the global market.

5. This discrepancy will be discussed further in chapter 10.
6. This will be discussed in more detail in Part III.

CHAPTER 3

1. Part of the basic information about the leadership of the three leaders is abstracted from Moon (2012c, f) and Parc, Park, and Moon (2012); this chapter then reorganized, added updated information, and extended the discussion by including additional analysis and implications from existing cases and examples.
2. See chapter 6 for more comprehensive analysis on the success of the three companies.

CHAPTER 4

1. The framework (or the ABCD model) introduced in this chapter was first proposed in Moon (2012a), and Moon (2012c) showed extensive case studies to support each component of this model; however, these cases centered more on Korea's past experiences. This chapter further updated these examples and cases by adding some internationally successful cases of Korea and other countries.
2. This is one of the most representative indices of customers' satisfaction. This index was introduced two years before the American Customer Satisfaction Index. The industries included in the evaluation account for 75% of Korea's domestic industry. In 2013, this included 111 manufacturing and service industries.
3. Apple scored a large victory in the United States. However, Samsung won the lawsuit against Apple in other countries.
4. Argentina's data is for 1962, due to the non-availability of 1961 data.

CHAPTER 5

1. New Confucian ethics was identified by Tu (1984) in the book titled *Confucian Ethics Today*, which emphasized the role of new Confucian ethics in East Asian countries' economic development; Song (1997) described five characteristics of Korea's new Confucian ethics and discussed how they were related to Korea's economic growth.
2. Fundamental policies cover stabilization of the macro-economy, high human capital, effective and secure financial systems, limitation of price distortions, openness to foreign technology, and agricultural development. Selective policies deal with financial repression, credit allocation, and the promotion of exports and target industries. Finally, institutional policies are used to insulate the influence of particular interest groups on policymakers while maintaining high-quality civil service and monitoring the effects of government interventions (World Bank 1993).
3. Some parts of the literature review of the four dominant theories on firm competitive advantages, and the limitation of these theories, are abstracted and extended from Moon, Yin, and Yim (2015).
4. The five forces model explains the five main factors influencing the industry attractiveness: rivalry among existing players, threat of new entrants, threat of substitutes, bargaining power of suppliers, and bargaining power of customers.
5. Eisenhardt and Martin (2000) argued that effective dynamic capabilities share commonalties, which are termed as "best practices." This implies that dynamic capabilities are repeatable and substitutable, and this violates the VRIN attributes of sustainable competitive advantages of the RBV assumption.

6. There is rich literature emphasizing the importance of agility—particularly "speed competitiveness." Most of them, however, are limited to the manufacturing sector (Sharifi and Zhang 1999), supply chain, and organizational management (e.g., Boehm and Turner 2004). Furthermore, these studies mostly focus on entering the market early to exploit first-mover advantages (Lieberman and Montgomery 1988). This book deals with a broader scope of agility than the existing studies.

7. Imitation can be linked to Porter's (1996) concept of operational effectiveness (OE), which means doing something better than rivals based on learning the current best practices, thereby reducing costs and increasing efficiency.

8. This concept, first introduced in economics (e.g., Panzar and Willig 1981), holds importance in business studies as well.

CHAPTER 6

1. Samsung Electronics Company, 12th; Hyundai Motor Company, 14th; POSCO, 37th (UNCTAD 2014b). Global firms are referred to as transnational corporations (TNCs) in UNCTAD.

2. This information is abstracted from POSCO's website.

3. The evaluation was performed by World Steel Dynamics (WSD), which assesses 36 steelmakers around the world (Lee 2015).

4. POSCO E&C was responsible for overall engineering and construction, while POSCO Energy took charge of constructing a steam power plant. Meanwhile, POSCO ICT established the EIC engineering and IT integrated system; POSCO CHEMTECH managed a processing facility for limestone and coke byproducts; and POSCO M-TECH built a factory to produce aluminum deoxidizers.

5. This information is abstracted from Samsung Electronics (2010).

6. The concept called *Mach Management* was first mentioned by CEO Lee Kun-hee in 2002: "If a jet is to double its speed, it not only needs to double its engine power, but also needs a whole new structure that spans across material engineering to physics" (*Business Korea* 2014).

7. Hyundai Motor Company was separated from the group early in 2000 and renamed as Hyundai Motor Group.

CHAPTER 7

1. The information for the case studies of the four countries (United States, Japan, China, and India) is abstracted and extended from Moon (2012c, e).

2. Gang of Four: a political faction composed of four Chinese Communist Party officials who seized power during the Cultural Revolution (1966–1976). The members were Jiang Qing (Mao Zedong's last wife), Zhang Chunqiao, Yao Wenyuan, and Wang Hongwen.

3. Before the 1980s, most foreign investors were from neighboring economies, such as Hong Kong, Macao, and Taiwan. However, since 1992 when China enhanced the scope and scale of internationalization, the home countries of investors became more diversified and firms from Europe and the United States also flew massively into the Guangdong area (Tuan and Ng 2006).

4. For more information, see "Commanding Heights: An Interview with Manmohan Singh," *PBS*, February 6, 2001. http://www.pbs.org/wgbh/commandingheights/shared/minitextlo/ int_manmohansingh.html. The abstract here is slightly modified from the original text for simplicity and better understanding.

5. Permit Raj: policy that controls all business transactions under government approval and regulation.
6. Petty's Law: the theory that describes the structural transformation of primary, secondary, and tertiary industries as the economy advances (Clark 1957; Li and Huang 1999). This development pattern was first suggested by William Petty (1690), and Colin Clark (1940) first labeled it as "Petty's Law" (Montresor and Marzetti 2011).
7. This study divided the economies into four groups depending on their level of national competitiveness and country size, which is measured by both population and land size. Therefore, if they are clustered in the same group, it means they share more similarities than differences with respect to national competitiveness and country size, and are more likely to compete with each other.

CHAPTER 8

1. The data of Samsung and Apple are obtained from their annual reports.
2. Multi-domestic firms independently operate in individual countries without global coordination across countries. See chapter 1 of Porter (1986: 15–60) for its concept and Moon (1994) for the critical evaluation of this concept.
3. Porter and Rivkin (2012) based their conclusions on an incorrect assumption because they did not distinguish domestic companies from multi-domestic companies.
4. A part of this section is adopted and reorganized from chapter 5 of Moon (2016); Jo, Moon, and Suh (2008); and Moon and Parc (2014).
5. For the debate, see Lee and Roland-Hoist (1998); Liu, Wang, and Wei (2001); Marchant, Cornell, and Koo (2002).

CHAPTER 9

1. The section related to the 1997 Asian Financial Crisis is abstracted and revised from Moon and Bark (2001).
2. In order to recover from the financial crisis, the three countries turned to the IMF for financial assistance. After review, the IMF approved Thailand, Indonesia, and Korea for loans of $3.9 billion, $10.1 billion, and $21 billion, respectively, under the conditions that the three countries adopt a series of structural adjustments.
3. The first-tier NIEs are Singapore, Hong Kong, Taiwan, and Korea, and the second-tier NIEs include Malaysia, Indonesia, Thailand, and Philippines.
4. Sun Tzu's *The Art of War* is one of the oldest military books in the world. Although the book was written by Sun Tzu 2,500 years ago, it is still studied as one of the most respected military strategies. Sun Tzu's teachings are not limited to military strategy, and his ideas have been widely adopted by business practitioners.
5. This part is abstracted and revised from Moon (2003a, b) and Moon and Parc (2014).
6. Computer system design; semiconductor manufacturing; Internet, telecommunications, data processing; architecture; computer equipment manufacturing; control instrument manufacturing; software publishers; and communication equipment manufacturing.
7. This part is abstracted and extended from Moon (2003a, 2012c).
8. There are five main reasons Hyundai made investments in Alabama: (1) increasing trade conflicts between Korea and the United States, (2) fluctuations in the

foreign exchange rate, (3) poor company image despite the enhanced quality of automobiles, (4) interference from strong labor unions, and (5) a package of incentives offered by the Alabama state government (e.g., tax abatement, a site preparation grant, and an access road and bridge) (Jo and You 2011).

9. This part is abstracted and extended from Moon (2004b, 2006).

CHAPTER 10

1. This company has larger than 300 employees and assets over $73 million for manufacturing and $27 million for services (Small and Medium Business Administration 2015).

2. The large and small firms can cooperate rather than compete when they form a business ecosystem, particularly in manufacturing industry, as explained in chapter 8.

3. As SMEs continue to play a dominant role in the service industries, they cannot be left out of discussion in the service sector (Jones 2009).

4. In 2014, the WEF Global Competitiveness Report ranked Korea 26th out of 144 countries. Economy and business-related areas held high rankings, such as macroeconomic environment.

5. In 2013, the IPS report ranked Korea 18th out of 62 countries. Economy and business-related areas held high rankings, such as domestic size (13th), demand quality (11th), and firm strategy (11th), whereas legal and institutional factors had low rankings, such as politicians (50th) and social context of entrepreneurs (38th).

6. This case study of the Sewol ferry disaster is abstracted and modified from Moon (2014b).

CHAPTER 11

1. See chapter 8 for details on business ecosystem.

2. Part of this chapter is abstracted and extended from Moon (2012c). Sections 11.1.1. and 11.2.1. show an important implication that a country can gain new competitiveness through the process of resolving the problems. For more discussions, see Porter (1990) and Cho and Moon (2013a).

3. For more literature review on the stage development of clusters and the importance of clusters on economic development, particularly of the developing countries, see Moon and Jung (2010) and Moon et al. (2013).

4. Regarding the Azerbaijan case, see Moon (2011c) about the implications for the efficient business strategy of firms from emerging countries (e.g., chaebol).

CHAPTER 12

1. The following explanation about the four types is abstracted and extended from Moon, Parc, and Yin (2012).

2. While Singapore and Hong Kong were more influenced by the United Kingdom than Japan, all of the NIEs learned industrial policies and technologies from Japan.

3. The case study of Apple is abstracted and reorganized from Moon (2010c, 2015). In particular, the convergence strategy of Apple is termed as "platform strategy." See Moon (2011a), for more detailed discussion on the concept and the success factors of platform strategy.

4. This section on general guidelines for followers and leaders is abstracted and reorganized from Moon (2014a, 2015).

REFERENCES

Akamai Technologies. 2014. "Akamai's State of the Internet." Q1 2014, Report 7, no. 1. https://www.akamai.com/us/en/multimedia/documents/content/akamai-state-of-the-internet-report-q4-2014.pdf.

Al Bawaba. 2013. "Middle East and North Africa Business Report." December 17.

Altbach, P. G. 1989. "Twisted Roots: Western Impact on Asian Higher Education." *Higher Education* 18, no. 1: 9–29.

Amsden, A. H. 1989. *Asia's Next Giant: South Korea and Late Industrialization*. New York: Oxford University Press.

Amsden, A. H. 1991. "Diffusion of Development: The Late-Industrializing Model and Greater East Asia." *American Economic Review* 81, no. 2: 282–286.

Amsden, A. H., and T. Hikino. 1994. "Project Execution Capability, Organizational Know-How and Conglomerate Corporate Growth in Late Industrialization." *Industrial and Corporate Change* 3, no. 1: 111–147.

Arestis, P., and P. Demetriades. 1997. "Financial Development and Economic Growth: Assessing the Evidence." *Economic Journal* 107, no. 442: 783–799.

Aryee, S., and Y. W. Chay. 1994. "An Examination of the Impact of Career-Oriented Mentoring on Work Commitment Attitudes and Career Satisfaction among Professional and Managerial Employees." *British Journal of Management* 5, no. 4: 241–249.

Auty, R. M. 2001. "The Political Economy of Resource-Driven Growth." *European Economic Review* 45, no. 4–6: 839–846.

Bae, K. H. 2014. *"Changjogyungjesidaeeh gazelles joongsokiupeui sunggongryul jego-leul wuihan sunggwagwanli bangan* [Performance Management to Raise the Success of Gazelles-Type SMEs in the Creative Economy Era]" [in Korean]. Korea Institute of Science and Technology Evaluation and Planning (KISTEP) Issue Paper, no. 2014-04. Seoul: KISTEP. http://www.kistep.re.kr/c3/sub3.jsp?brdType=R&bbIdx=7750.

Bandura, A. 1986. "The Explanatory and Predictive Scope of Self-Efficacy Theory." *Journal of Social and Clinical Psychology* 4, no. 3: 359–373.

Bandura, A. 1997. *Self-Efficacy: The Exercise of Control*. New York: Freeman.

Bank of Korea. 2015. "National Income and Growth Rate since the 1970s." https://ecos.bok.or.kr/.

Barkham, P. 2012. "Samsung: Olympic Smartphone Firm Aims for Big Global Wins." *Guardian*, August 9. http://www.theguardian.com/technology/2012/aug/09/samsung-olympic-smartphones-global-wins.

Barney, J. B. 1986. "Organizational Culture: Can It Be a Source of Sustained Competitive Advantage?" *Academy of Management Review* 11, no. 3: 656–665.

Barney, J. B. 1991. "Firm Resources and Sustained Competitive Advantage." *Journal of Management* 17, no. 1: 99–120.

Bartlett, C. A., and S. Ghoshal. 1989. *Managing across Borders: The Multinational Solution*. London: Harvard Business School Press.

Baumol, W. J., J. C. Panzer, and R. D. Willig. 1982. *Contestable Markets and the Theory of Industry Structure*. San Diego, CA: Harcourt Brace Jovanovich.

BBC. 2013a. "Q&A: Kaesong Industrial Complex." April 3, 2013. http://www.bbc.com/news/business-22011178.

BBC. 2013b. "Samsung Unveils 6.3 in Galaxy Mega Smartphone." April 11. http://www.bbc.com/news/technology-22107787.

Besanko, D., D. Dranove, S. Schaefer, and M. Shanley. 2009. *Economics of Strategy*. 5th International Student ed. New York: John Wiley.

Bianchi, P., and S. Labory. 2006. "From Old Industrial Policy to New Industrial Development Policies." In *International Handbook on Industrial Policy*, edited by P. Bianchi and S. Labory, 02–27. Cheltenham, UK: Edward Elgar.

Boehm, B., and R. Turner. 2004. *Balancing Agility and Discipline: A Guide for the Perplexed*. Boston, MA: Addison-Wesley Professional.

Booth, W. 2011. "Siesta? What Siesta? Mexican Work Longest Hours in World." *Washington Post*, May 1. https://www.washingtonpost.com/world/siesta-what-siesta-mexican-work-longest-hours-in-world/2011/04/27/AF3O0yTF_story.html.

Brondoni, S. M. 2012. "Innovation and Imitation: Corporate Strategies for Global Competition." *SYMPHONYA: Emerging Issues in Management* 1: 10–24.

Brouthers, K. D., and L. E. Brouthers. 2001. "Explaining the National Cultural Distance Paradox." *Journal of International Business Studies* 32, no. 1: 177–189.

Brown, W. 2012. "2012 Hyundai Azera: An Uncommon Touch." *Washington Post*, June 8. http://www.washingtonpost.com/cars/2012-hyundai-azera-an-uncommon-touch/2012/06/07/gJQAJNZCOV_story.html.

Business Korea. 2013. "Park Geun-hye Government Launched." February 26. http://www.businesskorea.co.kr/english/news/politics/1029-democracy-action-park-geun-hye-government-launched.

Business Korea. 2014. "Samsung Group Chairman: Will 'Mach Management' Accelerate Now that Tycoon Back in Korea?" April 18. http://www.businesskorea.co.kr/english/news/industry/4160-samsung-group-chairman-will-%E2%80%98mach-management%E2%80%99-accelerate-now-tycoon-back-korea.

Button, S. B., J. E. Mathieu, and D. M. Zajac. 1996. "Goal Orientation in Organizational Research: A Conceptual and Empirical Foundation." *Organizational Behavior and Human Decision Processes* 67, no. 1: 26–48.

Camp, R. C. 1989. "Benchmarking: The Search for Best Practices That Lead to Superior Performance. Part I: Benchmarking Defined." *Quality Progress* 22, no. 1: 61–68.

Central Intelligence Agency (CIA). 2013. *CIA World Factbook 2013–2014*. Washington, DC: Central Intelligence Agency. https://www.cia.gov/library/publications/the-world-factbook.

Chang, H. J., H. J. Park, and C. G. Yoo. 1998. "Interpreting the Korean Crisis: Financial Liberalization, Industrial Policy and Corporate Governance." *Cambridge Journal of Economics* 22, no. 6: 735–746.

Chang, P. W. 2005. *"Segyega jumokhaneun Hyundai jadongcha weh ganghanga* [Why Are Hyundai Cars Strong in the World?]" [in Korean]. Seoul: Screen M&B.

Chang, S. J. 2003a. *Financial Crisis and Transformation of Korean Business Groups: The Rise and Fall of Chaebols*. Cambridge: Cambridge University Press.

Chang, S. J. 2003b. "Ownership Structure, Expropriation, and Performance of Group-Affiliated Companies in Korea." *Academy of Management Journal* 46, no. 2: 238–253.

Chen, E. K. Y., and P. Lin. 2005. *Outward Foreign Direct Investment from Hong Kong*. Hong Kong: Lingnan University.

Chenery, H. B. 1975. "The Structuralist Approach to Development Policy." *American Economic Review* 65, no. 2: 310–316.

China Daily. 2009. "600,000 Migrant Workers Leave Guangdong amid Financial Crisis." January 1. http://www.chinadaily.com.cn/business/2009-01/08/content_7379756.htm.

China.org.cn. 1979. "We Can Develop a Market Economy under Socialism." November 26. http://www.china.org.cn/english/features/dengxiaoping/103388.htm.

Cho, D. S. 1994. "A Dynamic Approach to International Competitiveness: The Case of Korea." *Journal of Far Eastern Business* 1, no. 1: 17–36.

Cho, D. S., and H. C. Moon, eds. 2013a. *From Adam Smith to Michael Porter: Evolution of Competitive Theory*. Extended ed. Singapore: World Scientific Publishing.

Cho, D. S., and H. C. Moon. 2013b. *International Review of National Competitiveness: A Detailed Analysis of Sources and Rankings*. Cheltenham, UK: Edward Elgar.

Cho, S. 1994. *Dynamics of Korean Economic Development*. Washington, DC: Institute for International Economics.

Cho, Y. J., and J. K. Kim. 1995. *Credit Policies and the Industrialization of Korea*. Vol. 286. Washington, DC: World Bank Publications.

Choe, S. H. 2011. "Connected, Yes. Competitive, Maybe." *New York Times*, September 29. http://www.nytimes.com/2011/09/30/business/global/connected-yes-competitive-maybe.html?_r=0.

Choe, S. H. 2012. "After Verdict, Assessing the Samsung Strategy in South Korea." *New York Times*, September 2. http://www.nytimes.com/2012/09/03/technology/companies/south-korea-reassesses-samsung-after-battle-with-apple.html.

Choe, S. H., M. Fackler, A. L. Cowan, and S. Sayare. 2014. "In Ferry Deaths, a South Korean Tycoon's Downfall." *New York Times*, July 26. http://www.nytimes.com/2014/07/27/world/asia/in-ferry-deaths-a-south-korean-tycoons-downfall.html.

Choe, S. H., and M. Russell. 2012. "Bringing K-pop to the West." *New York Times*, March 4. http://www.nytimes.com/2012/03/05/business/global/using-social-media-to-bring-korean-pop-music-to-the-west.html.

Choi, N. S. 2013. "*Hanguk dekiupeui global gachisaseul hwakjangeul tonghan iljalee changchul* [Job Creation through Korea's Large Conglomerates' Global Value Chain Expansion" [in Korean]. Korea's Economic Research Institute (KERI) Brief, 13–25. http://www.keri.org/web/www/issue_02?p_p_id=EXT_BBS&p_p_lifecycle=0&p_p_state=normal&p_p_mode=view&_EXT_BBS_struts_action=%2Fext%2Fbbs%2Fview_message&_EXT_BBS_messageId=343971.

Chosun Daily. 2012. "*Hyundaicha, 91nyun chut dokjaengine gebal hoo eejen royalteebatneun hwesaro* [Hyundai Motor Receive Royalties for the First Time in Building Its Engine since 1991]" [in Korean]. January 26.

Chung, Y. I. 2007. *South Korea in the Fast Lane: Economic Development and Capital Formation*. Oxford: Oxford University Press.

Clark, C. 1940. *The Conditions of Economic Progress*. London: MacMillan.

Clark, C. 1957. *The Conditions of Economic Progress*. 3rd ed. London: MacMillan.

Clifford, M. L. 1994. *Troubled Tiger: Businessmen. Bureaucrats and Generals in South Korea*. Armonk, NY: M. E. Sharpe.

Coase, R. 1937. "The Nature of the Firm." *Economica* 4, no. 16: 386–405.

Coleman, J. S. 1988. "Social Capital in the Creation of Human Capital." *American Journal of Sociology* 94: S95–S120.

Collins, J. C. 2001. *Good to Great: Why Some Companies Make the Leap and Others Don't*. New York: Harper Business.

Collins, S. M., and B. Bosworth. 1996. "Economic Growth in East Asia: Accumulation versus Assimilation." *Brookings Papers on Economic Activity* 2: 135–203.

Connell, S. P. 2014. "Creating Korea's Future Economy: Innovation, Growth, and Korea–US Economic Relations." Asia Pacific Issues, No. 111. Honolulu, HI: East-West Center. http://www.eastwestcenter.org/sites/default/files/private/api111.pdf.

Daft, R. 1983. *Organization Theory and Design*. New York: West.

Dahlman, C. J., and L. E. Westphal. 1981. "The Meaning of Technological Mastery in Relation to Transfer of Technology." *Annals of the American Academy of Political and Social Science* 458, no. 1: 12–26.

D'Aveni, R. A. 1998. "Waking Up to the Era of Hypercompetition." *Washington Quarterly* 21, no. 1: 183–195.

Davis, G. F., K. A. Diekmann, and C. H. Tinsley. 1994. "The Decline and Fall of the Conglomerate Firm in the 1980s: The Deinstitutionalization of an Organizational Form." *American Sociological Review* 59, no. 4: 547–570.

Department of Homeland Security (DHS). 2011. "Testimony of Administrator Craig Fugate, Federal Emergency Management Agency." March 9. http://www.dhs.gov/news/2011/03/09/testimony-administrator-craig-fugate-federal-emergency-management-agency-united.

Dong-A Ilbo. 2012. "*[Insie Korea/ Brad Buck Walter] Geunmyunsungshileun 'hangukinmaneui DNA'* [Diligence and Hard Work Are Embedded in Koreans' DNA]" [in Korean]. July 6. http://news.donga.com/List/Series_70040100000101/3/70040100000101/20120706/47569025/1.

Dou. E. 2014. "Xiaomi Overtakes Samsung in China Smartphone Market." *Wall Street Journal*, August 4. http://blogs.wsj.com/digits/2014/08/04/xiaomi-overtakes-samsung-in-china-smartphone-market/.

Douglas, T. J., and W. Q. Judge. 2001. "Total Quality Management Implementation and Competitive Advantage: The Role of Structural Control and Exploration." *Academy Of Management Journal* 44, no. 1: 158–169.

Drucker, P. 1984. "The New Meaning of Corporate Social Responsibility." *California Management Review* 26, no. 2: 53–63.

Drucker, P. 1988. "The Coming of the New Organization." *Harvard Business Review* 66, no. 1: 45–53.

Duhigg, C., and K. Bradshier. 2012. "How the U.S. Lost Out on iPhone Work." *New York Times*, January 21. http://www.nytimes.com/2012/01/22/business/apple-america-and-a-squeezed-middle-class.html.

Dutta, S. 2015. "Why Xiaomi's New Phone Could Be in Your Hands Sooner than You Think." *Quartz India*, January 7. http://qz.com/322980/why-xiaomis-new-phone-could-be-in-your-hands-sooner-than-you-think/.

Dunning, J. H. 1976. *American Investment in British Manufacturing Industry*. New York: Arno Press.

Dunning, J. H. 2001. "The OLI Paradigm of International Production: Past, Present and Future." *International Journal of the Economics of Business* 8, no. 2: 173–190.

Dunning, J. H. 2003. "The Role of Foreign Direct Investment in Upgrading China's Competitiveness." *Journal of International Business and Economy* 4, no. 1: 1–13.

Dunning, J. H., and S. M. Lundan. 2008. "Institutions and the OLI Paradigm of the Multinational Enterprise." *Asia Pacific Journal of Management* 25, no. 4: 573–593.

Dweck, C. S. 1986. "Motivational Processes Affecting Learning." *American Psychologist* 41, no. 10: 1040–1048.

Economist. 2007. "Ten Years On." July 4. http://www.economist.com/node/9432495.

Economist. 2008. "Reflating the Dragon." November 13.

Economist. 2011. "What Do You Do When You Reach the Top?" November 12. http://www.economist.com/node/21538104.

Economist. 2015a. "From Minor to Major." March 14. http://www.economist.com/news/special-report/21645996-one-american-six-now-hispanic-up-small-minority-two-generations-ago.

Economist. 2015b. "Made in China?" March 14. http://www.economist.com/news/leaders/21646204-asias-dominance-manufacturing-will-endure-will-make-development-harder-others-made.

Economist. 2015c. "Now and Then." April 25. http://www.economist.com/news/science-and-technology/21649448-patent-records-reveal-way-inventions-are-made-has-changed-over.

Eichengreen, B., D. H. Perkins, and K. Shin. 2012. *From Miracle to Maturity: The Growth of the Korean Economy.* Cambridge, MA: Harvard University Press.

Eichengreen, B., and P. Gupta. 2009. "Two Waves of Service Sector Growth." NBER Working Paper, No. 14968. Cambridge, MA: National Bureau of Economic Research.

Elsenhardt, K. M., and J. A. Martin. 2000. "Dynamic Capabilities: What Are They." *Strategic Management Journal* 21, no. 1: 1105–1121.

Eun, K. S. 2007. "Lowest-Low Fertility in the Republic of Korea: Causes Consequences and Policy Responses." *Asia-Pacific Population Journal* 22, no. 2: 51–72.

Fackler, M. 2011 "Lessons Learned, South Korea Makes Quick Economic Recovery." *New York Times*, January 6. http://www.nytimes.com/2011/01/07/world/asia/07seoul.html.

Fagerberg, J., and B. Verspagen. 2002. "Technology-Gaps, Innovation-Diffusion and Transformation: An Evolutionary Interpretation." *Research Policy* 31, no. 8: 1291–1304.

Farr, J. L., D. A. Hofmann, and K. L. Ringenbach. 1993. "Goal Orientation and Action Control Theory: Implications for Industrial and Organizational Psychology." *International Review of Industrial and Organizational Psychology* 8, no. 2: 193–232.

Flynn, B. B., and B. Saladin. 2006. "Relevance of Baldrige Constructs in an International Context: A Study of National Culture." *Journal of Operations Management* 24, no. 5: 583–603.

Flannery, N. P. 2014. "Who Stands to Benefit from Obama's Immigration Plan?" *Forbes*, November 24. http://www.forbes.com/sites/nathanielparishflannery/2014/11/24/who-stands-to-benefit-from-obamas-immigration-plan/.

Fortes, D. 2011. "*Que tal imitar a Coreia?* [How about imitating Korea?]" [in Portuguese]. *Época Negócios*, September.

Fortune. 2014. Fortune 500 Ranking. http://fortune.com/fortune500/.

Fry, M. J. 1995. *Money, Interest and Banking in Economic Development.* 2nd ed. Baltimore, MD: Johns Hopkins University Press.

Gage, D. 2012. "The Venture Capital Secret: 3 Out of 4 Start-Ups Fail." *Wall Street Journal,* September 20. http://www.wsj.com/articles/SB10000872396390443 720204578004980476429190.

Ganzach, Y., A. Pazy, Y. Ohayun, and E. Brainin. 2002. "Social Exchange and Organizational Commitment: Decision-Making Training for Job Choice as an Alternative to the Realistic Job Preview." *Personnel Psychology* 55, no. 3: 613–637.

Gelb, A. H. 1989. *Financial Policies, Growth, and Efficiency.* Vol. 202. Washington, DC: World Bank Publications. http://wwwwds.worldbank.org/external/default/WDSContentServer/WDSP/IB/1989/06/01/000009265_ 3960928003618/Rendered/PDF/multi_page.pdf.

Gereffi, G., and D. L. Wyman. 1990. *Manufacturing Miracles: Paths of Industrialization in Latin America and East Asia.* Princeton, NJ: Princeton University Press.

Gist, M. E. 1987. "Self-Efficacy: Implications for Organizational Behavior and Human Resource Management." *Academy of Management Review* 12, no. 3: 472–485.

Grossman, G. M., and E. Helpman. 1994. "Endogenous Innovation in the Theory of Growth." *Journal of Economic Perspectives* 8, no. 1: 23–44.

Gupta, A. K., and V. Govindarajan. 2002. "Cultivating a Global Mindset." *Academy of Management Executive* 16, no. 1: 116–126.

Haggard, S. 1990. *Pathways from the Periphery: The Politics of Growth in the Newly Industrializing Countries.* Ithaca, NY: Cornell University Press.

Haggard, S., and C. I. Moon. 1990. "Institutions and Economic Policy: Theory and a Korean Case Study." *World Politics* 42, no. 2: 210–237.

Han, S. M. 2004. "The New Community Movement: Park Chung Hee and the Making of State Populism in Korea." *Pacific Affairs* 77, no. 1: 69–93.

Harvie, C., and H. H. Lee. 2005. "Korea's Fading Economic Miracle 1990–97." Working Paper, No. 05-09. Department of Economics, University of Wollongong. http://ro.uow.edu.au/cgi/viewcontent.cgi?article=1116&context=commwkpapers.

Harzing, A. W. 2000. "An Empirical Analysis and Extension of the Bartlett and Ghoshal Typology of Multinational Companies." *Journal of International Business Studies* 31, no. 1: 101–120.

Haynes, R. M., and D. M. Chalker. 1998. "The Making of a World-Class Elementary School." *Principal* 77, no. 3: 5–9.

Helfat, C. E., and M. A. Peteraf. 2003. "The Dynamic Resource-Based View: Capability Lifecycles." *Strategic Management Journal* 24, no. 10: 997–1010.

Helfat, C. E., and S. G. Winter. 2011. "Untangling Dynamic and Operational Capabilities: Strategy for the (N)Ever-Changing World." *Strategic Management Journal* 32, no. 11: 1243–1250.

Heller, P. S. 2006. "Is Asia Prepared for an Aging Population?" International Monetary Fund Working Paper, No. 06-272. Washington, DC: International Monetary Fund Publications. https://www.imf.org/external/pubs/ft/wp/2006/wp06272.pdf.

Henderson, R., and I. Cockburn. 1994. "Measuring Competence? Exploring Firm Effects in Pharmaceutical Research." *Strategic Management Journal* 15, no. 1: 63–84.

Hennart, J. F. 2009. "Down with MNE-Centric Theories! Market Entry and Expansion as the Bundling of MNE and Local Assets." *Journal of International Business Studies* 40, no. 9: 1432–1454.

Hill, C. W., and D. L. Deeds. 1996. "The Importance of Industry Structure for the Determination of Firm Profitability: A Neo-Austrian Perspective." *Journal of Management Studies* 33, no. 4: 429–451.

Hill, C. W. L., M. A. Hitt, and R. E. Hoskisson. 1992. "Cooperative versus Competitive Structures in Related and Unrelated Diversified Films." *Organization Science* 3: 501–521.

Hill, C. W. L., C. Wee, and K. Udayasanker. 2012. *International Business: An Asian Perspective.* Singapore: Mc-Graw Hill Education.

Hirschman, A. O. 1958. *The Strategy of Economic Development.* New Haven, CT: Yale University Press.

Hobday, M. 1994. "Export-Led Technology Development in the Four Dragons: The Case of Electronics." *Development and Change* 25, no. 2: 333–361.

Hobday, M. 1995a. "East Asian Latecomer Firms: Learning the Technology of Electronics." *World Development* 23, no. 7: 1171–1193.

Hobday, M. 1995b. *Innovation in East Asia: The Challenge of Japan.* Cheltenham, UK: Edward Elgar.

Hofstede, G. 1980. *Culture's Consequences: International Differences in Work-Related Values.* Beverly Hills, CA: Sage Publications.

Hofstede, G. 1983. "The Cultural Relativity of Organizational Practices and Theories." *Journal of International Business Studies* 14, no. 2: 75–89.

Hofstede, G., and M. H. Bond. 1988. "The Confucius Connection: From Cultural Roots to Economic Growth." *Organizational Dynamics* 16, no. 4: 5–21.

Hoj, J., M. Jimenez, M. Maher, G. Nicoletti, and M. Wise. 2007. "Product Market Competition in the OECD Countries: Taking Stock and Moving Forward." OECD Economics Department Working Paper, No. 575. Paris: OECD Publishing. http://dx.doi.org/10.1787/108734233645.

Hong, B. and H. Kim. 2009. "Retirement Type and Determinants of the Middle-Old Age." (Paper presented at the 1st Workshop of Korean Longitudinal Study of Ageing, Seoul, Korea, February 17, 2010).

Hong S. I. 2011. *"Hyundai junjaeui choo-uk* [The Memories of Hyundai Electronics]" [in Korean]. Joongang Ilbo Economic Research Institute. November 21. http://jeri.joins.com/viewissues/view_view.asp?idx=122.

Hoskisson, R. E., L. Eden, C. M. Lau, and M. Wright. 2000. "Strategy in Emerging Economies." *Academy of Management Journal* 43, no. 3: 249–267.

IBRD. 1968. *Current Economic Position and Prospects of Korea.* New York: United Nations Publication.

IBRD. 1969. *Current Economic Position and Prospects of Korea.* New York: United Nations Publication.

IHS Technology. 2014. "Global Semiconductor Market Set for Strongest Growth in Four Years in 2014." December 22. http://press.ihs.com/press-release/technology/global-semiconductor-market-set-strongest-growth-four-years-2014.

IMF. 2006. Republic of Korea: Selected Issues. International Monetary Fund (IMF). Washington D.C. https://www.imf.org/external/pubs/ft/scr/2006/cr06381.pdf.

Inglehart, R. 1997. *Modernization and Post-modernization: Cultural, Economic, and Political Change in 43 Societies.* Vol. 19. Princeton, NJ: Princeton University Press.

Institute of International Education website. http://www.iie.org/Services/Project-Atlas/United-States/International-Students-In-US.

International Institute for Management Development (IMD). 2014. *IMD World Competitiveness Yearbook, 2014*. Geneva: IMD.

Ito, K., and E. L. Rose. 2004. "An Emerging Structure of Corporations." *Multinational Business Review* 12, no. 3: 63–83.

Ito, T., and A. O. Krueger. 1995. *Growth Theories in Light of the East Asian Experience*. Chicago: University of Chicago Press.

Ivarsson, I., and C. G. Alvstam. 2005. "Technology Transfer from TNCs to Local Suppliers in Developing Countries: A Study of AB Volvo's Truck and Bus Plants in Brazil, China, India, and Mexico." *World Development* 33, no. 8: 1325–1344.

Jin, B., and H. C. Moon. 2006. "The Diamond Approach to the Competitiveness of Korea's Apparel Industry: Michael Porter and Beyond." *Journal of Fashion Marketing and Management* 10, no. 2: 195–208.

Jo, Y. T., H. C. Moon, and H. J. Suh. 2008. "Evaluation and Types of Foreign Direct Investment's Effects on National Competitiveness." *International Business Journal* 19, no. 4: 23–50.

Jo, H. J., and J. S. You. 2011. "Transferring Production Systems: An Institutionalist Account of Hyundai Motor Company in the United States." *Journal of East Asian Studies* 11: 41–73.

Johnson, C. 1987. "Political Institutions and Economic Performance: The Government–Business Relationship in Japan, South Korea, and Taiwan." In *The Political Economy of the New Asian Industrialism*, edited by Frederic Deyo, 136–164. Ithaca, NY: Cornell University Press.

Jones, G. R., and C. W. Hill. 1988. "Transaction Cost Analysis of Strategy-Structure Choice." *Strategic Management Journal* 9, no. 2: 159–172.

Jones, R. S. 2009. "Boosting Productivity in Korea's Service Sector." OECD Economics Department Working Papers, No. 673. Paris: OECD Publishing. http://dx.doi.org/10.1787/226625875038.

Jones, R. S. 2013. "Education Reform in Korea." OECD Economics Department Working Papers, No. 1067. OECD Publishing. http://dx.doi.org/10.1787/5k43nxs1t9vh-en.

Jones, R. S., and S. Urasawa. 2013. "Labour Market Policies to Promote Growth and Social Cohesion in Korea." OECD Economics Department Working Paper, No. 1068. Paris: OECD Publishing. http://dx.doi.org/10.1787/5k43nxrmq8xx-en.

Jung, L., and E. S. Woo. 2013. "*Segyega gamtanhan seosan ganchukjee 'Chung Ju-yung gongbup*' [The World Admired for 'Chung Ju-yung Method of Construction' in Sosan Reclaimed Land" [in Korean]. *Newsis*, May 25. http://www.newsis.com/ar_detail/view.html?cID=&ar_id=NISX20130524_0012109387.

Jwa, S. H. 2004. "The Chaebol, Corporate Policy and Korea's Development Paradigm." In *Competition and Corporate Governance in Korea: Reforming and Restructuring the Chaebol*, edited by I. K. Lee, chapter 1. Cheltenham, UK: Edward Elgar.

Kahn, W. A. 1990. "Psychological Conditions of Personal Engagement and Disengagement at Work." *Academy of Management Journal* 33, no. 4: 692–724.

Kang, P. J. 2012. "*Olympic taegeuk junsaga numuhyahal byuk 'Korea*' [Korean Olympics Platers Must Challenge Their Own Name]" [in Korean]. DAUM Sports. July 26. http://sports.media.daum.net/sports/newsview?newsId=20120726083203534.

KDI. 2012. *New Research on Saemaul Undong: Lessons and Insights from Korea's Development Experience.* Seoul: Korea Saemaulundong Center of KDI School. http://cid.kdi.re.kr/report/report_aview.jsp?pub_no=13378.

Keaveney, S. M. 1995. "Customer Switching Behaviour in Service Industries: An Exploratory Study." *Journal of Marketing* 59, no. 2: 71–82.

Kee, K. B. 2013. "Investing in Korea: Staying Rational despite Samsung's Halo Effect." *BeyondProxy*, June 5.

Keese, M. 2003. "Reversing the Tide: Preliminary Lessons from the OECD's Older Worker Thematic Review." (Paper presented at the International Conference on Labor Market Policies in an Aging Era: Korea's Cases – Seoul, Korea, October 23, 2003).

Khanna, T., and K. Palepu. 1997. "Why Focused Strategies May Be Wrong For Emerging Markets." *Harvard Business Review* 75, no. 4: 41–54.

Kim, E. M. 1997. *Big Business, Strong State: Collusion and Conflict in South Korean Development, 1960–1990.* New York: State University of New York Press.

Kim, E. M., and G. S. Park. 2011. "The Chaebol." In *The Park Chung Hee Era: The Transformation of South Korea*, edited by B. K. Kim and E. F. Vogel, 265–294. Cambridge, MA: Harvard University Press.

Kim, H. C. 2004. *Japanese Companies and Japanese Marketing.* Seoul: Bupmunsa.

Kim, I. K. 1992. "*Hangukgwa ilboneui ingoobyunhwa byunchun bigyo* [A Comparative Study of Demographic Transition between Korea and Japan]" [in Korean]. *Dongguk Journal of Sociology* 1: 43–78.

Kim, I. K., J. Liang, K. O. Rhee, and C. S. Kim. 1996. "Population Aging in Korea: Changes since the 1960s." *Journal of Cross-Cultural Gerontology* 11, no. 4: 369–388.

Kim, J. H. 2014. "*Hyundaicah mi·il kisul jehyuro sijakhe segue chaecho susocha yangsan daeguk deungjang* [Hyundai Motor, the First Automaker of Mass Production for the Hydrogen-Fuel Cell Car, through the Technology Alliance with the US and Japan]" [in Korean]. *Asiatoday*, July 09. http://www.asiatoday.co.kr/view.php?key=20140708010004854.

Kim, J. I., and L. Lau. 1994. "The Sources of Economic Growth of the East Asian Newly Industrialized Countries." *Journal of the Japanese and International Economies* 8, no. 3: 235–271.

Kim, J. K., S. D. Shim, and J. I. Kim. 1995. "The Role of the Government in Promoting Industrialization and Human Capital Accumulation in Korea." In *Growth Theories in Light of the East Asian Experience*, NBER-EASE, Vol. 4, edited by Takatoshi Ito and Anne O. Krueger, 181–200. Chicago: University of Chicago Press.

Kim, K. 2007. "A Great Leap Forward to Excellence in Research at Seoul National University, 1994–2006." *Asia Pacific Education Review* 8, no. 1: 1–11.

Kim, S. I. 2010. "*De·joongsokiup sengsansung bunsukgwa dongbansungjang banghyang* [The Productivity Analysis of LEs-SMEs and the Cooperation Policy Direction]" [in Korean]. *Korean Academy of High Potential Enterprises* 1, no. 2: 85–99.

Kim, S. T. 2007. *Prospects for Increasing Labor Market Flexibility: Korea's Economy 2007.* Washington, DC: Korea Economic Institute.

Kim, W. C., and R. Mauborgne. 2005. *Blue Ocean Strategy: How to Create Uncontested Market Space and Make Competition Irrelevant.* Cambridge, MA: Harvard Business Press.

Kim, Y., T. Kelly, and S. Raja. 2010. "Building Broadband: Strategies and Policies for the Developing World." Global Information and Communication Technologies

Department, January 2010. Washington, DC: World Bank Publications. http://hdl.handle.net/10986/2469.

Kim, Y. C. 2014. "Samsung CEO to Present IOT Strategy at CES." *Korea Times*, December 29. http://www.koreatimes.co.kr/www/news/tech/2014/12/133_170723.html.

Kim, Y. W. 2013. "Samsung Targets Faster Decision-Making in 2014." *Korea Herald*, December 24. http://www.koreaherald.com/view.php?ud=20131224000674.

King, R. G., and R. Levine. 1993. "Finance, Entrepreneurship and Growth." *Journal of Monetary Economics* 32, no. 3: 513–542.

Klayman, B. 2014. "Toyota Tells U.S. Agency Seat Issue Could Lead to Recall." *Reuters*, January 30. http://www.reuters.com/article/2014/01/31/us-autos-toyota-nhtsa-idUSBREA0U03I20140131.

Koh, Y., S. Kim, C. Kim, Y. Lee, J. Kim, S. Lee, and Y. Kim. 2010. "The Growth of Korean Economy and the Role of Government." In *Social Policy in the Korean Economy: Six Decades of Growth and Development*, edited by K. I. Sa and Y. Koh. Seoul: Korea Development Institute.

Koh, Y. S. 2008. "*Hangukgungjeeui sungjanggwa jungbooeui yukhwal: gwagu, hyunje, mirae* [Korea's Economic Growth and the Role of the Government: The Past, Present, and Future]" [in Korean]. Korea Development Institute Research Report. http://cid.kdi.re.kr/cid_eng/public/report_read05.jsp?1=1&pub_no=10642.

Korean Statistical Service Database. 2015. http://kosis.kr/index/index.jsp.

Koske, I., I. Wanner, R. Bitetti, and O. Barbiero. 2014. "The 2013 Update of the OECD Product Market Regulation Indicators: Policy Insights for OECD and Non-OECD Countries." OECD Economics Department Working Papers. Paris: OECD Publishing. http://dx.doi.org/10.1787/5js3f5d3n2vl-en.

KOSTAT. 2013. "*Yunglibupin giupche hengjungtonggye Q&A* [Q&A for Administrative Statistics on Profit Enterprises]" [in Korean]. Seoul: Statistics Korea (KOSTAT). http://kostat.go.kr/portal/korea/kor_nw/2/8/7/index.board?bmode=download&bSeq=&aSeq=310802&ord=9.

Krugman, P. 1992. *Geography and Trade*. Cambridge, MA: MIT Press.

Krugman, P. 1994. "Myth of Asia's Miracle." *Foreign Affairs* 73 (November/December): 62–77.

Kumaraswamy, A., R. Mudambi, H. Saranga, and A. Tripathy. 2012. "Catch-up Strategies in the Indian Auto Components Industry: Domestic Firms' Responses to Market Liberalization." *Journal of International Business Studies* 43 (May): 368–395.

Kuznets, P. W. 1988. "An East Asian Model of Economic Development: Japan, Taiwan, and South Korea." *Economic Development and Cultural Change* 36, no. 3: S11–S43.

Kuznets, S. 1966. *Modern Economic Growth: Rate, Structure and Spread*. New Haven, CT: Yale University Press.

Kwon, H. J., and I. Yi. 2009. "Economic Development and Poverty Reduction in Korea: Governing Multifunctional Institutions." *Development and Change* 40, no. 4: 769–792.

Kye, B., E. Arenas, G. Teruel, and L. Rubalcava. 2014. "Education, Elderly Health, and Differential Population Aging in South Korea: A Demographic Approach." *Education* 30, no. 26: 753–794.

Lakhal, L. 2009. "Impact of Quality on Competitive Advantage and Organizational Performance." *Journal of the Operational Research Society* 60, no. 5: 637–645.

Lawrence, R. Z., and D. E. Weinstein. 1999. "Trade and Growth: Import-Led or Export-Led? Evidence from Japan and Korea." NBER Working Paper Series, No. 7264. Cambridge, MA: National Bureau of Economic Research. http://www.nber.org/papers/w7264.

Lee, B. H., B. I. Cho, and Y. M. Kim. 2007. *"Woorinara service-upeui jinipjangbyuk hyunhwang bunsuk* [Analysis of Entry Barriers to the Service Industry]" [in Korean]. *Research Paper of the Bank of Korea*, 2007–28. Seoul: Bank of Korea. http://public.bokeducation.or.kr/ecostudy/publishList.do?&contentId=2651&mode=view.

Lee, C. H., K. Lee, and K. Lee. 2002. "Chaebols, Financial Liberalization and Economic Crisis: Transformation of Quasi-Internal Organization in Korea." *Asian Economic Journal* 16, no. 1: 17–35.

Lee, H., and D. W. Roland-Hoist, eds. 1998. *Economic Development and Cooperation in the Pacific Basin: Trade, Investment, and Environmental Issues.* Cambridge: Cambridge University Press.

Lee, H. 2008. *"Jubail hangbangongsaro joongdongsinhwa sijak* [The Start of Miracle in Middle East through the Jubail Harbor Project]" [in Korean]. *Korea Daily*, November 7.

Lee, H. J. 2013. *"Samsung 5de sinsujong saup bujin. Lee Kun-heeeui gyuldaneun?* [Poor Performance of Samsung in 5 New Business. . .The Deicions of Lee Kun-hee?]" [in Korean]. *CEO ScoreDaily* http://www.ceoscoredaily.com/news/article.html?no=3129.

Lee, H. J., R. M. O'Keefe, and K. Yun. 2003. "The Growth of Broadband and Electric Commerce in South Korea: Contributing Factors." *The Information Society: An International Journal* 19, no. 1: 81–92.

Lee, H. K. 2013. *"Joongsokiupeui joongkyun·dekiupeuloeui sungjang doingingwa jungchek gwaje* [Motives and Policy Guideline for SME Growth]" [in Korean]. *KERI Policy Research* 2013-06. Seoul: Korea Economic Research Institute (KERI). http://www.kefplaza.com/labor/manage/man_view.jsp?nodeid=290&idx=13867.

Lee, J. W. 2005. "Human Capital and Productivity for Korea's Sustained Economic Growth." *Journal of Asian Economics* 16, no. 4: 663–687.

Lee, O. F., J. A. Tan, and R. Javalgi. 2010. "Goal Orientation and Organizational Commitment: Individual Difference Predictors of Job Performance." *International Journal of Organizational Analysis* 18, no. 1: 129–150.

Lee, S. H. 2015. "Steelmaker Rankings POSCO Named World's Most Competitive Steelmaker for 6 Straight Years." *Business Korea*, June 10. http://www.businesskorea.co.kr/english/features/focus/10977-steelmaker-rankings-posco-named-world%E2%80%99s-most-competitive-steelmaker-6-straight.

Lee, S. J. 2011. "Dynamic Capabilities at Samsung Electronics: Analysis of Its Growth Strategy in Semiconductors." KDI School Working Paper Series, No. 11-07. Seoul: KDI School of Public Policy and Management. http://www.kdischool.ac.kr/new/data/WP2011-07.pdf.

Lee, S. J., and E. H. Lee. 2009. "Case Study of POSCO: Analysis of its Growth Strategy and Key Success Factors." KDI School Working Paper Series, No. 09-13. Seoul: KDI School of Public Policy and Management. http://www.kdischool.ac.kr/new/data/w09-13.pdf.

Levy, S. 2000. *Insanely Great: The Life and Times of Macintosh, the Computer that Changed Everything.* New York: Penguin Books.

Lewellen, W. G. 1971. *The Ownership Income of Management*. New York: Columbia University Press.

Lewis, L., and H. A. Patrinos. 2011. "Framework for Engaging the Private Sector in Education: System Assessment and Benchmarking Education for Results (SABER)." Washington, DC: World Bank Publications. http://saber.worldbank.org/index.cfm?indx=11&tb=12.

Lewis, W. A. 1954. "Economic Development with Unlimited Supplies of Labour." *The Manchester School* 22, no. 2: 139–191.

Lewis, W. W. 2004. *The Power of Productivity*. Chicago: University of Chicago Press.

Li, J., and S. J. Huang. 1999. "Research on the Evolution of Tertiary Industry in the Major Cities in China." *Service Industries Journal* 19, no. 3: 187–202.

Li, X., and X. Liu. 2005. "Foreign Direct Investment and Economic Growth: An Increasingly Endogenous Relationship." *World Development* 33, no. 3: 393–407.

Lieberman, M. B., and D. B. Montgomery. 1988. "First-Mover Advantages." Special issue, *Strategic Management Journal* 9: 41–58.

Lin, S. C., and J. N. Chang. 2005. "Goal Orientation and Organizational Commitment as Explanatory Factors of Employees' Mobility." *Personnel Review* 34, no. 3: 331–353.

Lipsey, R. E. 2000. "Inward FDI and Economic Growth in Developing Countries." *Transnational Corporations* 9, no. 1: 67–96.

Liu, X., C. Wang, and Y. Wei. 2001. "Causal Links between Foreign Direct Investment and Trade in China." *China Economic Review* 12, no. 2–3: 190–202.

Lloyd, G., ed. 1983. *Hippocratic Writings*. 2nd ed. London: Penguin Books.

Lucas, R. E. 1988. "On the Mechanics of Development." *Journal of Monetary Economics* 22: 3–42.

Makadok, R. 2001. "Toward a Synthesis of the Resource-Based and Dynamic-Capability Views of Rent Creation." *Strategic Management Journal* 22, no. 5: 387–401.

Mann, A. and Nunes, T. 2009. "After the Dot-Com Bubble: Silicon Valley High-Tech Employment and Wages in 2001 and 2008." Regional Report Summary, No. 09-08. Washington, DC: Office of Publications and Special Studies. http://www.bls.gov/opub/regional_reports/200908_silicon_valley_high_tech.htm.

Marchant, M. A., D. N. Cornell, and W. Koo. 2002. "International Trade and Foreign Direct Investment: Substitutes or Complements?" *Journal of Agricultural and Applied Economies* 34, no. 2: 289–302.

Markham, J. W. 1973. *Conglomerate Enterprise and Economic Performance*. Cambridge, MA: Harvard University Press.

Markides, C. C., and P. J. Williamson. 1996. "Corporate Diversification and Organizational Structure: A Resource-Based View." *Academy of Management Journal* 39, no. 2: 340–367.

Mason, A. 1997. "Population and the Asian Economic Miracle." *Asia-Pacific Population & Policy*, no. 43: 01–04. http://www.eastwestcenter.org/fileadmin/stored/pdfs/p&p043.pdf.

Mason, E. S. 1980. *The Economic and Social Modernization of the Republic of Korea*. Cambridge, MA: Harvard University Press.

Massa, S., and S. Testa. 2004. "Innovation or Imitation? Benchmarking: A Knowledge-Management Process to Innovate Services." *Benchmarking: An International Journal* 11, no. 6: 610–620.

McDonald, P. 2000. "Gender Equity in Theories of Fertility Transition." *Population and Development Review* 26, no. 3: 427–440.

Ministry of Science, ICT and Future Planning of Korea 2013. *"Kisulmooyuk simcheung-boonseok mit jungchekbangahn* [The In-Depth Analysis and Policy Directions on Technology Trade]" [in Korean]. http://www.nstc.go.kr/c3/sub3_2_view.jsp?regIdx=628&keyWord=&keyField=.

Ministry of Strategy and Finance of Korea (MOSF). 2012. "Korean Taxation." Seoul: Ministry of Strategy and Finance, Tax Treaties Division. https://www.nts.go.kr/eng/data/KOREANTAXATION2012.pdf.

Moffett, S., K. Anderson-Gillespie, and R. McAdam. 2008. "Benchmarking and Performance Measurement: A Statistical Analysis." *Benchmarking: An International Journal* 15, no. 4: 368–381.

Montgomery, C. A. 1994. "Corporate Diversification." *Journal of Economic Perspectives* 8, no. 3: 163–178.

Montresor, S., and G. V. Marzetti. 2011. "The Deindustrialisation/Tertiarisation Hypothesis Reconsidered: A Subsystem Application to the OECD7." *Cambridge Journal of Economics* 35: 401–421.

Moon, H. C. 1994. "A Revised Framework of Global Strategy: Extending the Coordination-Configuration Framework." *International Executive* 36, no. 5: 557–573.

Moon, H. C. 1999. "Education and Competitiveness of Japanese Firms in a Changing Global Economy." In *Restructuring Japanese Business for Growth: Strategy, Finance, Management, and Marketing Perspective*, edited by Raj Aggarwal, 31–41. Boston, MA: Kluwer Academic Publishers.

Moon, H. C. 2001. *"Muleun 21segieui jawonjunlyak* [Water is the Strategic Resource in the 21st Century]" [in Korean]. *Korea Economic Daily*, July 2.

Moon, H. C. 2003a. *"Segyehwaga kungjenglyukeui beegyul* [Internationalization is the Secret of Competitiveness" [in Korean]. *Korean Economic Daily*, August 27.

Moon, H. C. 2003b. *"Wyegookin nodongja jungchekbanghyang* [Policy Directions for Dealing with the Foreign Workers]" [in Korean]. *Korean Economic Daily*, November 21.

Moon, H. C. 2004a. "Cooperation among Japan, Korea, and China through Sharing Business and Cultural Advantages." *Review of Business History* 19, no. 1: 33–48.

Moon, H. C. 2004b. *"Gyujechulpega woosun* [Deregulation Should Come First]" [in Korean]. *Korean Economic Daily*, September 6.

Moon, H. C. 2005a. "Economic Cooperation between Vietnam and Korea through Foreign Direct Investment." *Southeast Asian Review* 15, no. 2: 341–363.

Moon, H. C. 2005b. "The New Organization of Global Firms: From Transnational Solutions to Dynamic Globalization." *International Journal of Performability Engineering* 1, no. 2: 131–143.

Moon, H. C. 2006. *"Screen quotaeh dehan jalmotdwen senggak* [The Misunderstanding on the Screen Quota]" [in Korean]. *Korean Economic Daily*, February 10.

Moon, H. C. 2010a. *Global Business Strategy: Asian Perspective*. Singapore: World Scientific Publishing.

Moon, H. C. 2010b. *"Red ocean + α > blue ocean* [Red Ocean + α > Blue Ocean.]" [in Korean]. *Dong-A Business Review* 60, no. 1: 80–83.

Moon, H. C. 2010c. *"Steve Jobs, jakseun yakjumee maneun gangjumeul garyuyo* [Steve Jobs, the Strengths are Veiled by a Small Weakness]" [in Korean]. *Dong-A Business Review* 63, no. 2: 70–73.

Moon, H. C. 2011a. *"Ecosystem junjengsidae: Kyungjengjunlyakdo jinhwahanda* [The Evolution of Competitive Strategy in the New Period of Competition Based on Ecosystem]" [in Korean]. *Dong-A Business Review* 88, no. 1: 20–28.

Moon, H. C. 2011b. "*Seroeun gwanjumehsuh barabon hangook gyungjeeui baljun model* [The Success Model of Korea's Economic Development in New Perspective]" [in Korean]. *Shinhan Monthly Review*, March: 2–7.

Moon, H. C. 2011c. "*Nobelsik gyungyunggwa hangukeui chaebol gyungjung* [The Nobel-Style of Business Strategy and Korea's Chaebol Management]" [in Korean]. *Dong-A Business Review* 75, no. 1: 20–28.

Moon, H. C. 2012a. "*Minchup+benchmarking+yoonghap+junnyum=K-Strategy* [Agility + Benchmarking + Convergence + Dedication = K-Strategy]" [in Korean]. *Dong-A Business Review* 112, no. 1: 36–39.

Moon, H. C. 2012b. "*Good to Smart* [Good to Smart]" [in Korean]. Seoul: Rainmaker.

Moon, H. C. 2012c. "*K-Jeonryak:Hanguksik sungjang junlyak model* [K-Strategy: Korea's Growth Model]" [in Korean]. Seoul: Miraebook.

Moon, H. C. 2012d. "*Porter gyosoodo mot bon global trend: Dajoong gachee saseul* [The Multi-Domestic Value Chain: The Global Trend Porter Overlooked]" [in Korean]. *Dong-A Business Review* 105, no. 1: 40–43.

Moon, H. C. 2012e. "*Gukjehwa+becnmarking= gukga gosoksungjang* [The Secret of National Growth: Internationalization and Benchmarking]" [in Korean]. *Dong-A Business Review* 107, no. 2: 40–43.

Moon, H. C. 2012f. "*Yungwoongehsuh gisooljaro boonsukheya* [Shifting the Analysis from Hero to Engineering]" [in Korean]. *Dong-A Business Review* 110, no. 1: 56–59.

Moon, H. C. 2012g. "*Hoobalja woowui junlyakee bitcheul balhaldde* [When the Strategy of Latecomer Advantage Shines]" [in Korean]. *Dong-A Business Review* 70, no. 1: 92–95.

Moon, H. C. 2014a. "The ABCD Framework of K-Strategy: The Secret to Korea's Success." Presentation at Stanford University. http://ksp.stanford.edu/events/the_abcd_framework_of_kstrategy_the_secret_to_koreas_success/.

Moon, H. C. 2014b. "*Minchup+benchmarking+yoonghap+junnyum=K-Strategy: Titanicgwa dareun sewolho de-eung, baggulgil itdda* [Agility + Benchmarking + Convergence + Dedication = K-Strategy: The Different Response to the Titanic and Sewol and Solution]" [in Korean]. *Dong-A Business Review* 160, no. 1: 107–113.

Moon, H. C. 2015. "*Kyungjenglyukeul nopeeneun seroeun junlyak* [The New Strategy of Enhancing Competitiveness]" [in Korean]. *Shinhan Monthly Review*, January, 2–7.

Moon, H. C. 2016. *Foreign Direct Investment: A Global Perspective*. Singapore: World Scientific Publishing.

Moon, H. C., and T. Bark. 2001. "Asian Economic Crisis, Foreign Direct Investment, and Stabilized Economic Growth: Crisis Revisited and Implications for APEC Member Countries." *Journal of International Business and Economy* 2, no. 1: 39–55.

Moon, H. C. and E. Choi. 2001. "Cultural Impact on National Competitiveness." *Journal of International and Area Studies* 8, no. 2: 21–36.

Moon, H. C., Y. K. Hur, W. Yin, and C. Helm. 2014. "Extending Porter's Generic Strategies: From Three to Eight." *European Journal of International Management* 8, no. 2: 205–225.

Moon, H. C., and J. S. Jung. 2010. "Northeast Asian Cluster through Business and Cultural Cooperation." *Journal of Korea Trade* 14, no. 2: 29–53.

Moon, H. C., and M. Y. Kim. 2006a. "Cooperation among APEC Member Economies: An Interdisciplinary Approach of Economic and Cultural Perspectives." APEC Study Series 06-01. Seoul: Korea Institute for Industrial Economic Policy.

Moon, H. C., and M. Y. Kim. 2006b. "Enhancing Cooperation between Korea and Japan: An Interdisciplinary Approach of Business Competitiveness and Culture." *Hitotsubashi Journal of Commerce and Management* 40, no. 1: 19–33.

Moon, H. C., and M. Y. Kim. 2008. "A New Framework for Global Expansion: A Dynamic Diversification-Coordination (DDC) Model." *Management Decision* 46, no. 1: 131–151.

Moon, H. C., and D. Lee. 2004. "The Competitiveness of Multinational Firms: A Case Study of Samsung Electronics and SONY." *Journal of International and Area Studies* 11, no. 1: 1–21.

Moon, H. C., and Y. W. Lee. 2014. "Corporate Social Responsibility: Peter Drucker, Michael Porter and Beyond." *Journal of Creativity and Innovation* 7, no. 2: 45–72.

Moon, H. C., and J. Parc. 2014. *"Hewejikjuptoojaeui gyungjejuk hyogwa: Samsungjunjaeui hwudepon boomoon sarereul joongshimeuro* [The Economic Effects of Outward Foreign Direct Investment: A Case Study of Samsung Electronics Co]" [in Korean]. *Korea Business Review* 18, no. 3: 125–145.

Moon, H. C., J. Parc, S. H. Yim, and W. Yin. 2013. "Enhancing Performability through Domestic and International Clustering: A Case Study of Samsung Electronics Corporation (SEC)." *International Journal of Performability Engineering* 9, no. 1: 75–84.

Moon, H. C., J. Parc, and W. Yin. 2012. *"Gookgawoonyungcheje boonlyuwa seroeun kyungjebaljun modeleui jesi: Hangookeui kyungjebaljun sareleul joongshineuro* [Types of Nation's Operating System and a New Economic Development Model: A Case Study of Korea's Economic Development" [in Korean]. *Review of International Area Studies*, 21, no. 2: 1–30.

Moon, H. C., and T. W. Roehl. 2001. "Unconventional Foreign Direct Investment and the Imbalance Theory." *International Business Review* 10, no. 2: 197–215.

Moon, H. C., A. M. Rugman, and A. Verbeke. 1995. "The Generalized Double Diamond Approach to International Competitiveness." In *Research in Global Strategic Management*, vol. 5, *Beyond the Diamond*, edited by A. M. Rugman, J. V. Den Broeck, and A. Verbeke, 97–114. Greenwich, CT: JAI Press.

Moon, H. C., A. M. Rugman, and A. Verbeke. 1998. "A Generalized Double Diamond Approach to the Global Competitiveness of Korea and Singapore." *International Business Review* 7, no. 2: 135–150.

Moon, H. C., and S. Yim. 2014. "Re-interpreting Ownership Advantages and Re-categorizing Investment Motivations of Multinational Corporations: From the Perspective of Imbalance Theory." *Journal of International and Area Studies* 21, no. 1: 87–99.

Moon, H. C., W. Yin, and S. H. Yim. 2015. "Latecomers' Growth Strategy: The ABCD Framework and Its Application to Samsung Electronics." Presented in the 2015 AIB Annual Conference, Bengaluru, India, June 28–30.

Morikawa, H. 1992. *Zaibatsu: The rise and fall of family enterprise groups in Japan.* University of Tokyo Press.

Nakata, C., and K. Sivakumar. 1996. "National Culture and New Product Development: An Integrative Review." *Journal of Marketing* 60, no. 1: 61–72.

Naor, M., K. Linderman, and R. Schroeder. 2010. "The Globalization of Operations in Eastern and Western Countries: Unpacking the Relationship between National and Organizational Culture and Its Impact on Manufacturing Performance." *Journal of Operations Management* 28: 194–205.

Nayyar, P. R. 1992. "On the Measurement of Corporate Diversification Strategy: Evidence from Large US Service Firms." *Strategic Management Journal* 13, no. 3: 219–235.

Ncube, F., and S. Jerie. 2012. "Leveraging Employee Engagement for Competitive Advantage in the Hospitality Industry: A Comparative Study of Hotels A and B in Zimbabwe." *Journal of Emerging Trends in Economics and Management Sciences* 3, no. 4: 380–388.

Nicolas, F., S. Thomsen, and M. Bang. 2013. "Lessons from Investment Policy Reform in Korea." OECD Working Papers on International Investment, No. 2013-2. Paris: OECD Publishing. http://dx.doi.org/10.1787/5k4376zqcpf1-en.

Nicoletti, G. 2001. "Regulation in Services: OECD Patterns and Economic Implications." OECD Economics Department Working Paper, No. 287. Paris: OECD Publishing. http://dx.doi.org/10.1787/223766183220.

Nicoletti, G., and S. Scarpetta. 2005. "Regulation and Economic Performance: Product Market Reforms and Productivity in the OECD." OECD Economics Department Working Paper, No. 460. Paris: OECD Publishing. http://dx.doi.org/10.1787/726517007575.

Noland, M. 2012. "Korea's Growth Performance: Past and Future." *Asian Economic Policy Review* 7, no. 1: 20–42.

Nurkse, R. 1952. "Some International Aspects of the Problem of Economic Development." *American Economic Review* 42, no. 2: 571–583.

Nurkse, R. 1953. *Problems of Capital Formation in Underdeveloped Countries.* London: Oxford University Press.

OECD. 2007. "Globalization and Structural Adjustment: Summary Report of the Study on Globalization and Innovation in the Business Services Sector." Paris: OECD Publishing. http://www.oecd.org/sti/38619867.pdf.

OECD. 2013a. "Average Annual Hours Actually Worked Per Worker—Korea, Mexico." https://stats.oecd.org/Index.aspx?DataSetCode=ANHRS.

OECD. 2013b. *Entrepreneurship at a Glance 2013.* Paris: OECD Publishing. http://dx.doi.org/10.1787/entrepreneur_aag-2013-en.

OECD. 2013c. *Interconnected Economies: Benefiting from Global Value Chains.* Paris: OECD Publishing. http://www.oecd.org/sti/ind/interconnected-economies-GVCs-synthesis.pdf.

OECD. 2013d. "StatExtracts: Average Annual Hours Actually Worked per Worker, Korea." https://stats.oecd.org/Index.aspx?DataSetCode=ANHRS.

OECD. 2014a. *OECD Economic Surveys: KOREA.* Paris: OECD Publishing. http://www.oecd.org/eco/surveys/Overview_Korea_2014.pdf.

OECD. 2014b. PISA 2012 Results: What Students Know and Can Do—Student Performance in Mathematics, Reading and Science. Vol. 1. Revised ed. PISA OECD Publishing. ttp://www.oecd-ilibrary.org/education/pisa-2012-results-what-students-know-and-can-do-volume-i-revised-edition-february-2014_9789264208780-en.

Organization of the Petroleum Exporting Countries (OPEC). 2013. "OPEC Annual Statistics Bulletin 2013." Vienna: Austria. http://www.opec.org/opec_web/static_files_project/media/downloads/publications/ASB2013.pdf.

Oliver, C., and N. Hume. 2012. "POSCO to Invest in Australian Mining Venture." *Financial Times*, January 17. http://www.ft.com/intl/cms/s/0/d079ed0c-411a-11e1-8c33-00144feab49a.html.

Olson, P. 2014. "It May Be Crushing Samsung in China, but Xiaomi Barely Makes a Profit." *Forbes*, December 15. http://www.forbes.com/sites/parmyolson/2014/12/15/xiaomi-profit-margins-samsung-china/.

Pack, H. 1994. "Endogenous Growth Theory: Intellectual Appeal and Empirical Shortcomings." *Journal of Economic Perspectives* 8, no. 1: 55–72.

Pack, H., and J. M. Page. 1994. "Accumulation, Exports and Growth in the High Performing Asian Economies." *Carnegie-Rochester Conference Series on Public Policy*, no. 40: 199–235.

Page, J. M. 1994. "The East Asian Miracle: An Introduction." *World Development* 22, no. 4: 615–625.

Panzar, J. C., and R. D. Willig. 1981. "Economies of Scope." *American Economic Review* 71, no. 2: 268–272.

Parc, J., N. Park, and H. C. Moon. 2012. "*Diamond modeleui jupgeunbupeul hwalyonghan gyungyungineui leadership wonchuneh dehan gochal: Hyundaigroupeui Jungjuyung hwejanggwa Samsunggroupeui Leebyungchul hwejangeh dehan sare yungoo* [A Diamond Model Approach to the Analysis of Leadership: Case Studies on Chung, Ju-yung of Hyundai Group and Lee, Byung-chull of Samsung Group]" [in Korean]. *Journal of Professional Management* 15, no. 2: 1–19.

Park, B. Y., W. Chae, J. M. Lee, K. Lee, and S. C. Lee. 2007. "*Hangook kyungjebaljungyung-humeui de gedogook jukyong ganeungsung* [Reinterpretation of Korea's Economic Development and Lessons for Developing Countries]" [in Korean]. Seoul: Korea Institute for International Economic Policy. https://www.kiep.go.kr/include/filedown.jsp?fname=PAIK200713.pdf.

Park, G. H. 2013. "The 18th Presidential Inaugural Address: Opening a New Era of Hope." February 25. http://www.korea.net/Government/Briefing-Room/Presidential-Speeches/view?articleId=105853.

Park, S. C. 2009. "FDI in Services and the Productivity of Manufacturing: The Case of Korea." *International Commerce Research* 14, no. 2: 93–110.

Park, S. S. 2014. "POSCO Wins 'World's Most Competitive Steelmaker' Award." *Korea Times*, June 17. http://www2.koreatimes.co.kr/www/news/biz/2015/07/123_159297.html.

Patrinos, H. A., F. B. Osorio, and J. Guáqueta. 2009. *The Role and Impact of Public–Private Partnerships in Education*. Washington, DC: World Bank Publications. http://www.ungei.org/resources/files/Role_Impact_PPP_Education.pdf.

PBS. 2001. "Commanding Heights: An Interview with Manmohan Singh." February 6. http://www.pbs.org/wgbh/commandingheights/shared/minitextlo/int_manmohansingh.html.

Peng, M. W. 2002. "Towards an Institution-Based View of Business Strategy." *Asia Pacific Journal of Management* 19, no. 2: 251–267.

Peng, M. W. 2006. *Global Strategy*. Cincinnati, OH: South-Western Thomson.

Peng, M. W., S. L. Sun, B. Pinkham, and H. Chen. 2009. "The Institution-Based View as a Third Leg for a Strategy Tripod." *Academy of Management Perspectives* 23, no. 3: 63–81.

Peng, M. W., D. Y. Wang, and Y. Jiang. 2008. "An Institution-Based View of International Business Strategy: A Focus on Emerging Economies." *Journal of International Business Studies* 39, no. 5: 920–936.

Penrose, E. T. 1959. *The Theory of the Growth of the Firm*. New York: John Wiley.

Perlmutter, H. V. 1969. "The Tortuous Evolution of the Multinational Corporation." *Columbia Journal of World Business* 4, no. 4: 9–18.

Perry, S. R. 1998. "A Meta-Analytic Review of the Diversification-Performance Relationship: Aggregating Findings in Strategic Management." PhD dissertation, Florida Atlantic University.

Peteraf, M., G. D. Stefano, and G. Verona. 2013. "The Elephant in the Room of Dynamic Capabilities: Bringing Two Diverging Conversations Together." *Strategic Management Journal* 34, no. 12: 1389–1410.

Peteraf, M. A. 1993. "The Cornerstones of Competitive Advantage: A Resource-Based View." *Strategic Management Journal* 14, no. 3: 179–191.

Pfeffer, J. 1994. *Competitive Advantage through People*. Cambridge, MA: Harvard Business School Press.

Porter, L. W., and E. E. Lawler. 1968. *Managerial Attitudes and Performance*. Homewood, IL: Irwin-Dorsey.

Porter, M. E. 1980. *Competitive Strategy*. New York: Free Press.

Porter, M. E. 1986. *Competition in Global Industries*. Cambridge, MA: Harvard Business School Press.

Porter, M. E. 1990. *The Competitive Advantage of Nations*. New York: Free Press.

Porter, M. E. 1996. "What Is Strategy?" *Harvard Business Review* 74, no. 6: 61–78.

Porter, M. E. 1998a. "Cluster and the New Economics of Competition." *Harvard Business Review* 76, no. 6: 77–90.

Porter, M. E. 1998b. *On Competition*. Boston, MA: Harvard Business School Press.

Porter, M. E. 2000a. "Attitudes, Values, Beliefs, and the Microeconomics of Prosperity." In *Culture Matters: How Values Shape Human Progress*, edited by L. E. Harrison and S. P. Luntington, 14–28. New York: Basic Books.

Porter, M. E. 2000b. "Location, Competition, and Economic Development: Local Clusters in a Global Economy." *Economic Development Quarterly* 14, no. 1: 15–34.

Porter, M. E., and M. R. Kramer. 2002. "The Competitive Advantage of Corporate Philanthropy." *Harvard Business Review* 80, no. 12: 56–68.

Porter, M. E., and M. R. Kramer. 2006. "The Link between Competitive Advantage and Corporate Social Responsibility." *Harvard Business Review* 84, no. 12: 78–92.

Porter, M. E., and M. R. Kramer. 2011. "Creating Shared Value." *Harvard Business Review* 89, no. 1/2: 62–77.

Porter, M. E., and J. W. Rivkin. 2012. "Restoring U.S. Competitiveness." *Harvard Business Review* 90, no. 3: 81–93.

POSCO. 2013. "POSCO Annual Report 2013." Seoul: POSCO.

POSCO. 2015. POSCO Website. http://www.posco.com.pl/pages/39.

POSCO ICT. "Total Solution for Steel Manufacturing." https://www.poscoict.co.kr/download/catalog/en/steel_manufacturing_en.pdf.

Powell, T. C. 1995. "Total Quality Management as Competitive Advantage: A Review and Empirical Study." *Strategic Management Journal* 16, no. 1: 15–37.

Prahalad, C. K., and Y. L. Doz. 1987. *The Multinational Mission: Balancing Global Integration with Local Responsiveness*. New York: Free Press.

Prahalad, C. K., and G. Hamel. 1990. "The Core Competence of the Corporation." *Harvard Business Review* 90, no. 3: 79–91.

Priem, R. L., and J. E. Butler. 2001. "Is the Resource-Based 'View' a Useful Perspective for Strategic Management Research?" *Academy of Management Review* 26, no. 1: 22–40.

Ramaswamy, K., M. Li, and B. S. P. Petitt. 2004. "Who Drives Unrelated Diversification? A Study of Indian Manufacturing Firms." *Asia Pacific Journal of Management* 21, no. 4: 403–423.

Ramírez, L. F., and J. E. Rubio. 2010. "Culture, Government and Development in South Korea." *Asian Culture and History* 2, no. 1: 71–81.

Rashid, H. A., A. Asad, and M. M. Ashraf. 2011. "Factors Persuading Employee Engagement and Linkage of EE to Personal & Organizational Performance." *Interdisciplinary Journal of Contemporary Research in Business* 3, no. 5: 98–108.

Rechtin, M. 2004. "Hyundai Soars in Power Quality Rating." *Automotive News*, April 28. http://www.autonews.com/article/20040428/SUB/404280701/hyundai-soars-in-power-quality-ratings.

Reich, R. B. 1990. "Who Is Us?" *Harvard Business Review* 68, no. 1: 53–64.

Reich, R. B. 1991. "Who Is Them?" *Harvard Business Review* 69, no. 2: 77–88.

Reuters. 2013. "Xiaomi CEO: Don't Call Us China's Apple." August 15. http://www.reuters.com/video/2013/08/15/xiaomi-ceo-dont-call-us-chinas-apple?videoId=249009264.

Rodrick, D. 2004. "Industrial Policy for the Twenty-First Century." KSG Working Paper, No. RWP04-047.

Rosenstein-Rodan, P. N. 1943. "Problems of Industrialization of Eastern and South-Eastern Europe." *Economic Journal* 53, no. 210/211: 202–211.

Rostow, W. W. 1959. "The Stages of Economic Growth." *Economic History Review* 12, no. 1: 1–16.

Rostow, W. W. 1960. *The Stages of Economic Growth: A Non-Communist Manifesto.* Cambridge: Cambridge University Press.

Rostow, W. W. 1990. *The Stages of Economic Growth: A Non-Communist Manifesto.* 3rd ed. Cambridge: Cambridge University Press.

Roubini, N., and X. Sala-i-Martin. 1992. "Financial Repression and Economic Growth." *Journal of Development Economics* 39, no. 1: 5–30.

Rugman, A. M. 1991. "Diamond in the Rough." *Business Quarterly* 55, no. 3: 61–64.

Rugman, A. M., and J. R. D'Cruz. 1993. "The Double Diamond Model of International Competitiveness: The Canadian Experience." Special issue, *Management International Review* 33, no. 2: 17–39.

Salomon, R. M., and J. M. Shaver. 2005. "Learning by Exporting: New Insights from Examining Firm Innovation." *Journal of Economics and Management Strategy* 14, no. 2: 431–460.

Samsung Electronics. 2010. *"Samsung junja 40nyun sung-gongbeehwa: 1969–2009* [40 Years of Samsung Electronics' History: From 1969 to 2009]" [in Korean]. Suwon: Samsung Electronics.

Samsung Electronics. 2013. "Annual Report 2013." Seoul: Samsung Electronics.

Schnaars, S. P. 1994. *Managing Imitation Strategies: How Late Entrants Seize Marketing from Pioneers.* New York: Free Press.

Schumpeter, J. 1934. *The Theory of Economic Development: An Inquiry into Profits, Capital, Credit, Interest, and the Business Cycle.* Herndon, VA: Transaction Publishers.

Science and Technology Policy Institutes (STEPI). 2012. *"Hangooj hyukshincheje-eui dongteboonsukgwa baljunjunlyak* [The Dynamic Analysis of Korea's Innovation System and Development Strategy]" [in Korean]. Policy Research 2012–14. http://www.stepi.re.kr/app/report/view.jsp?cmsCd=CM0012&categCd=A0201&ntNo=741&sort=PUBDATE.

Scott, W. R. 2008. *Institutions and Organizations: Ideas and Interests.* 3rd ed. Thousand Oaks, CA: Sage Publications.

Selznick, P. 1957. *Leadership in Administration: A Sociological Perspective.* New York: Harper & Row.

Seo, K. G. 2011. *"Chulgwang wang* [The Steel King]" [in Korean]. Seoul: Hanul.

SERI. 2014. *"Hangook daegee-upeui global gyungjenglyukgwa goyong junlyak* [The Global Competitiveness of Korean Large Firms and the Strategy of Job Creation]" [in Korean]. Consulting Report. Samsung Electronic Research Institute (SERI).

Seth, M. J. 2002. *Education Fever: Society, Politics, and the Pursuit of Schooling in South Korea*. Honolulu: University of Hawaii Press.

Sharifi, H., and Z. Zhang. 1999. "A Methodology for Achieving Agility in Manufacturing Organisations: An Introduction." *International Journal of Production Economics* 62, no. 1: 7–22.

Shenkar, O. 2010. "Copycats: How Smart Companies Use Imitation to Gain a Strategic Edge." *Strategic Direction* 26, no. 10: 3–5.

Shin, G. W. and J. N. Choi. 2015. *Global Talent: Skilled Labor as Social Capital in Korea*. Stanford, CA: Stanford University Press.

Shin, J. C., M. J. Kim, and H. B. Park. 2007. *"Dehakeui jayulsungeh gwanhan jungboo mit dehak ganeui insikchaeui* [Perceptional Differences between Government and Universities on Institutional Autonomy]" [in Korean]. *Korean Journal of Educational Administration* 25, no. 3: 243–269.

Shinohara, M., T. Yanagihara, and K. W. Kim. 1983. "The Japanese and Korean Experiences in Managing Development." World Bank Staff Working Papers, No. 574. Management and Development Series, No. 1. http://documents.worldbank. org/curated/en/1983/07/440826/japanese-korean-experiences-managing-development.

Singer, H. W. 1964. *International Development: Growth and Change*. New York: McGraw-Hill.

Small and Medium Business Administration. 2015. "Criteria for Korean SMEs." http://www.smba.go.kr/eng/smes/scope.do?mc=usr0001146.

Smith, A. [1776] 1937. *An Inquiry into the Nature and Cause of the Wealth of Nations*. Edited by C. W. Eliot. The Harvard Classics. New York: P. F. Collier.

Solow, R. M. 1956. "A Contribution to the Theory of Economic Growth." *Quarterly Journal of Economics* 70, no. 1: 65–94.

Solow, R. M. 1962. "Technical Progress, Capital Formation, and Economic Growth." *American Economic Review* 52, no. 2: 76–86.

Song, B. N. 1997. *The Rise of the Korean Economy*. New York: Oxford University Press.

Song, J. Y., and K. M. Lee. 2014. *The Samsung Way*. New York: McGraw-Hill.

Song, I. H. and M. H. Park. (2012). *"Goryungjawa jungoryungjaeui chyupgyuljungyoin beegyogunsuk* [Comparative Analysis on Working Decision between the Aged and the Semi-Aged Person]" [in Korean]. *Social Science Studies* 19, no. 2: 7–26.

Sony. 2001. "Annual Report 2001." Tokyo: Sony Corporation.

Sony. 2013. "Annual Report 2013." Tokyo: Sony Corporation.

Stalk, G. 1988. "Time—The Next Source of Competitive Advantage." *Harvard Business Review* 66, no. 4: 41–51.

Statista. 2015. "Leading Motor Vehicle Manufacturers Worldwide in 2014, Based on Global Sales (in Million Units)." http://www.statista.com/statistics/275520/ranking-of-car-manufacturers-based-on-global-sales/.

Teece, D. 1983. "Technological and Organizational Factors in the Theory of Multinational Enterprise." In *Growth of International Business*, edited by M. Casson, 51–62. London: Allen and Unwin.

Teece, D. J. 2007. "Explicating Dynamic Capabilities: The Nature and Microfoundations of (Sustainable) Enterprise Performance." *Strategic Management Journal* 28, no. 13: 1319–1350.

Teece, D. J., G. Pisano, and A. Shuen. 1997. "Dynamic Capabilities and Strategic Management." *Strategic Management Journal* 18, no. 7: 509–533.

Thomson, S. D. 1989. "How Much Do Americans Value Schooling?" *NASSP Bulletin* 73, no. 519: 51–67.

Toussaint, E. 2006. "South Korea: The Miracle Unmasked." *Economic and Political Weekly* 41, no. 39: 4211–4219.

Troianovski, A. and S. Grundberg. 2012. "Nokia's Bad Call on Smartphones." *Wall Street Journal*, July 18. http://www.wsj.com/articles/SB10001424052702304 3880045775310025913155494.

Tu, H. S., S. Y. Kim, and S. E. Sullivan. 2002. "Global Strategy Lessons from Japanese and Korean Business Groups." *Business Horizons* 45, no. 2: 39–46.

Tu, W. M. 1984. *Confucian Ethics Today: The Singapore Challenge*. Singapore: Curriculum Development Institute of Singapore.

Tuan, C., and L. F. Ng. 2006. "The Place of FDI in China's Regional Economic Development: Emergence of the Globalized Delta Economies." Presented at International Conference on Globalization and Regional Economic Development, organized by KEBA, RCIE, and KIET in Korea. https://faculty. washington.edu/karyiu/confer/GJ06/papers/tuan-ng.pdf.

UNCTAD. 2005. "World Investment Report 2005: Transnational Corporations and the Internationalization of R&D." New York: United Nations Publication. http://unctad.org/en/Docs/wir2005_en.pdf.

UNCTAD. 2006. "World Investment Report 2006: FDI from Developing and Transition Economies: Implications for Development." New York: United Nations Publication. http://unctad.org/en/docs/wir2006_en.pdf.

UNCTAD. 2012. *Twenty Years of India's Liberalization: Experiences and Lessons*. New York: United Nations Publication. http://unctad.org/en/ PublicationsLibrary/osg2012d1_en.pdf.

UNCTAD. 2013. ""World Investment Report 2013: Global value chains- Investment and trade for development." New York: United Nations Publication. http:// unctad.org/en/PublicationsLibrary/wir2013_en.pdf.

UNCTAD. 2014. "World Investment Report 2014: Investing in the SDGs: An action plan." New York: United Nations Publication. http://unctad.org/en/ PublicationsLibrary/wir2014_en.pdf.

UNCTAD Statistics. 2015. http:// unctad.org/ en/ Pages/ Statistics.aspx.

UNESCO. 2000. "The EFA 2000 Assessment: Country Report, Republic of Korea." Seoul: Korean National Commission for UNESCO.

UNESCO. 2012. "The Archives of Saemaul Undong (New Community Movement) (Republic of Korea)." http://www.unesco.org/new/fileadmin/MULTIMEDIA/ HQ/CI/CI/pdf/mow/Korea_Saemaul_Undong.pdf.

UN Statistics Division. 2013. *Demographic Yearbook*. New York: United Nations Publication.

United States Congress. 1986. "The Korean Economy in Congressional Perspective." A study prepared for the use of the Joint Economic Committee Congress of the United States. 99th Cong., 2nd sess. Report 990185. Washington: U.S. Government Printing Office.

US International Trade Commission. 1985. *Analysis of the International Competitiveness of the U.S. Commercial Shipbuilding and Repair Industries.* Washington, DC: US International Trade Commission.

VandeWalle, D., S. P. Brown, W. L. Cron, and J. W. Slocum, Jr. 1999. "The Influence of Goal Orientation and Self-Regulation Tactics on Sales Performance: A Longitudinal Field Test." *Journal of Applied Psychology* 84, no. 2: 249–259.

Verge. 2012. "Samsung Galaxy Note II Review." October 8. http://www.theverge.com/2012/10/8/3464212/samsung-galaxy-note-ii-review.

Vogel, E. F. 1991. *The Four Little Dragons: The Spread of Industrialization in East Asia.* Vol. 3. Cambridge, MA: Harvard University Press.

Westphal, L. E. 1990. "Industrial Policy in an Export Propelled Economy: Lessons from South Korea's Experience." *Journal of Economic Perspectives* 4, no. 3: 41–59.

Williamson, O. E. 1975. "Transaction-Cost Economics: The Governance of Contractual Relations." *Journal of Law and Economics* 22, no. 2: 233–261.

Winter, S. G. 2003. "Understanding Dynamic Capabilities." *Strategic Management Journal* 24, no. 10: 991–995.

Wohlsen, M. 2015. "Xiaomi's Great New Phone Is a Lot Like an iPhone. Apple Should Take Note." *Wired*, February 26. http://www.wired.com/2015/02/xiaomis-great-new-phone-lot-like-iphone-apple-take-note/.

Woo, J. E. 1991. *Race to the Swift: State and Finance in Korean Industrialization.* New York: Columbia University Press.

Woolcock, M. 1998. "Social Capital and Economic Development: Toward a Theoretical Synthesis and Policy Framework." *Theory and Society* 27, no. 2: 151–208.

World Bank. 1989. "Country Reports: Korea." http://www.unesco.org/education/wef/countryreports/korea/contents.html.

World Bank. 1993. *East Asian Miracle: Economic Growth and Public Policy.* New York: Oxford University Press.

World Bank. 2013. "GDP (current US$) Data." http://data.worldbank.org/indicator/NY.GDP.MKTP.CD.

World Bank. 2015. "Doing Business." http://www.doingbusiness.org/rankings.

World Economic Forum (WEF). 2014. "The Global Competitiveness Report 2014–2015." Geneva: World Economic Forum. http://www3.weforum.org/docs/WEF_GlobalCompetitivenessReport_2014-15.pdf.

Xing, Y., and N. Detert. 2010. "How the iPhone Widens the United States Trade Deficit with the People's Republic of China." ADBI Working Paper Series, No. 257. Tokyo: Asian Development Bank Institute. http://www.adb.org/sites/default/files/publication/156112/adbi-wp257.pdf.

Yanikkaya, H. 2003. "Trade Openness and Economic Growth: A Cross-Country Empirical Investigation." *Journal of Development Economics* 72: 57–89.

Yim, J. Y. 2011. "Korea's Balanced Recovery." *Wall Street Journal*, June 3. http://www.wsj.com/articles/SB10001424052702303657404576361023375944348.

Young, A. 1992. "A Tale of Two Cities: Factor Accumulation and Technical Change in Hong Kong and Singapore." In *NBER Macroeconomics Annual*, edited by O. Blanchard and S. Fischer, 13–53. Cambridge, MA: MIT Press.

Young, A. 1994a. "Accumulation, Exports and Growth in the High Performing Asian Economies: A Comment." *Carnegie-Rochester Conference Series on Public Policy*, no. 40: 237–250.

Young, A. 1994b. "Lessons from the East Asian NICs: A Contrarian View." *European Economic Review Papers and Proceedings* 38, no. 3–4: 964–973.

YTN News. 2004. "*Hangooksonsilnodongilsoo sunjingookeui chego 111be* [Korea's Work Days Loss over 111 Times Greater than Advanced Countries]" [in Korean]. July 25. http://www.ytn.co.kr/_ln/0102_200407251339011870.

Zhou, Y. M. 2011. "Synergy, Coordination Costs, and Diversification Choices." *Strategic Management Journal* 32, no. 6: 624–639.

Zollo, M., and S. G. Winter. 2002. "Deliberate Learning and the Evolution of Dynamic Capabilities." *Organization Science* 13, no. 3: 339–351.

INDEX